The Undercover Philosopher

The Undercover Philosopher

A guide to detecting shams, lies, and delusions

Michael Philips

ONEWORLD
OXFORD

A Oneworld Paperback Original

Published by Oneworld Publications 2008

Copyright © Michael Philips 2008

ISBN 978–1–85168–581–3

Typeset by Jayvee, Trivandrum, India
Cover design by by D.R.Ink
Printed and bound in the United States of America
by Thomson-Shore-Inc

Oneworld Publications
185 Banbury Road
Oxford OX2 7AR
England
www.oneworld-publications.com

To my father, Seymour Philips, who was as kind and compassionate as they come, but nobody's fool.

Contents

Acknowledgments

I would like to thank Mike Harpley, my editor at Oneworld Publications, for his helpful criticisms and comments. They have made this a better book. I am also grateful to the anonymous reader for his suggestions, and to my friends Trink Morimitsu, Tom McClaren, Rachel Gaffney, and Larry Bowlden for their comments and encouragement. I am particularly grateful to my friend Ilene O'Malley, who read much of the manuscript, and made many useful stylistic suggestions.

Introduction

In the realm of belief we are all hostages to fortune. Had we been born in a different era, culture, or social class – had we been educated at different schools, raised in a different neighborhood, or born with a different temperament – many of our beliefs would be different than they are. So, unless we are unbelievably lucky, we all enter adulthood saddled with false beliefs, even about the most important matters. The prevalence of false beliefs is also obvious from the fact that human beings disagree so much. Disagreement about matters large and small is a permanent and pervasive fact of life. We disagree about whether science tells the whole story and what exactly your mother meant by *that*, about how much choice homosexuals have about being gay and what the fastest route is from point A to point B, about whether we all deserve to suffer from Adam's sin and whether retinol prevents wrinkles. Whenever two people disagree about a question to which there is a correct answer, at least one of them is wrong. So, again, we are wrong about a lot of things. Why? How could it be that we – *Homo sapiens*, rational animals – are so very fallible? And what can we do about it?

Of course, we also agree on many things. Without a lot of agreement, societies could not reproduce themselves from one day to the next. The fact that we agree does not necessarily mean we are right. But, clearly, we are right about a lot of things too. We can fly at incredible speeds, and send messages across the globe almost instantaneously. We know how plants reproduce, and how fish breathe. We fill encyclopedias without scratching the surface of our knowledge. But this book is more about our tendencies to get things wrong than our capacity to get things right. It's about the obstacles and hazards we face on the road to an accurate view of the world. The main goal is to help us answer the questions that motivated René Descartes, David Hume, and other great epistemologists in the philosophical tradition: by what methods, or on the basis of what principles, can we determine which of our beliefs are worth retaining and which are not? These questions are obviously vitally important. We don't want to live lives based on illusions or make decisions based on false beliefs. Fortunately, given advances in psychology, sociology, history, biology, and philosophy since the seventeenth and eighteenth centuries, we are now in a much better position to address these questions than even the greatest philosophers of past centuries.

These questions were introduced in their most dramatic form by Descartes, who is also often called the father of modern epistemology (a.k.a. the theory of knowledge). Disturbed by the widespread disagreement on almost every important topic of his day, Descartes set out to discover what we can know and how we can know it. To assure that knowledge rests on a secure foundation, he decided not to accept any proposition he could find any reason to doubt. According to his official story, at least, he had reason to doubt everything except the fact that he had certain conscious experiences (roughly, he calls these "ideas"), and whatever else he could infer from that fact (first and most famously, his own existence: "I think therefore I am"). His problem was to build a system of knowledge from this meager foundation. Although all he had to go on were the properties of the ideas themselves, he produced an astonishing array of systematically related conclusions about God, minds, and the universe, including the most prominent system of physics in Europe before Newton. But, as every philosopher now agrees, several key arguments that got him there are seriously flawed. If you have only the properties of your own immediate experience to go by, it is notoriously difficult to prove that you are not dreaming, that a world exists independently of your experiences, and that other people exist with minds of their own.

Unfortunately, although most twentieth-century theorists of knowledge rejected Descartes's arguments, they continued to accept his starting point and devoted enormous amounts of time and energy trying to solve the problems that starting point created. Accordingly, many philosophers devoted much of their professional careers to showing that we really do have good reasons to believe that other people have conscious experiences (now known as "the Zombie problem"), and that trees actually do fall in the forest when nobody is there to experience them. This project, known as "answering the skeptic," was widely regarded as *the* central problem of the theory of knowledge in the last century. This is because philosophers are nothing if not systematic and methodical. First things first: we need proof that there is a world out there before it makes sense to worry about how to know it. These persistent, even obsessive attempts to prove what only crazy people doubt explains why so many people are so bewildered and frustrated by philosophy. It also explains why twentieth-century philosophers of knowledge have done so little to meet Descartes's central objective. To the extent we are obsessed with proving or disproving that there is a world out there in the first place, we are not figuring out how to know it. Descartes hoped to eliminate confusion from the world by providing us with tools to decide which of our beliefs are worthy of retaining and which are not. That is a noble objective, but it was largely derailed in twentieth-century (English-language) philosophy in favor of an attempt to prove what every sane person takes for granted.

If we are to revive Descartes's objective, we need to amend his starting point. First, we need to get rid of the idea that we can make headway by thinking about a single person – oneself – and generalize what we find to all humanity. When it comes to our capacity to err and to know, there are obviously important differences between us (for example, in intelligence, in training, and in degree of sanity). Second, we need to consider the social basis of knowledge. Except for some beliefs about our own past, relatively few of our beliefs are based entirely on our own experience. In fact, we learn almost everything we know from others – parents, teachers, historians, scientists, cartographers, doctors, journalists, and the rest, who themselves also learn from others. Sometimes we stand on the shoulders of giants who stand on solid ground; sometimes we stand on the shoulders of dwarfs who stand in a mire. But when it comes to beliefs and knowledge, we almost never stand alone. The individual in the "state of nature," that old philosophical conceit, will learn even less than a child raised by wolves. Knowledge is social.

This means that our biggest problem as knowledge-seeking human beings is deciding whom to trust and when to trust them. When should we trust the M.D. and when (if at all) the naturopath, when the *New York Times* and when Noam Chomsky, when the materialist philosopher and when the spiritualist? In the last part of the twentieth century, some Anglo-American philosophers started to pay attention to such problems. This is a good thing, but, unfortunately, with a few exceptions, they have managed to generate a typical academic literature – abstract, theoretical, defensive, self-referential, inaccessible to nonprofessionals, and (with a few exceptions) not primarily directed by the interests of living people facing real-world problems. As an academic in recovery, I will try to produce something more useful.

Because most of us have lives, we don't have the time and energy to evaluate *all* our sources carefully (or even very many of them). Of course, we have attitudes ("You heard it on Fox News? Come on!"). But usually these reflect our self-concepts, loyalties, and affiliations more than some fierce love of truth. And usually, when we have nothing personal at stake, we slip comfortably into the pleasant and familiar bathwater of authoritative sources and accept the various official stories on the basis of which we and our fellows distinguish between the reasonable and the unreasonable, the sane and the crazy. Every society has such stories and provides incentives to accept them. Dissenters are marginalized as kooky, weird, or downright dangerous and sometimes jailed or tortured or burned at the stake. There are differences of degree, but all human groups expect conformity on certain basic issues: "If you are one of us, you must think as we do." Of course, as societies fracture, fragment, and polarize along class, religious, ideological, and other lines, the territory of authoritative sources diminishes, and what counts as authoritative is increasingly contested. What is authoritative for one group is often not authoritative for another.

As this suggests, "authoritative" does not necessarily imply "accurate." From the standpoint of a philosopher, one of the more depressing facts about human history is the way authoritative sources claim knowledge that far exceeds their resources and capabilities. Every known human society, every known tribe, has an official story about how the universe began. Pause for a moment to think about that. Human beings just seem to have a hard time saying, "I don't know." Until relatively recently, the history of human expertise has included a long succession of people adorned in masks, feathers, body paint, or gem-embossed robes dancing, chanting, burning incense, sacrificing animals, and pulling the beating hearts out of other human beings to combat disease, end famine and drought, guarantee safe sea crossings and military victories, advance various personal agendas, and so on. In Greek and Roman times such highly trained paid professionals read omens and portents in the flights of birds, the guts of animals, and the positions of the stars. Have all of the human tendencies that generated the widespread acceptance of these practices been extinguished in the last few centuries? Do the various safeguards now in place in the scientific community and other communities of knowledge seekers effectively filter them out? Or do they continue to surge and surface unrecognized in areas most of us regard now safe and secure? Yes, things have gotten better since the days of the Sumerians, but, as we shall see, there is still much room for improvement.

It's not surprising that Descartes ignored and other seventeenth- and eighteenth-century philosophers neglected the social basis of knowledge. There were few or no professional research communities in those days. All the significant intellectual advances were made by individuals working alone or in correspondence with a handful of others. Also, when thinking about the reliability of our beliefs, it does make sense to focus on the individual first. It's not just that individuals must decide what to accept and reject from authoritative sources. In addition, and more importantly, authoritative sources are individuals or communities of individuals. To work effectively, these communities must be organized in ways that avoid or overcome our tendencies to err as human beings (for example, to see what we expect to see, to believe what we want to believe, and to manufacture "memories" of a fictionalized past). Evolutionary psychologists and biologists struggle to explain these tendencies. Psychotherapists try to help us overcome them. Novelists and playwrights explore the tragedy and comedy they produce in our lives. Professional research communities must find ways to guard against them. Unless we know what these tendencies are, we won't be in a position to determine where they fail and where they succeed at this.

So we will begin with our fallibilities as individuals. A century of psychological and social psychological research has unearthed many problems in the way human beings acquire, record, process, and retrieve information. Sometimes we misperceive what is right before our eyes. Sometimes we misremember and fictionalize the past. Most of us also jump to conclusions, generalize from small samples, and create sweeping theories on the merest wisps of evidence. The majority of us also ignore essential information when we calculate risks and benefits. Many of us also tend to look for evidence that confirms what we already believe and ignore evidence that disconfirms it. These errors are responsible for all manner of mistaken beliefs resulting in all manner of personal, social, and political problems – marital breakdowns, mistaken medical diagnoses, false eyewitness identifications, ill-conceived military initiatives, the proliferation of religious cults, and so forth. But many of these errors are avoidable or can be reduced significantly with understanding and vigilance. These are the subject of the first part of this book.

This portrait of the individual is bleaker than those offered by some recent celebrants of human cognition. Perhaps the best known of these is Malcolm Gladwell, whose blockbuster bestseller *Blink: The Power of Thinking without Thinking*, advertises itself as a tribute to the insightfulness of intuition and snap judgments (as he calls them). Gladwell acknowledges that intuition is fallible. But he thinks that it errs mainly when we are misled or distracted by "our emotions, or interests or sentiments," and when we use it "out of context" (an idea he never explains). Oddly, though, almost all of his examples and case studies of successful intuitive thinking involve extraordinary people who owe their success to *accurate beliefs* about the world which the rest of us lack. In most of these cases, *their* intuitions work astonishingly well, while *our* intuitions work badly (as Gladwell himself acknowledges). This is not because these extraordinary people have a more highly developed faculty of intuition than the rest of us. And it is not because, as Gladwell suggests, the rest of us are misled by our emotions, or interests or sentiments, or that we make judgments "out of context." Roughly, it's because *they* know something about the world that *we* don't; that is, they have true beliefs in areas where we are ignorant or mistaken. These true beliefs are what make their unconscious processing successful. Whether we are consciously evaluating data or arguments, or making intuitive judgments, our conclusions can be no more accurate than the background theories and beliefs on which they rely (that is, unless we are amazingly lucky and our errors cancel each other out). I will say more about this, and the reliability of intuition in general, in Chapter 2.

The second part of this book will deal with attempts of communities of investigators to achieve reliable beliefs. To succeed, they need to avoid or overcome the problems we have as individuals, and otherwise do things right. Roughly, communities of investigators include any group, organization, or set of practitioners we rely on as sources of credible information about the world. Because all such communities take data (raw materials) from the world and turn those data into conclusions (finished products), we can think of them as "Knowledge Machines." Our problem is to determine how to decide when these machines produce and effectively distribute reliable products. This is not an easy problem. For one thing, there are many different kinds of Knowledge Machines producing many different kinds of conclusions. Some, like physics, produce general theories of how the world works. Others, like doctors, produce plans for identifying and fixing particular problems of particular individuals. Still others, like historians, produce descriptions, explanations, and interpretations of phenomena in the past. All these differences do and should affect the ways these various kinds of practitioners go about their business. Despite all of these differences, though, there is a very general level at which all Knowledge Machines share a common set of problems (this makes it possible to have a theory about Knowledge Machines). Since they all gather data from the world, all Knowledge Machines need rules and procedures for gathering and filtering that data. Since they all work that data up into conclusions, they also need methods and techniques for doing that. Finally, they need ways to get their products to the rest of us in good condition. To ask to what extent an authoritative source is reliable is to ask to what extent it does these things well. Does it allow false or misleading data into the mix? Does it exclude relevant data? Do its methods for arriving at conclusions produce theories that outrun the data? Do the ways it publicizes the conclusions mislead?

The Knowledge Machine analogy is just an analogy, and it's not a perfect one. For one thing, it suggests that data are gathered first and processed later. It does sometimes happen this way. For example, that's what meteorologists do to predict the weather. But sometimes it doesn't. Police trying to solve crimes may move back and forth between data gathering and provisional conclusions any number of times. So may scientists trying to solve a particular problem. Also, in some cases, experimental scientists may do their most important thinking and theorizing *before* they gather any data at all. In particular, they think and theorize about what data – what experimental results – would help answer their question and how to design experiments to get those data. The significance of the experimental result – the data – is understood before the data are gathered.

Both data gathering and data "processing" can go wrong in three ways. First, our established ways of doing things – our accepted methods and procedures – may be flawed (problems of design). Second, our established ways of doing things, though fine, may not be followed (problems of compliance). Finally, both stages of the process may be based on mistaken beliefs and theories. Most of us expect some problems of compliance. We know that our trusted authorities are human with all the frailties and vulnerabilities that implies. We expect a certain amount of laziness, sloppiness, incompetence, and dishonesty. We are not surprised when people take shortcuts to fame and fortune, or cave in to political and economic pressures. Such is the way of the world. What is surprising is the weakness of the safeguards in place to deter, detect, and punish these transgressions, which may and sometimes do have disastrous

consequences. I will discuss examples from science, accounting, survey research, and journalism in some detail. Problems
of design seem more surprising. Although history abounds
with examples of omen-readers in high places, we tend to
think that these are relics of our benighted past vanquished in
our scientific age. This exceptionalism of the present is unwarranted. We will consider examples of this from medicine, the
criminal justice system, brokerage houses, cosmology, and
brain science.

Problems of design are often rooted in false theories, beliefs,
or assumptions about how the world works. In fact, both data
gathering and the move from data to conclusions depend heavily on our preexisting beliefs, theories, and assumptions. If
those theories are mistaken we will be saddled with bad data
and/or bad conclusions. Pathologists, for example, diagnose
diseases by looking at tissue samples or fluid samples under a
microscope. These samples are their data. But they can serve as
data for pathologists only because pathologists have certain
beliefs about optics, microorganisms, and diseases (for example, that there are such things as bacteria, they look like *that*
under a microscope, and they cause certain diseases). If these
theories are false, what appears on the slide might not even be
relevant to their diagnosis. The corresponding point holds for
the move from data to conclusions. Cosmologists, for example,
move from data gathered by telescopes to conclusions about
the origins of the universe with the help of a rich and highly
complicated set of theories and beliefs about the nature of
matter, radiation, gravity, and other phenomena. If these
theories turn out to be false, so (almost certainly) do the cosmologists' conclusions. As this suggests, the success of our
present intellectual efforts is greatly influenced by the beliefs
and theories we inherit from the past. But, as the history of

science reminds us again and again, some of these theories may well be false.

From a practical standpoint, this might seem like useless information. After all, if the experts in a field can't tell that they are working with false theories, how can we? Well, often we can't; we simply die before the verdict of history is delivered. But sometimes we can. Sometimes one Knowledge Machine provides us with very strong reasons for rejecting the theories and assumptions of another, reasons that are clear to any impartial person. And sometimes the flawed machine is slow to adjust. In fact, as we will see, such Knowledge Machines are sometimes able to resist change for decades.

One reason for this is specialization. Although specialization in the pursuit of knowledge was partly responsible for the knowledge explosion in the twentieth century, it is also responsible for the persistence of obsolete and unreliable methods and practices. All Knowledge Machines – from academic disciplines, to medicine, to the jury system – have their own organizational structures, methods, and traditions. This often makes them slow to accept research from other fields, especially research that calls for changes in these methods and standards. This slowness and reluctance are not entirely attributable to pride, arrogance, turf struggles, rivalry, laziness, inertia, and plain stubbornness. They are also a result of the way social organizations work. Practitioners in any field – members of any organization – tend to trust their own methods and superstars more than they trust outsiders. This is partly for psychological reasons: many practitioners have invested much of their lives in their work, and no one wants to believe that they've spent twenty years barking up the wrong tree. But it is also partly for career-related reasons: people who challenge the methods, techniques, or assumptions of their own field based on work done in other fields have a harder time even getting their work published in the journals of their own field. Often, they are marginalized. Sometimes they are viewed as traitors. Of course, this isn't always so. The rate at which Knowledge Machines assimilate the results of other Knowledge Machines varies from case to case. But resistance to outside research is common.

Where does this leave us? How skeptical and pessimistic should we be about our attempts to understand the world? This is the sort of question that gets asked at not very useful academic conferences. On one side of this debate are the skeptics. Skepticism about rationality has a long and distinguished pedigree in the Western tradition. Although Plato believed that reason could unveil the essence of all things, he also believed that reason was a hothouse plant that needed constant nurturing, and that it could get that nurturing only in a utopian political or social environment. In actual societies, it tends to be trampled underfoot. St. Augustine, strongly influenced by Plato, introduced a still more pessimistic picture into mainstream Christian theology. According to Augustine we are weak and corrupt heirs to Adam's sin driven by greed, pride, and bodily appetites, all of which distort and dominate our thinking. We cannot rely on ourselves to find truth. We must rely on the grace of God. A more secular tradition of skepticism with ancient roots came to full flower in the last century, in response to the massive organized madness of those years (the trench warfare, the genocides, the totalitarian propaganda, the religious fundamentalism, and all the rest). This tradition attributes the causes of irrationality to hegemonic social and economic forces (the Frankfurt School, Foucault, and others), psychological mechanisms (Freud and the Freudians), and even language itself (Derrida and his followers). They come together in various versions of post-modernism, which, in its more dramatic versions, attacks the very idea of an accurate view of the world. Because we are "situated" by our historical position, our culture, our religion, our ethnicity, our class, our gender, and even our language, post-modernists argue, we are forever limited to partial and distorted perspectives.

The apostles of rationality also have a distinguished pedigree. Aristotle famously defined human beings as rational animals. According to his picture, every normal, well-raised member of a well-ordered human community will become rational in thought and action. This picture of human nature entered the Christian tradition through St. Thomas Aquinas, probably the most influential theologian in the history of Christianity, who consistently refers to Aristotle "the Philosopher." According to St. Thomas, reason is a God-given natural power that is fully capable of understanding the natural world and even certain aspects of the divine. This optimistic picture of reason has many other sources as well. Descartes, Leibniz, and Spinoza argued that we can understand the fundamental truths about the nature of the universe by reason alone. Economists since Adam Smith have based their understanding of markets on the assumption that we make rational economic choices. And positivists since Comte have argued that we can discover truths about human societies and the natural world by applying the method of science. Philosophers of action also tend to be defenders of the more optimistic view. Despite all the madness, chaos, and confusion in the world, they argue, we are purpose-driven creatures who act to promote our interests or satisfy our desires. We do this thousands of times each day. All other things being equal, if I want to leave the room, I go to the door. If I want to open the door, I turn the knob. One way or another, rationality manifests itself in every purposeful act (even by lunatics).

These debates between the rationalists and the skeptics tend to be formulaic, pointless, and tiresome. The deflationary truth of the matter is that there are ways in which we are rational, and ways in which we aren't, and that our capacity for and use of rationality may vary with our circumstances. So, instead of arguing about whether human beings deserve some ill-defined honorific like "rational animal," we would do better to investigate how and when we think well, and how and when we don't. Thinkers on both sides of the issue are well stocked with examples. This book focuses mainly on ways thinking goes wrong. But it is important to remind ourselves how often thinking goes right. It's a good bet that even most skeptics get X-rayed to check for broken bones, fly airplanes to travel, have high-speed internet connections, and so on. But how can one trust these technologies without trusting the theories and beliefs on which they are based? Did we just get incredibly lucky?

That said, both sides of this debate have interesting and compelling points to make. Their debates are tiresome because they make them over and over again and fail to engage each other. What is needed, philosophically at least, is a theory of knowledge that synthesizes the strong points of each side while transcending the opposition (as Kant synthesized the strong points of rationalism and empiricism in the eighteenth century). How can we do justice to the obvious limitations imposed on us by history, culture, race, class, gender, and personal circumstances while at the same time acknowledging our evident capacity to learn about the world? This, I think, is among the most pressing philosophical questions of the present century. I do not try to address it here. The focus of this book is more practical. Still, some of the discussions about cognition, authoritative sources, and reasonable belief policies in this book may supply pieces of the puzzle.

Finally, what is the reader to do with all this information about how things go wrong?

The obvious answer is "use it." We all have an obvious interest in avoiding obstacles and hazards on the road to an accurate view of the world. False beliefs can lead us in bad directions and even kill us. On the other hand, avoiding false beliefs has a price. How much time and energy should each of us spend to determine whether there really were weapons of mass destruction in Iraq, what the stock market will do next week, whether retinol really does work to reduce wrinkles, or who said what to whom at the last family Christmas dinner? Some bits of information are obviously more important to us than others, but how much time and energy should we invest in even important information? On the one hand, all of us have beliefs we could shore up with a day or two of research in the library. On the other hand, one could spend one's entire life in the library. What does wisdom dictate here? What is our responsibility to others? What is our responsibility to ourselves? What attitude should we adopt toward people who do little or nothing to get their beliefs straight, or people who always trust the authorities, or people who simply believe whatever makes them feel good? What should our attitude be toward people who rarely if ever trust authoritative sources (like most conspiracy theorists)? There is an intricate web of related questions here. They will be the subject of my final chapter.

CHAPTER 1

Seeing What Isn't There and Remembering What Never Happened

Although we get most of our beliefs from others, many of our beliefs are also based on personal experience. In fact, many of us base some of our most important beliefs wholly or partly on what we've seen, heard, and felt (or thought we've seen, heard, and felt). The religious among us may have felt the spirit of the Lord or witnessed faith healings and other miracles. Others may have had compelling sessions with psychic readers and spiritualists, witnessed acts of telekinesis (like spoon bending), had good results from homeopathic medicines or various herbal cures, or vividly remembered (under hypnosis) being abducted by aliens or being sexually assaulted by their parents. These experiences may lead us to reject sources most others regard as authoritative, to question the prevailing scientific worldview, and to understand our past in an entirely new and frightening way. But how trustworthy are these experiences? To what degree and under what conditions can we trust our memories and perceptions? We need to answer these questions not only to evaluate our own beliefs but also to determine what kinds of mistakes communities of investigators must guard against.

Perception

Most of us believe that the world is revealed to us through our senses. We take it for granted that the solid, colored objects we see would exist as they are even if we were not around to see them. The red roses would still be red and smell as sweet, and their thorns would be as sharp. The sky would still rumble and crack when it thundered. Before we think about it, we simply assume that colors, textures, sounds, and tastes are independent features of the natural world, the world as it is in itself. And we have access to that world through our sense organs.

This picture, however, is too simple. First of all, our sense organs by themselves reveal nothing. They work in conjunction with our brains, and it is our brains that convert the information they accumulate into our experience of colors, tastes, sounds, and so on. Without brains we would have no experience, no consciousness, at all. In the second place, our brains convert this information from the senses into the kind of experiences they do because our brains are structured the way they are. If our brains were constructed differently, they would convert that information into different kinds of experiences. Strictly speaking, for example, our eyes detect light waves, our ears detect vibrations in the air (sound waves), and our noses detect molecules in the air. If our brains were built differently, we might experience light waves of various frequencies differently than we do. We might experience a wider or narrower range of colors, or no colors at all. Instead of experiencing light waves as color we might experience them as various kinds of tingles, or heat, or in some way we can't even imagine (as people blind from birth can't imagine colors). In short, the world as it appears to us through the senses is not the world as it is in itself but rather a consequence of the world as it is in itself interacting with sense organs and brains like our own. In addition, our senses detect only some aspects of that world. Unlike electric fish, we don't sense objects entering electric fields. Unlike bees, we don't directly sense ultraviolet light.

This means that a deep knowledge of the physical world requires getting beyond the way the world discloses itself to us in perceptual experience. The goal of physics is to describe the world that underlies perception and the world to which we have no perceptual access at all. Theoretically, we could share our understanding of that world – our science – with aliens who have none of our sense organs and whose own sense organs are attuned to completely different features of the world (magnetic attraction, cellphone signals, colonies of viruses, and so on).

The practical problems we face as knowers take place within the perceptual world we share, or mostly share, with each other (I say "mostly share" because there are differences between individuals as well). But even in this world our brain produces a world of experience that goes well beyond the information presented to the brain by the senses. The brain ceaselessly edits and elaborates on that information. What we see, for example, is always both more and less than what meets the eye. This is true not only when we hallucinate, but also in normal perception.

For one thing, the brain is highly selective. When I walk through the park my eyes record all the shapes and colors in my visual field, all the subtle differences of light and shadow, hue and saturation. But unless I stop and take a close and careful look I am unaware of most of this. If I am preoccupied with a philosophical problem, I am hardly aware that there are flowers and trees. What we actually experience is determined by our goals, interests, and concerns. It is even influenced by our state of mind. When I am happy, the colors of the world are more vibrant. This is all the work of my brain.

The brain also makes corrections and fills in missing information. If it simply reproduced the information recorded on the retina, we would see the world upside down, and have a big black hole in our visual field (the blind spot). The brain also sees to it that the color of the objects we see remains relatively constant despite big changes in the color of the light in which we see them. A leaf looks green to us at midday, when the illumination is white sunlight, and also at sunset, when the illumination is mainly red (a phenomenon called "color constancy"). The brain also fills in color at the periphery of our visual field. Our color receptors (cones) are concentrated in a small area in the center of our retina called the fovea (which, as one researcher put it, occupies about as much space in the retina as the moon in the night sky). The small size of the fovea makes it impossible for the cones to receive color information at the periphery of our visual field. The fact that we see color at the periphery is a result of the brain filling in on the basis of the information it has.

For the most part, the brain selects, corrects, and fills in without misleading us about the world. In some cases, though, the normal workings of the sense organs and the brain present us with misleading pictures. Because we are familiar with some of these distortions we are not taken in by them. We don't think the stick half submerged in the pool of water is really bent or that a moving picture is anything but a series of stills projected at a high enough speed. In other cases, we are protected against false conclusions by the context. We don't believe the stage magician really pulled that big green parrot out of that six-year-old volunteer's ear or that the man in the "antigravity house" really is standing at a forty-five-degree angle from the wall. But it is easy to see how sleight of hand and optical illusions could be used to exploit the gullible (and no doubt were by the "magicians" and "sorcerers" of yore). I was quite surprised to discover just how wide a variety of optical illusions there are. On his webpage, researcher Michael Bach (www.michaelbach.de/ot) provides sixty-one examples involving color, shape, and motion.

Charlatans can exploit these normal operations of our sense organs and brains to support all manner of beliefs involving occult or supernatural forces. The Amazing Randi, a stage magician, made a second career for himself duplicating "demonstrations" of spoon bending and other paranormal phenomena by tricking the brain. Randi's duplications don't *prove* that the original demonstrations were faked. Stage magicians can also use these techniques to make us believe they are doing something amazing that people actually can do (e.g. saw people in half and multiply long sequences of big numbers in their heads). But what Randi's demonstrations do prove is that "I saw him do it myself" is not proof that the original demonstrations were genuine. But we don't need charlatans to be fooled by what we "see." We do a pretty good job of that all by ourselves. When the information we receive from the senses is vague, sketchy, or ambiguous, the brain often interprets that information on the basis of what we believe, what we expect, what we fear, what we hope for, or what we have been prompted to look for. As a result, we may "see" all kinds of things that aren't really there and hear things that aren't really said.

These phenomena of the brain are the basis of periodolia, the tendency to make sense of sketchy or ambiguous data. Many of us get a frightening dose of this as children when the large, terrifying man who appears in our bedroom at night turns out to be a shirt hanging on a closet door. But periodolia does not end with childhood. Among other things, periodolia is also responsible for "sightings" of bridges on the moon, evidence of life on Mars (a stone face, a canal system, and a pyramid), and at least some sightings of alien spacecraft. It is probably no coincidence that large numbers of these sightings occur when the skies are active (as they did on March 3, 1968, when the rocket used to launch the Soviet Zond 4 spacecraft reentered the atmosphere and broke into luminous fragments). Some of these sightings were quite detailed (e.g. a cigar-shaped spacecraft with many lighted windows). Reports of U.F.O.'s have also been based on meteor fireballs, and even on advertising aircraft equipped with strings of electric lights (viewed at an oblique angle). Again, this does not prove that alien spacecraft have not entered our atmosphere. But it does give us reason to doubt many first-hand reports.

Perception is also quite vulnerable to suggestion. Under hypnosis, where we are most suggestible, we can be made to feel hot, cold, heavy, light, itchy, and touched by angels without any change in external conditions. Hypnotists can also induce temporary color blindness, tunnel vision, and visual hallucinations. But perception may be influenced by suggestion without the help of a hypnotist. Some of us are just highly suggestible. If we read about a disease we may find ourselves experiencing sensations that are symptoms of that disease (that is, sensations produced by the mind). If we spend enough time reading about diseases, this may happen even to those of us who are not particularly suggestible. This happens regularly to second-year medical students, who spend that year immersed in diseases and their symptoms. According to one study report seventy percent of them suffer from transient hypochondriasis.[1]

Suggestion often produces expectations, and expectations may also powerfully shape perception. If we expect to see a friend at a party, we may momentarily misidentify someone else as that friend (especially from behind, from across the room, or in bad lighting). If we are told by experimenters to walk down a corridor until we see a light flash, some of us will indeed "see" the light flash even when it doesn't. Expectations can also cause us to miss things that are there, especially when they blend in. In a famous experiment performed by John S. Brunner and Leo Postman, subjects were shown a group of playing cards for a few seconds and asked how many aces of spades they saw. Most reported seeing three. In fact, there were five. Two of the aces of spades were colored red instead of black. The subjects missed seeing them because they expected aces of spades to be black (although some people may have not reported the red aces because they thought that aces of spades are black by definition).[2]

Our tendency to see and hear what we expect is responsible for some awkward moments and interpersonal misunderstandings. If we think our lover is angry at us but trying not to show it, we may well hear suppressed anger in her voice or see it in her face. If we are fearful or suspicious of someone, we may misread his facial expression, body language, or tone of voice as threatening or deceitful. On the other hand, if we expect someone to be truthful, we may miss the normal but subtle signs of deception in her tone of voice or face. Skilled

salespeople take advantage of this tendency by selling themselves to us (as honest and caring) even before they sell their
product. Expecting them to be honest, we may miss cues we
would pick up on if we expected them to be dishonest.

Probably the most dramatic cases of the power of expectations are the placebo and nocebo effects. In the placebo effect, a
patient's symptoms and/or underlying condition are allevi-
ated or eliminated by a treatment because or partly because the
patient believes that treatment will work. Sometimes these
symptoms are bodily sensations (which I will treat as perceptions for the moment, since we use them to make inferences
about our physical condition). In one experiment, for example,
morphine relieved pain fifty percent more effectively when
patients were told they were getting it. In another experiment,
patients whose pain had been controlled by morphine for
several days were given a saline solution they believed to be
morphine. In this situation, the saline solution worked just as
well to relieve pain.[3,4] The placebo effect is so powerful that
medical research into the effectiveness of a treatment must
include both a group that actually gets the treatment and a control group that gets a placebo, with neither the subjects nor the
people administering the placebo knowing who gets which.
Otherwise, researchers can't tell whether the drug itself or
the patient's expectation achieved the alleviation of symptoms
or cure.

In the nocebo effect, sometimes referred to as "the evil twin"
of the placebo effect, expectations cause rather than alleviate
symptoms or even medical conditions. In one study, two
groups of heart patients taking aspirin as a blood thinner were
warned by their doctors that aspirin might cause gastrointesti-
nal problems. A third group did not receive this warning.
Although the risk factors were the same for all three groups,

patients in the first two groups were three times as likely to suffer the bodily sensations associated with these problems as patients in the third.[5] The placebo and nocebo effects should affect the way doctors present treatments to their patients (but that is a topic for another book).

It is worth noting that expectations may also affect the perceptions of trained scientists. Shortly after the discovery of X-rays, the distinguished French physicist René Blondlot announced the discovery of another form of radiation he called "N-rays." N-rays were supposed to be emitted by certain metals, increase the brightness of a spark, and help the eye to see better in dim light. When directed at objects coated with luminous paint, they were supposed to make the object brighter. Dozens of research studies in France "confirmed" Blondlot's discovery and even extended it. But both the discovery and its confirmations relied on eyewitness reports that (among other things) the painted objects did get brighter in the presence of N-rays. Scientists outside France could not duplicate these findings. Blondlot and his colleagues rejected and resented their skepticism. The truth of the matter was brought to light by the resourceful American physicist Robert Wood. In a visit to Blondlot's lab, Wood rigged one of Blondlot's experiments. According to Blondlot's theory, N-rays were blocked by lead. In the experiment in question, Wood was responsible for positioning a lead sheet in front of the object at which N-rays were supposedly aimed. Wood told Blondlot and his colleagues that the sheet was in place when it really wasn't and that it wasn't in place when it really was. Blondlot "saw" the object grow brighter with the shield down and dimmer with the shield up.[6] The fact that perceptions can be influenced by expectations in this way is one reason scientists now use instruments to measure phenomena like heat and brightness.

In another more recent case, a sociologist at Syracuse University popularized a technique that allegedly enabled people to communicate who were otherwise unable to do so. This technique, called Facilitated Communication, was supposed to open new worlds for the severely autistic, the brain-damaged, and victims of cerebral palsy (among others). In Facilitated Communication the patient communicates by guiding the hand of a facilitator to keys on a keyboard (with the help of the patient's hand, wrist, or shoulder). As a result of some apparent successes, centers for Facilitated Communication spread across the U.S. in the early 1990s. But a series of controlled experiments soon demonstrated that in at least many cases it is the facilitator who does the communicating. In response, the American Psychological Association issued a position paper on Facilitated Communication concluding that there is "no scientifically demonstrated support of its efficacy."[7] Still, not even the most hardened skeptics questioned the sincerity of the facilitators. Instead, they concluded that the facilitators imagined pressure coming from the "communicator" caused by the facilitators' expectations of what the "communicator" would want to say (not unlike a Ouija board). (This does not prove that Facilitated Communication is *never* effective. In fact, there seem to be a few cases in which people taught by this technique have learned to communicate without the help of a facilitator.[8] But the studies show that this is not usually how it goes.)

Finally, and perhaps most frightening, there is a sense in which what we believe may determine what we perceive. If I believe in God and believe that God is sending me a sign I may see an image of Jesus where others see only a stain on a shower curtain. In addition to shower curtains, the face of Jesus has "miraculously" appeared to believers on cooked tortillas, trees and walls, a rose petal, a muddy towel, and the Hubble photograph of the Eagle Nebula. You can find pictures of most of these "sightings" at www.thefolklorist.com (where you will also find images of Mother Theresa in a cinnamon bun and Rasputin in a kitten's ear). In some of these sightings, the resemblance to Jesus is so tenuous that nonbelievers dispute it even when believers point it out ("Oh, come on. That doesn't look anything like a mouth at all"). In other cases, though, nonbelievers can recognize the similarity and might even have noticed it on their own ("Look at the bole of that tree; doesn't that look like Jesus?"). In these cases, there is a sense in which the nonbeliever sees the same thing as the believer and a sense in which she or he doesn't. Both see a natural object that resembles Jesus. The believer sees it as a sign from God, the nonbeliever as an accident of nature.

Because there is a sense in which both see the same thing, some philosophers will argue that this is not really a case in which our beliefs determine what we see. Rather, it's a case in which the beliefs determine how we interpret what we see. On the other hand, there is a sense in which all normal perception is "interpretive." Normally, we don't experience the world as a boom and buzz of colors, shapes, sounds, odors, and so on. We experience it as a collection of things and events. For example, we *see* someone paying for an apple at a grocery store. We see this because we have the concepts of money, grocery store, etc. In normal perception, our brain applies those concepts to the information it receives from our senses and presents that "finished product" to us in consciousness. We experience – or directly perceive – the person paying for the apple. We don't consciously make an inference that that is happening based on the colors, shapes, and sounds we hear and see. Arguably, one could say the same about the image of Jesus in the tree bole.

That is, one could say that the believer may experience it directly as a sign from God. For our present purposes, it doesn't much matter on which side of this philosophical divide we find ourselves, so we don't need to untangle the complicated web of philosophical issues raised by this controversy. Whatever we decide, the important point is the same. What we believe on the basis of observation – what we believe we have observed – depends on our beliefs and assumptions about the world. This is important, since those observations may turn out to be false. For many centuries, for example, Europeans believed they saw the sun making its daily revolution around the earth each day. During much of the sixteenth and seventeenth centuries, witch hunters believed they saw marks of Satan and signs of demon possession in the actions of those they burned (there were, in fact, detailed diagnostic manuals explaining what to look for).

In sum, although many of us tend to take what we see at face value – seeing is believing – there are often good reasons to doubt what we see. We may be fooled by perceptual illusions and our tendency to impose order on sketchy and ambiguous perceptual data (periodolia). We may be misled by suggestion and by what we expect to see. And what we see – or think we see – may be determined by beliefs and assumptions about the world that turn out to be false. In many cases, believing is also seeing.

Memory

Many of our most important beliefs are based on memory. We rely mostly on memory for our pictures of what our childhoods were like, what our parents were like, what our first fumbling romances were like, where our marriages went wrong, and the rest. As this suggests, our knowledge of ourselves – our version of who we are – depends heavily on what we remember. To the extent that our memories are mistaken, then, the stories we tell ourselves and others about who we are and what we're like are false. The results can be tragic. We may reject what is good for us and repeat past mistakes. We may burden ourselves with misplaced guilt, unwarranted pride, unjustified resentments, and baseless gratitude. We may provide our doctors with false information about past medical symptoms, and our therapists and marriage counselors false information about our psychological history. The problems produced by false memories are social as well as personal. Faulty memories may move us to bear false witness against our neighbors, lovers, parents, and friends in private and public contexts (for example, in court). And, if we are participants in important events, they may distort the historical record (since journalists and historians depend partly on what participants tell them).

Most of us think that our memories of events are more accurate than they are. We tend to think that events are captured and stored in memory the way images are captured and stored on a camera card. Unlike images on a camera card, we realize that some of these memories may be hard to retrieve. Still, we tend to believe that they are *all* recoverable, especially with the help of special techniques like hypnosis. Let's call this the camera analogy (some memory researchers call it "the storehouse view"). Although the camera analogy has been undermined by more than a century of research findings, studies strongly suggest that most educated people continue to accept it. In 1980, Elizabeth Loftus and G. R. Loftus asked a group of subjects which of the following statements best reflected their view of how memory works:

1) Everything we learn is permanently stored in the mind, although sometimes particular details are not accessible. With hypnosis or other special techniques these inaccessible details could eventually be recovered.

2) Some details that we learn may be permanently lost from memory. Such details would not be able to be recovered by hypnosis, or any other special technique because those details are simply no longer there.

The subjects included seventy-five people with graduate training in psychology and ninety-four people from a variety of other backgrounds. Eighty-four percent of the psychologists and sixty-nine percent of the non-psychologists selected the first option.[9] This finding was reproduced in more recent studies. In a 1997 study nearly two-thirds of the persons interviewed (graduate students from a variety of disciplines) agreed that once an event is experienced it is permanently stored in the brain.[10] Despite what certain researchers say, these studies don't prove that people believe our memories are usually *accurate*. Strictly speaking, one could agree with the first statement and still believe that our memories often mislead us (there may be problems in the retrieval process). Nonetheless, the camera analogy seems to capture many people's idea of how memory works. That is why eyewitness testimony is so compelling in the courtroom.

Before we look at the research that undermines the camera analogy it's worth wondering why so many people buy it. It's not supported by experimental evidence or by first-hand experience. Our experience is that memories fade and disappear and that people at the same event often remember key facts differently (as often happens at my family reunions). In addition, it's just wildly implausible. Why in the world should we *assume* that every smile, every cough, every tender touch, every dust mote dancing in a shaft of light, every trampled flower and falling leaf, every kind word, every lame joke is stored somewhere in memory? The story is even weirder if we also assume that what get stored are *accurate* representations of events. As we have seen, perception is *interpretive* and sometimes inaccurate. So the view that memories are accurate pictures of events implies that we sometimes remember something other than what we perceive (for example, that inaccurate perceptions get corrected by the brain before they are stored as memories). In view of all this, how do we explain the appeal of the camera analogy? Since we rely so heavily on our memories for our understanding of ourselves and our world, perhaps the thought that memory may misrepresent events is just too threatening to us. If we can't trust our memories, how can we construct plausible narratives of our lives? Perhaps also the popularity of the camera analogy is another depressing example of our tendency to accept uncritically what most people take for granted.

If I am trying to understand my life or some episode of my life, I need to decide which memories to trust. To believe that a memory of an event is trustworthy, I must believe four things: (1) that I accurately recorded the event; (2) that my memory record of it has not degraded or decayed (the universal condition of storage devices); (3) that I can retrieve that memory without distorting it or changing it (for example, my retrieval is not affected by my current mood or life circumstances); and (4) that I can distinguish between genuine memories of events and pseudo-memories produced by suggestion or imagination. False memories are produced when something goes wrong in at least one of these areas. As we will see, it's pretty clear that something can go wrong in each of them.

If we misperceive something, it is hard to imagine that we record it as it really is. That would mean that our brain some-how has the true picture, which it records in memory, while it produces a false picture in consciousness. Furthermore, not everything we perceive gets recorded. For example, not every-thing in short-term memory gets transferred to long-term memory. In the case of diseased or injured brains, very little may get transferred. But even healthy brains have their prob-lems. For example, every adult American has seen pennies thousands of times. Nickerson and Adams showed their sub-jects fifteen different images of the heads side of a penny and asked them to identify the correct one. The majority of their subjects could not do it.[11] This experiment has been replicated many times.

There are also problems with storage. As we all know, mem-ories fade with time. One could think of this as a problem of retrieval rather than storage; the further in the past the mem-ories are, the harder they are to retrieve. But all information recorded in physical systems degrades with time (including information on CDs, DVDs, and hard drives). So it would be rather amazing if that didn't happen in the brain. In fact, we know it happens. Memories are lost as a result of brain injuries, brain lesions, brain plaque, and so on. All physical systems break down (entropy) and the information that they store may be lost as a consequence. There are also obvious problems with retrieval. These are evident every time we have difficulty remembering something that we later remember.

It is often hard to distinguish in practice between problems of storage (decay, degradation) and problems of retrieval. Most memory research involves asking people to remember something and later testing them on what they remember. This strategy helps us to discover the conditions under which false memories are generated. But it does not tell us how, that is, where in the process, false memories arise (bad storage or retrieval problems). In a typical study, for example, subjects were asked to remember a series of sentences on which they were later to be tested. The test consisted of a second series of sentences that they were supposed to identify as either new (that is, not part of the original list) or old (that is, part of the original list). Many subjects identified as old sentences that were *implied* by the original sentences and sentences that combined ideas contained in the original sentences (even though they were not on the original list).[12] In a related experiment, subjects were asked to memorize a list of words related to sleep ("bed," "rest," "tired," "night," "doze," etc.). The word "sleep" did not appear on the list but when the subjects were later tested they identified it as "old" as often as they correctly identified items that had actually appeared on the list.[13] Are these problems of recording, storage, or retrieval? Without a better understanding of how the brain works, we can only speculate.

For our purposes, though, it really doesn't matter where in the process memory fails. What concerns us are the conditions under which it fails; that is, the kinds of causes *outside* the brain that produce memory failure. These are the kinds of conditions we can guard against in our personal lives and in the organization of our knowledge-seeking communities.

That our memories of events are sometimes false is obvious to us all. We've all experienced cases where two witnesses have conflicting memories of the same events (e.g. in marital arguments). Still, we are often convinced that our vivid and detailed memories of important events must be true. Unfortunately, the research says otherwise. For many years memory researcher

Ulric Neisser had a clear picture of where he was when Pearl Harbor was attacked. He was at home in bed listening to a radio broadcast of a major league baseball game which was dramatically interrupted by an emergency news report. He told that story many times; that is, until it finally dawned on him that there is no major league baseball in December. Many years later Neisser and his collaborator Harsch tried to discover how common false memories of memorable events are. One day after the *Challenger* disaster, they asked a group of people how they learned of the event. They asked the same people the same question three years later. In almost every case, there were differences. In a third of the cases, there were very big differences. But in all cases, the people they interviewed were just as confident in their three-year-old "memory" as they were in their memory one day after the event.[14]

As this illustrates, our memories of an event can be influenced by what happens *after* the event itself. Some of these post-event influences have been extensively studied. Among the most important of these is post-event information. In one well-known experiment, Elizabeth Loftus showed subjects a videotape of an automobile accident. The accident occurred at an intersection with a stop sign. Subjects later read a narrative of the accident that identified the sign as a yield sign. When asked later what they remembered from the videotape, many subjects reported remembering a yield sign. According to Loftus "hundreds of studies have been published documenting memory distortion induced by exposure to [later] misinformation." Loftus calls this the "misinformation effect."[15] In another experiment, paired subjects each watched a different video of a theft, under the mistaken impression that they were watching the same video. In fact, the two videos were filmed from slightly different angles such that some details in the first were not visible in the second (for example, the woman actually stealing the money). The subjects were asked to discuss what they saw before they were tested on their memories. The majority of these subjects (seventy-one percent) reported remembering things they could not have remembered from the videos they had watched but must have learned from the discussion with their partner.[16] Some researchers have questioned these results, suggesting that subjects in these experiments remember correctly but do not trust their memories as much as they trust the post-event information (e.g. in the written narratives). But the subjects in these experiments were asked to remember what they *saw*, not to report what they believed to be true, and they had nothing to gain by misrepresentation.

Post-event information also affects our memory of information. In one experiment, subjects read a fictional passage about a fictional dictator called Gerald Martin. Later some of them were told that the passage was actually about Adolf Hitler. When later tested on the passage, these subjects mistakenly identified a number of sentences that were true of Hitler as part of the narrative (e.g. that Gerald Martin persecuted Jews).[17] Their memory of the narrative was influenced by post-event information. Similar results were achieved in another well-known study. Subjects read a passage about a woman called Betty K. which included information about Betty's social life. After reading the narrative, half the subjects were told that Betty was now a lesbian and the other half were told that she was now heterosexual. In a multiple-choice recall test a week later, subjects told that she was a lesbian made errors consistent with their assumptions about lesbians (for example, that she never dated men in high school).[18]

Our present circumstances or point of view can also influence our memory of our past. In some cases, at least, we have a tendency to remember the past as more like the present than it actually was. In one study, for example, G. B. Marcus found that people remembered the political attitudes they held nine years ago as closer to their current attitudes than they actually were.[19] Still another study suggests that this can happen over a much shorter time span.[20] In this one, high school students were subjected to a process intended to change their position on the use of school bussing to combat de facto segregation. Within two weeks of completing that process, they were asked to recall their earlier attitudes. That recall was, on average, highly distorted. Again, students tended to believe that their old views were much closer to their new views than they actually were. (Since researchers reminded them that their older views were on record, they were not just trying to seem less foolish.)

This same tendency to minimize the distance between the past and the present also occurs in medical contexts and in personal contexts. In one study doctors interviewed chronic headache patients in a pain management program about the intensity of their past pain. Patients suffering from intense pain at the time of the interview tended to overestimate their past pain (which had been recorded); patients suffering from only mild pain at the time of the interview tended to underestimate it.[21] Another study found that people's retrospective reports of tobacco, marijuana, and alcohol use were heavily influenced by their use levels at the time of the interview.[22] Still another found that our current attitudes about dating partners and significant others influence our memories. In one study researchers had subjects record their impressions of their dating partners at the beginning and the end of a two-month interval. Subjects whose impressions became more favorable over time remembered their initial evaluations as more positive than they originally reported them to be. Subjects whose impressions became less positive recalled more negative evaluations.[23] Similarly, men whose attitudes toward their wives had become more negative over time remembered early interactions with their wives as less positive than they initially reported them to be.[24]

These studies suggest that our current emotional states, attitudes, and physical conditions can affect our memories of the past. In addition, our memories are (in some contexts) influenced by our beliefs. In one experiment subjects with known views on nuclear power read a narrative about a fire at a nuclear power plant. After a week or two they were tested on what they'd read. In addition to statements taken from the narrative, the test contained pro- and anti-nuclear-power distortions. Subjects were asked both whether these statements were consistent with the original narrative and how confident they were of that. Subjects from both groups were often confident that the distorted facts were consistent with the narrative.[25]

Finally, it perhaps goes without saying that what we remember about the past depends on our mood. When we are depressed, we tend to remember depressing things. When we are angry at someone, we tend to remember a litany of bad things about them (all the other ways they betrayed or exploited us). When we are happy or in love, on the other hand, our memories are sunnier. These obvious facts, by themselves, should make it clear that we remember the past from the point of view of the present.

Up to now we have been discussing how post-event happenings can affect memories of events that actually happened. As it turns out, we also have memories (or pseudo-memories) of events that never occurred. These "memories" can be implanted by suggestion. The most powerful form of suggestion is hypnosis. During the 1980s hypnosis was frequently used by psychotherapists to "recover" memories of traumatic events. In one such case, a Missouri woman named Beth Rutherford "recovered" memories that her father, a clergyman, regularly raped her from the age of seven to fourteen, sometimes with the help of her mother. She remembered twice becoming pregnant as a result and being forced to abort the fetus herself with a coat hanger (these accusations became public and her father was forced to resign his position). Later medical examinations revealed that the woman had never been pregnant and, in fact, that she was still a virgin at twenty-two (she sued her therapist and won a million-dollar settlement in 1996).[26] Of course, these kinds of cases do not prove that recovered memories are *never* accurate. But, together with the research on the role of suggestion in memory, they persuaded key professional organizations in North America and Europe to issue position papers concluding that recovered memories are often pseudo-memories created by suggestion.[27] We will discuss this in some detail in Chapter 3. It is worth noting that people under hypnosis also recover "memories" of alien abductions and past lives.

Memories may also be implanted by less powerful forms of suggestion. Sometimes just reading or hearing about an event is enough. In one study, subjects were presented with descriptions of four events from their childhood, three accurate and one fictional (being lost in a shopping mall as a small child and found by a stranger). In three separate interviews, experimenters asked their subjects how much detail they could remember about these events. At the end of the first interview, seven of the twenty-four subjects claimed wholly or partly to remember the fictional event. In the two later interviews the number dropped to six.[28] Other studies also demonstrate the power of suggestion to create memories.[29] Not surprisingly, this tendency seems particularly strong in children. In one study suggestions made by researchers led children to report events that had not occurred during a medical examination (for example, that the doctor looked in their ears).[30] In a related study, children's reports were influenced by questions like "How many times did the doctor kiss you?"[31] (It's possible that these children were not reporting what they remembered but rather what they thought the researcher wanted to hear.)

Studies indicate that we can confuse events that actually occurred with events we have only imagined. In one experiment, for example, subjects had a difficult time distinguishing between words spoken by the experimenter and words they were asked to imagine the experimenter speaking. In another, experimenters read subjects a list of actions. The subjects were told to perform some of them, imagine some of them, and do nothing in relation to the others. In a second session they were asked just to imagine actions they had not performed. In the final session they were asked which actions they had performed in the first session. Some subjects named actions they had only imagined. It's not entirely clear exactly what implications studies like these have for memory outside the laboratory. But they do show that we cannot always tell the difference between what we remember and what we imagine.[32]

It's also hard sometimes for us to distinguish between what we remember and what we infer. We have already seen examples of that with respect to information (the word list experiments). It also happens in relation to events. Perhaps for this reason, one memory researcher has written that memories of events are less like pictures than they are like a book written from fragmentary notes. According to researcher Norbert Schwartz, when we report the frequency of past symptoms to doctors we do not relive them in memory (imagine what that

would be like). Although it seems to us that we are remembering, we are really making estimates based on what seems to
make sense at the time. According to Schwartz, "retrospective
frequency reports are fraught with uncertainty. In particular
when the behavior is frequent, mundane and irregular, respondents can only arrive at a frequency report by relying on an esti-
mation strategy. Unfortunately, many of the behaviors that
health researchers are interested in fit these characteristics."
When we are reporting past symptoms to our physicians we
need to keep this in mind (and perhaps remind our doctors
as well).[33]

All of these forms of distortion should give us pause when
we construct our versions of the past. The good news is that
experimental results show strong individual variations. So
some people's memories of the past are more accurate than
others. This is common sense. Some people mythologize their
past, populating it with heroes, villains, and epic struggles and
become greatly exercised when their versions of the events are
challenged. Others tend to be deflationary or aggressively
matter of fact, to speak soberly and suck all the drama out of
life. If we are seriously interested in understanding ourselves,
we need to have some idea of our own tendencies. One way to
do this is to keep a journal and compare our later memories of
events to what we recorded there. That way we can get a better
sense of our own personal tendencies to rewrite the past as well
as the distance between our past and present selves.

Of course, we should be interested in memory not only
because we are each the star of our own movie, endlessly fasci-
nated with ourselves, and eager not to repeat past mistakes.
There are also public contexts in which the accuracy of memory
is of great concern. One example of this is the criminal justice
system. The most compelling courtroom evidence tends to be

eyewitness testimony. It is now clear that a lot of eyewitness identifications are false. The Innocence Project, an American organization that works to free innocent people convicted of serious crimes, has freed 192 people in fifteen years. Most of them were convicted of rapes and murders and exonerated on the basis of D.N.A. evidence. About seventy-seven percent of them were convicted wholly or partly on the basis of eyewitness testimony. Other wrongly convicted people have been exonerated by the work of private attorneys or the confessions of the guilty parties. Did the eyewitnesses who helped bring about these convictions lie under oath? Well, maybe a few. But psychologists have been studying eyewitness testimony for close to a century and the consensus is clear: regardless of the sincerity and the confidence of eyewitnesses, their testimony is unreliable in many cases.

Part of the problem is rooted in perception. Social psychologists who stage fake crimes in the classroom discover considerable variations in how their students describe the perpetrator (their height, weight, clothing, etc.). Since these descriptions occur very close to the time of the staged event, the variations are probably not the result of memory problems (although one can't rule out that possibility completely).

But many problems with eyewitness testimony are rooted in memory. A lot of time elapses between a crime and a criminal trial. Often witnesses are asked to swear that someone they'd seen briefly just one time, more than a year before, is the person sitting at the defendant's table. There is plenty of time here for post-event happenings to affect memory (for example, newspaper stories about the suspect). Typically, eyewitnesses make their initial identification by picking the defendant out of a lineup or from a book of mugshots. Little is done in these sessions to protect against the power of suggestion (even pressure). These sessions are conducted by police officers investigating the crime. These officers know which person in the lineup is the suspect (or which mugshot is the suspect's, if they already have a suspect when they display the mugshots). Often, they were the ones who arrested and interrogated the suspect, and they are convinced (or hopeful) that they have the right person. Accordingly, they may very much want the witness to identify that person. In some documented cases, the police have purposely arranged the lineup or the array of mugshots so that the suspect stands out. Even when they don't do this intentionally, they may stack the deck against the suspect without being aware of it. And even when the lineup or mugshot array is fair, the officers may intentionally or unintentionally reveal who the suspect is (tone of voice, facial expression, body language, etc.). These suggestions may influence what the witness remembers. And once the witness has identified the suspect the witness has a stake in the correctness of that identification. For these reasons, some memory researchers have argued that lineups should be conducted by people who don't know who the suspect is. In fact, to protect witnesses from police pressure to make an identification (even when they are unsure) some researchers have argued that lineups should not be conducted by the police at all. Instead, they should be contracted out to people familiar with the psychological literature on memory and perception.

Reflections

Perception and memory are less reliable than most people assume. When we organize ourselves collectively to pursue knowledge, we need to guard against the ways they mislead us.

The sciences do this by relying on instrument readings rather than sensory observation reports whenever possible. When they can't rely on instruments, they typically require observations by many people. But when it comes to filtering out unreliable data, this is just a partial solution. As we have seen, there is a sense in which what we observe depends on what we believe. In particular, it depends on the concepts we use to understand the world. Many Knowledge Machines, especially in the sciences, have their own sets of concepts – their own vocabularies – and will accept observations as data only if they are described in that vocabulary. Because European and American biologists, physiologists, and doctors don't include chi energy among their concepts, they don't accept observation reports from acupuncture patients and practitioners of t'ai chi and chi qong about the movement of chi energy in their bodies (which is something the patients and practitioners say they feel).

We do roughly the same thing as individuals. We each have our own set of concepts – our own vocabulary – for describing what is, and we don't take observation reports seriously if they fall outside that vocabulary. If we don't believe in ghosts or spirits, for example, we don't take reports of alleged sightings of ghosts and spirits at face value. If we don't believe in demonic possession, we don't believe people who claim to see evil shining in the eyes of someone ranting on a street corner. Overall, the research on perception and memory makes it easier for skeptics of religion, the occult, and the paranormal to discount observation reports intended to support such beliefs. Skeptics can always explain these away as the effects of suggestion, expectancy, periodolia, hallucination, and outright fraud. After all, stage magicians make their living by creating illusions that appear to violate the laws of nature. They can get us to "see" all kinds of things to which believers in miracles, the occult, and the paranormal appeal to justify their beliefs. Again, this doesn't prove that observations of spoon bending, ghosts, weeping Madonnas, and the like are always false or faked. Stage magicians can also create the illusion of doing amazing things that people can actually do. But the fact they can create convincing illusions of violating the laws of nature does weaken the force of "I know it's true because I saw it with my own eyes."

Some skeptics argue that this means it's always irrational to trust such observations. But matters are more complicated than that. After all, one could dismiss any observation of something that doesn't fit into one's worldview by attributing it to suggestion, expectancy, or outright fraud that exploits perceptual illusion. Consider the case of Alex, the African grey parrot. Alex not only mimicked human speech; he understood the meanings of many words for objects, shapes, colors, and numbers. He could also understand and make requests. Since almost no biologists believed a bird brain capable of this, it took many years for his trainer – Irene Pepperberg – to convince the scientific community of this. Many people had to see Alex in action and elaborate measures had to be taken to eliminate alternative explanations of Alex's apparent abilities. At what stage in this process was it reasonable for one to trust what one observed, viz. a genuine talking parrot? Suppose that instead of being a scientist with respectable credentials, Irene Pepperberg had been your slightly ditzy next-door neighbor. And suppose she invited you in to show you what Alex could do. Would it have been unreasonable for you to believe what you observed (or thought you observed)? The point is that the same arguments used to undermine observation reports of ghosts, demons, stigmata, and alien spaceships can be used against observations of anything that is radically surprising, i.e. anything that conflicts with our ideas of how the world works and what is possible. To reject all such observations because they might be attributable to fakery and/or perceptual illusion seems dogmatic.

The questions about memory raised in this chapter have less to do with big metaphysical and worldview issues and more to do with our personal and social lives. Our tendency to see our past selves as more like our present selves than they were, and to otherwise minimize the gap between our present and our past, interferes with our efforts to understand the arc of our lives. It also impedes our ability to provide accurate information about past symptoms to our doctors, and past relationships to our new loves or therapists. If we want accurate autobiographical memories we need to keep journals. Even then, of course, our entries are only as accurate as our perceptions and interpretations of each day's events, which will inevitably be colored by our moods and emotions (among other things). It may be that our autobiographical tales reveal at least as much about who we are and what we want in the present as they reveal about who we were in the past.

The problems with memory we've discussed also suggest how hard it often is to reach an accurate version of the past when our memories conflict. This can be a big problem. The need for agreement can be strong. People with grievances often need others to acknowledge what they've done before they can forgive them. But in many cases personal conflicts and grievances are rooted in conflicting memories about matters like who said what to whom, when, and in what tone of voice. Often, we act as if the first step in addressing *these* grievances is achieving a shared version of the past. And often the result is a struggle in which each tries to make their own version the official story. Since there is typically no independent evidence in these cases, there is typically no way to arrive at the truth. This means that any agreement is either imposed or accepted just to make peace. Usually, this does not dispel resentments. They just go underground. (Where there is documentary or other independent evidence, the situation is more complicated.)

These facts about memory make life more difficult for those historians and biographers who rely on interviews, memoirs, and the like to reconstruct the past – especially those conducted or written long after the event in question. The further we are from an event, the more room there is for post-event information and happenings to affect our memory of it. Such memories can't be accepted at face value. To whatever extent possible, they must be compared with other evidence (for example, quotations, letters, and other writings from the person in question and from others). Those quotations and letters, of course, may also post-date the event in question. Even if they don't, they represent one person's version of things. Historians and biographers pepper their accounts with quotations, letters, and other writings that support their own interpretation of the past. We readers of history and biography can only guess how representative those documents are, and what documents historians leave out.

CHAPTER 2

What We Think We
Know about Thinking

When I was a student I was often told that human beings are distinct from other animals because we think and they don't. But a large body of research on animal cognition has shattered this conceit. This same research has moved some to ask what thinking really is. That question has no correct answer. The English word "thinking" has many different uses and meanings. If we are studying thinking, we may want to pick one of these and make it more precise for the purposes of delimiting our subject matter. But when we do that we are trying to formulate the definition that best helps get us where we want to go. We are not trying to discover what thinking really is (the essence of thinking).

This chapter examines some important ways in which thinking goes awry. For that purpose, it's better to begin not with a definition, but rather with a list of the kinds of activities we wonder about when we wonder about how well we think. In no particular order, these include classifying, inferring, explaining, calculating, estimating, interpreting, appraising, representing, organizing, comparing, verifying and falsifying hypotheses, and updating beliefs in relation to new data, among others. All of these activities help produce our pictures of the world. A general theory about thinking that tells us how it goes awry must consider them all. Such a theory would also explore the relationship between these activities and almost certainly end up treating some of them as special cases or combinations of others (thereby greatly reducing the number of categories). After that, we might come up with a useful definition of thinking that expressed what all those activities have in common.

But don't expect a general theory of thinking anytime soon. Sadly, we don't know nearly enough about these activities to make much headway there. The research on them is far too scant, narrowly focused, and unsystematic. It focuses on only some of those activities – or certain aspects of them – and ignores the rest. The emergence of cognitive psychology will almost certainly improve our prospects, but the field is still young. Still, researchers have produced some very interesting and important work on certain aspects of thinking, and we will discuss those in this chapter. In particular we will discuss work on estimating probabilities, updating beliefs in response to new evidence, and verifying and falsifying hypotheses. We will also discuss some gaps and questionable research results. In particular, we will look at work on thinking that is not directed at seeking truth but rather at reaching particular conclusions and work on the relationship between thinking and feeling.

Before we get to this research, though, I need to say something about the relationship between conscious and nonconscious thinking. As all psychologists now agree, most of our thinking is not conscious. That is obvious when we make split-second decisions, for example, on the basketball or tennis court. We don't say to ourself, "Given that the ball will cross the net at a seventy-degree angle, traveling about sixty miles an hour, and turning with a top spin of six rotations a second, I need to move three feet behind the baseline." We just move. And if we are good, we move intelligently. The processing that makes this possible happens outside consciousness.

In fact, non-conscious processing is pervasive. For example, it governs every social interaction. You say something, and I immediately respond. My response is based on how I read you; whether I think you're joking or sincere, hurt or amused, defensive or open-hearted, suspicious or trusting, comfortable or insecure, deceitful or truthful, and so on. And my impressions of your state of mind (motives and intentions) is based on the content of what you say, your tone of voice, your facial expression, your body language, my assumptions about your psychology, and so on. But I don't arrive at these impressions consciously. That is, I don't say to myself, "Her gaze is lowered, therefore . . ." or "Her voice is pitched higher than usual, therefore . . ." I process this and other information outside consciousness. This processing also generates my response. For example, I don't say to myself, "Well, she's being defensive and I want to put her at ease. Given what I know about her, a good joke should do it. But I'd better be careful because she's also a little touchy about these things. Let's see . . ." No, I process all this non-consciously in a split second and make my joke. If my background beliefs and assumptions are true, I usually succeed.

In fact, non-conscious processing goes on even when we are thinking consciously. We speak and write in grammatical sentences without consciously consulting the rules of grammar (the way an adult just learning a language might). When we write a good paragraph or tell a good story, our sentences follow each other in an orderly, purposeful way. But we don't usually plan or consider their relationship to each other. For example, while we are in the midst of excitedly entertaining our friends with an amusing anecdote we rarely say things to ourselves like, "I think I need to build a little more suspense in the next sentence. Maybe if I . . ." In fact, as we learned in Chapter 1, non-conscious processing makes conscious experience what it is. What we see and how we interpret what we see, for example, are affected by our interests, hopes, desires, expectations, and background beliefs about the world. And that all happens outside consciousness as well.

The upshot is that any complete theory of reliable thinking will tell us when to trust and distrust our non-conscious processes. We are a long way from such a theory now. But this much is clear. Non-conscious processing is, to a significant extent, based on our background beliefs and theories about the world, and can be only as accurate as they are (again, except in the rare and fortunate cases our mistakes cancel each other out). The best strategy we have for improving non-conscious processes, then, is to make those beliefs as accurate as we can and to train ourselves to "activate" them in our non-conscious thinking. In some cases, it is reasonably easy to identify those beliefs. In other cases, it isn't. In both, though, the real test of our non-conscious processing in various areas is our track record.

This take on non-conscious thinking runs counter to some recent popular thinking on the subject, most notably Malcolm Gladwell's thesis in *Blink: The Power of Thinking without Thinking*.[1] Gladwell argues that in many cases non-conscious thinking is better than conscious thinking. As we've just seen, though, this sharp contrast between conscious and non-conscious thinking is an oversimplification, since even conscious thinking rests on non-conscious processes. Still, what really interests Gladwell is the difference between snap judgments and intuitive thinking, on the one hand, and conscious evaluation of data and arguments, on the other. In particular, he wants to know when should we trust one and when should we trust the other. Although his title and many of his comments enthusiastically endorse intuitive thinking and snap judgments, he spends a lot of time discussing cases in which they go wrong. For the most part, though, he treats intuitive thinking and snap judgments as if they work perfectly well unless they are misused or interfered with in some way. They are misused when we use them "out of context" (he never explains this idea). They are interfered with when we are distracted or misled by our "emotions, or interests, or sentiments."

Gladwell's celebration of intuitive thinking rests heavily on cases studies and examples. But almost all of his examples involve extraordinary people with extraordinary abilities. These include John Gottman, who can tell whether couples will stay together by listening to small snippets of their conversations (about relationship issues), and John Ekman, who can see behind our social masks, identify what we are really feeling, and tell with amazing accuracy whether we are lying. But, clearly, the successes of such people are not evidence of the power of intuitive thinking *in general*. Gottman, Ekman, and the other people Gladwell discusses can do something the rest of us can't. *Our* intuitions in these cases are either absent or unreliable. Of course, we can improve. But the explanation of how we improve is consistent with my account, not Gladwell's.

Gladwell thinks Gottman, Ekman, and others succeed because they do what he calls "thin-slicing;" that is, they can reach conclusions almost instantly (in a blink) with very little exposure to data. He is right about this. That is exactly what they do. But Gladwell doesn't understand why thin-slicing works. There is nothing magical or mysterious about it. It's a matter of knowing how the relevant part of the world works, and training ourselves to activate that knowledge. We can do this because the world is orderly. Roughly speaking, this is because events have causes. More accurately it is because some properties or events in the world are very highly correlated with and there-fore highly reliable indicators of others. When we spot these indicator events, we know immediately that the events they indicate are either there or will be there. We can thin-slice when we know which events are indicators of what other events, and we can detect those indicator events; that is, when we know and can attend to what really matters. John Gottman can predict whether couples will stay together because he knows what to look for in their conversations (defensiveness, stonewalling, criticism, and, most important of all, contempt). After years of research and analysis, he discovered that these were the indica-tors of marital failure, and he trained himself to spot them. John Ekman can read faces and detect liars for the same reason. After painstaking analyses of videotapes and the like, Ekman and his coworker Wallace Friesen discovered the specific involuntary muscle contractions involved in genuine expressions of emo-tion and trained themselves to notice them (despite the fact that they are often highly fleeting). In fact, once we know how Gottman, Ekman, and others do what they do, there is some-thing strained about saying that they make snap judgments or rely on intuitions. They rely on knowledge and training. If we have that, our "intuitions" will be good. If we lack it, our intu-itions will be unreliable or just plain absent.

Although both Ekman and Gottman have explicit and artic-ulate knowledge of what matters in most cases of successful intuitive thinking, we don't. Tennis coach Vic Braden, for example, can predict whether a server will double-fault just before his or her racquet contacts the ball. Braden doesn't have any idea how he knows this. He just knows it. But this too is a matter of having the right background beliefs. Braden is responding to indicator events. He is attuned to what matters. This knowledge can be made explicit, and Braden is, in fact, trying to do that. With the help of experts in biomechanics, he carefully analyzes videos and films of tennis players, trying to identify the feature of the world to which he is already responding. There is no reason to think he can't succeed. Like all extraordinary abilities, Braden's talent is amazing. But really it's no different in kind from what the rest of us do. We all have and activate knowledge that we can't articulate. We can tell that a sentence is ungrammatical by hearing it, without being about to cite the rule of grammar it violates. We can say funny things without being able to explain how (or even why) they are funny. We can ride bicycles without being about to say how we keep our balance.

Because successful intuitive responses depend on accurate background beliefs and theories, much of the answer to Gladwell's question is clear. We can trust our intuitive judgments when they are *based on* accurate background beliefs and theories. Usually, we are not consciously aware of those beliefs and theories. In the overwhelming majority of cases, we acquire them "automatically," that is, without special effort or training. As young children, for example, we absorb the rules of our native language, and learn to read social situations primarily by exposure. In these and most other cases, we are rarely able to articulate what we know. The accuracy or inaccuracy of our background beliefs and theories is measured by how often our intuitive judgments succeed and fail. If we notice that they fail too often, we try to replace them with accurate beliefs and theories that we learn to activate. If we have trouble speaking or writing grammatically, for example, we may need to learn the rules of grammar explicitly, and train ourselves to use them. In addition, like Gottman and Ekman, we may make explicit discoveries about the world which enable us to improve our judgment, or to thin-slice in new ways. Often we can train ourselves (or be trained) to internalize this new knowledge so that it is activated non-consciously. Ekman, for example, has developed a successful training tape and Gottman has taught others to hear what he hears.

Sometimes there is a disconnect between our explicit, conscious beliefs and the background beliefs and theories that generate our "blink" responses. That is, what we say we believe, and how we immediately and intuitively understand the world may be two different things (psychotherapists see a lot of this). When we become aware of this, we need to decide which of the conflicting beliefs are more accurate. It's not always the conscious ones (for example, our official stories about our lives are not always true). But when the conscious ones are more accurate, we should, of course, try to activate them. This isn't always easy or even possible, but psychologists do have techniques that are successful in some cases. For example, they are good at reducing or eliminating certain phobias with the help of hypnosis and desentization techniques (e.g. fear of flying). Since the client generally realizes the phobia is irrational, the therapist is helping him or her to internalize and activate what he or she consciously believes to be true (e.g. that flying is safer than driving).

In the end, though, the proof of the pudding is in the eating. The accuracy of our non-conscious beliefs and theories in an area is measured by how often we get things right. To judge the accuracy of our intuitive responses, we have to rely on our track record. Sometimes we have enough information to do this (for example, we may have a reasonably good idea of how well we can spot ungrammatical sentences). But often we don't. Since most of us don't keep records of our intuitive hits and misses in various areas of our lives, we must rely on our memories, and our memories may not be accurate. In fact, as discussion later in this chapter suggests, we can easily be fooled about our abilities in this and other areas (which is why pool hustlers and professional poker players make a living). The problem of getting accurate assessment of our abilities is also complicated by the fact that (as Gladwell says) our intuitive responses may be distorted at times by our emotions and interests. As we will see later in this chapter, they may go wrong in other ways as well. The background beliefs and theories that normally direct our non-conscious processing may be deactivated or replaced by others. What normally seems non-threatening, for example, may seem very threatening to someone when he panics. As our knowledge of the brain increases, we will have a better understanding of how all this works.

We are now almost ready to get to the research on thinking. Before we do, I want to briefly explain why this chapter includes no discussion of formal logic or informal logic. I taught formal logic for many years, and I think it's a wonderful intellectual achievement. I also think people who study it seriously do improve their ability to think systematically and that they become more sensitive to certain important nuances and distinctions. But, as with playing the piano, those benefits come from hard work and practice. Learning the rules of formal logic is not by itself particularly helpful. You have to do the exercises. In addition, a little formal logic can be a dangerous thing.[2]

During the last fifty years or so universities in the U.S. have been under increasing pressure to offer courses that improve critical thinking skills. Because they recognized that formal logic classes are not very effective at this, philosophy departments tried to meet this demand by offering classes in informal logic. Informal logic helps us evaluate one kind of thinking, viz. the kind that occurs in arguments in natural languages. But there is no standard format or set of techniques for doing this. Most books on informal logic do it by trying to help students identify what are called "informal fallacies." But there is no one agreed list of informal fallacies, and there is no set of methods or rules for identifying them. Also, there is no indication at all how often we are taken in by which of them.

The list of informal fallacies can be daunting. Some informal logic books list thirty to forty of them (usually under five or six major categories). The "List of Fallacies" in *Wikipedia* includes nearly fifty. Most of the items on these lists are already familiar to us (though not under their fancy Latin names, which often begin "argumentum ad . . ."). They include illegitimate appeals to authority ("It's true because I'm your father and I said so"), appeals to power ("It's true because I've got a gun and I'll kill you if you disagree"), various kinds of appeals to emotion ("That can't be true. It's just too sad"), and even (on at least one list) the fallacy of dealing with an opposing argument by making a joke (a fallacy of distraction, if you will). Accompanied by many clever exercises, exposure to lists of informal fallacies may sensitize some readers to certain sleazy rhetorical tricks of politicians, public relations people, advertisers, and others (I say "may" because I'm mildly skeptical having taught informal logic twice). But simply reading over these lists is not going to help anyone. Again it's like playing the piano. You need to practice your scales. If you want to do that, you have many books on informal logic from which to choose. Since the differences between them are largely pedagogic, my advice is to find one written in a style that works best for you.

I now turn to the research on thinking.

Estimating Probabilities: Ignoring Base Rates

In the 1970s Amos Tversky and Daniel Kahneman started a hugely influential research program on mistakes we make when we estimate probabilities. They found that, instead of calculating probabilities the way scientists and statisticians do, most of us employ shortcuts or rules of thumb they call "heuristics." We don't consciously employ these heuristics but they shape our thinking much as the rules of grammar shape our speech (also generally without our conscious awareness). Often, these heuristics serve us well. But often they don't.

Tversky and Kahneman describe three broad categories of heuristics: representativeness, availability, and anchoring.[3] Roughly, we use the representativeness heuristic when we base our judgments of the likelihood of A, given B, on how closely A resembles B in our mind. For example, on the basis of a certain description we might judge that someone is more likely to be the first violinist of a major orchestra than a high school math teacher because that description better fits our image of a first violinist (despite the fact that there are tens of thousands of times more high school math teachers than there are first violinists). Some critics complain that Tversky and Kahneman's definition of representativeness is too vague, and I agree. But one of the tendencies they take to be an instance of it is surprising and important. That is our tendency to ignore base rates. Roughly, the base rate of an event or phenomenon is the frequency with which it occurs. For example, the base rate of breast cancer among women with suspicious mammograms is the percentage of women with suspicious mammograms who have breast cancer. As we will see, because they ignore base rates, doctors often misunderstand the results of the tests they order and misinform patients of the likelihood that they have the disease for which they were tested. Often doctors are off by a factor of ten.

Tversky and Kahneman argue that, instead of estimating probabilities by consulting base rates, we estimate them on the basis of how well they match some stereotype. In one famous experiment they gave two groups several brief personality descriptions and asked them to decide whether the person described was a lawyer or an engineer. They told one group that the descriptions were randomly drawn from a group that consisted of seventy lawyers and thirty engineers. They told the other the opposite (seventy engineers and thirty lawyers). Both groups made essentially the same selections. They were not influenced by base rates at all. In a related experiment, Tversky and Kahneman asked their two groups to decide whether someone who fitted the following completely undiagnostic description was a lawyer or an engineer: "Dick is a thirty year old man. He is married with no children. A man of high ability and high motivation, he promises to be quite successful in his field. He is well liked by his colleagues." Again, one group was told the description was randomly drawn from a group of seventy lawyers and thirty engineers and the other was told the opposite. In this case, both groups decided that the probability of his being an engineer or a lawyer was fifty percent. Apparently, because the description was neutral between stereotypes, they treated the choice as a flip of the coin and completely ignored base rates.[4]

The tendency to ignore base rates has been repeatedly demonstrated in many practical contexts.[5] Although Tversky and Kahneman's explanation of that tendency is not convincing in all these cases, there is no doubt that the tendency itself exists and that it is responsible for errors that seriously affect our lives. Let's return to the shocking example of medical diagnosis. Suppose you are tested for a rare cancer and the results are positive. Your doctor tells you that the test is ninety percent accurate. What are the chances that you have that disease? You might think, well, ninety percent. But in fact it's impossible to tell from the information given. To begin with, tests like this don't have a single measure of accuracy. They have two measures. People who have the disease can test negative (false negatives) and people who don't have the disease can test positive (false positives). So the unqualified statement that the test is ninety percent accurate doesn't give us enough information to make a judgment.

But neither does just knowing the rate of false positives and false negatives. Suppose that ninety percent of people who have the disease test positive and that ninety percent of the people who don't have it test negative (i.e. there are ten percent false positives and ten percent false negatives). Now what are the chances that you have the disease? As studies show, most people (including most doctors) think they can answer this question. But the truth is that you can't. You still don't have enough information (I'll explain in a moment). As a result most people and most doctors get the wrong answer (as studies also establish).[6] And that means that most doctors cannot accurately tell you the chances that you have a disease based on test results. It's not really the doctors' fault. Again, we all have a strong tendency to ignore base rates. What is astonishing is that medical schools don't teach medical students how to guard against this tendency. Since diagnosing diseases is so central to medical practice, this is disgraceful.

To calculate the chances that you have a disease, you need to know what percentage of people in the population with your symptoms have that disease. That percentage is the base rate. If we assume that a representative sample of the population with your symptoms gets tested for the disease, the base rate is the percentage of people who have been tested who have the disease. If ten thousand people have been tested and two hundred of them have the disease, the base rate is two percent. Statisticians calculate the probability you have the disease by plugging the base rate and the percentages of false positives and false negatives into a daunting mathematical formula. But you don't need a complicated formula to calculate the probability. You can do it with common sense and simple arithmetic. Let's say that fifty thousand people are tested for this disease and five hundred of them have it. That's a base rate of one percent. Since the test has ten percent false negatives, ten percent of these five hundred people will test negative (fifty) and ninety percent of these people will test positive (450). *But these aren't the only people who test positive. In fact, they are a small percentage of those people.* Since only five hundred of the fifty thousand people tested have the disease, 49,500 of them don't have it. How many of these will test positive? Well, since the test has a ten percent rate of false positives, ten percent of them will – that's 4,950 people. In other words, *for every person who tests positive and has the disease, there are more than ten people who test positive and do not.* So, given this base rate, your chance of having the disease if you test positive is less than ten percent (despite the fact that the test is ninety percent accurate with respect to false positives and false negatives).

Since this is so important, let me explain it in a slightly different, step-by-step way. You can follow this even if you're mathphobic. It's just simple arithmetic. Basically, we're just trying to find out what percentage of people who test positive for the disease have it by comparing the number of people who test positive and have it with the number of people who test positive and don't. Here's how we do it. Step one: learn the base rate (the percentage of people tested who have the disease). Step two: choose a big number that's easy to work with, say ten thousand (it doesn't matter what number you actually choose, since we'll be dealing with percentages or ratios and they'll be the same whatever the number). Step three: given the base rate, calculate how many of those ten thousand people have the disease (if the base rate is two percent, two hundred of them will). Step four: calculate how many of those people – the ones with the disease – will test positive for it (since there are ten percent false negatives, twenty of them will test negative so 180 will test positive). Step five: calculate how many disease-free people also took the test (since two hundred people have the disease, the remaining 9,800 people are disease free). Step six: calculate how many of those disease-free people test positive (since there are ten percent false positives, 980 of them will). Step seven: calculate the total number of people who test positive (add the result of steps four and seven, which comes to 1,160). Finally, step eight: divide the number from step four (the 180 who test positive and have the disease) by the number in step seven (the 1,160 who test positive). That comes to about 15.5%. Of course, you can use this same technique no matter what the base rate are or the rates of false positives and false negatives.

In a poll of doctors conducted by psychologist David Eddy, ninety-five out of one hundred doctors were unable to do this kind of calculation.[7] His test concerned the probability that a woman who tested positive on a mammogram had breast cancer. From the numbers Eddy supplied, most doctors estimated the chances to be around seventy-five percent. The right answer for that population is around seven percent. It's frightening to imagine how many women have chosen to have breast surgeries they might not have chosen had they been given the right numbers. Again, the reason that doctors are so bad at this is that they are human and almost all of us ignore base rates in cases like this (again, the scandal is that medical schools do so bad a job immunizing doctors against this tendency).

This result is just one example of a general principle. Whenever we use an imperfect test – that is, a test with false positives or false negatives – to detect any property, event, or phenomenon, we need to consider base rates. Suppose you are trying to determine the probability that a job applicant uses illegal drugs. Suppose you have a test that is ninety percent accurate with respect to both positives and negatives. And suppose your applicant tests positive. What are the chances that she or he uses illegal drugs? It's exactly the same problem as the disease case. You need to know how many applicants have taken the test and how many of those turned out to be illegal drug users. My guess is that employers ignore base rates at least as often as doctors do, and overestimate the probabilities in the same way. Barring unlikely coincidences, ignoring base rates always leads to bad probability judgments, which lead to bad and sometimes even fatal decision-making.

Tversky and Kahneman's second heuristics is called "the availability heuristic." This one is also a bit vague but clear enough to be useful. We use the availability heuristic when we base a probability judgment on the ease with which the target event or phenomenon comes to mind (the vagueness comes in because ease is hard to measure). In one study, for example, subjects were asked whether more words begin with "r" or have an "r" in the third position. Although the "third position" is the right answer, most people chose the first alternative, presumably because it's easier to think of words that begin with "r."[8] Availability also affects our mathematical reasoning. In another study subjects were asked to estimate how many two-member committees and how many eight-member committees could be formed from a group of ten people. The median estimate for two-member committees was seventy; the medium estimate for eight-member committees was twenty. In fact, the right answer in both cases is forty-five. It is the same in both cases because whenever you make a two-member group from a pool of ten, you have also made an eight-member group (the ones left over) and vice versa. Presumably, people miss this because they try to imagine two-member groups and eight-member groups and it's much easier to imagine the former.[9]

Research also suggests that the availability heuristic generates serious mistakes in many practical contexts.[10] Because we are influenced by availability, for example, we tend to overestimate risks and dangers that easily come to mind, and to underestimate risks and dangers that don't. Since well-publicized events more easily come to mind, we tend to overestimate the chances we will die of causes we hear or read a lot about and underestimate the chances we will die of causes that appear less often in the news or conversation. Since the ones we more often read and talk about are often not as frequent as the ones we less frequently read and talk about, we are often wrong about the degree of danger they pose.[11]

Particularly dramatic events – especially recent ones – also increase availability. Since crime stories are almost always big news, most of us tend to overestimate the chances that we will be victims of crimes. Once, on a train ride to Los Angeles, I sat next to a woman reporter on the *Los Angeles Times* who was anxious about returning to the city, which was then in the grip of a particularly brutal string of well-publicized rape-murders. There had been five of them in the preceding two months, all presumably by the same man. In response, many women were taking special security precautions, some quite expensive and elaborate, often at the urging of their male friends and family members. Many women would not go out alone and many bought guns. But how much danger was there really? Assuming that the rape-murders continued at their current rate for an entire year, there would have been a total of thirty victims. By comparison there were at least five hundred traffic fatalities in Los Angeles that year and more than eighteen hundred murders. The publicized cases increased the murder rate by less than two percent.

Availability influences our thinking in other unhappy ways as well. It causes us to make all kinds of unsubstantiated generalizations that affect our attitudes and actions. This can happen in several ways. First, since the impact of events in our lives tends to fade with time, the most recent events – the freshest, the most available – tend to have a disproportionate effect on our thinking. Being mugged or even short-changed at the grocery store can change one's entire view of human nature for a while, or at least erode one's trust of strangers (although it adds just one more mugging to a mugging-rich world). Being divorced or even dumped by a casual boyfriend or girlfriend can lead to blizzards of wildly unfair condemnations of the other gender (and dampen our enthusiasm for another go). Second, things that happen to *us* are always more vivid and available than things that happen to other people, so we tend to give disproportionate weight to our own personal experience. If you try a weird herbal concoction and your symptoms disappear a day later, you believe in the efficacy of that cure despite the fact that it's been proven ineffective in serious studies. If you've worked hard to overcome the burdens of an impoverished childhood and you succeeded, you may well believe that everyone who tries can succeed. Too often, because it is so vivid to me, my own case rules.

The availability heuristic affects not only ordinary people but also experts and professionals. Studies have shown, for example, that doctors also make too much of recent events and their own personal experience. Surgeons in dangerous specialties like neurology overestimate the number of people who die on operating tables while surgeons in less dangerous specialties like cosmetic surgery underestimate that number. Doctors who have recently treated a condition are more likely to incorrectly diagnose that condition in new patients than doctors who have not recently treated it. Doctors also tend to overestimate the lethality of diseases that have recently received a lot of attention in medical journals.[12]

Finally and most frightening of all, the availability heuristic is a major tool of one of the most dangerous technological developments of the twentieth century, viz. the quantum leap in the technology of persuasion. Propagandists, politicians, marketers, public relations firms, and advertising agencies all push their agendas by promoting the availability of their favored images and messages. If one can keep a vivid image, slogan, or message before the public eye, one can influence the way the public thinks whether or not that image or slogan bears any relation to the facts. Just as our judgments about human nature may be disproportionately colored by a recent encounter with a conman, so may our opinions of ethnic groups, religious groups, political parties, corporations, and products be influenced by frequent exposure to vivid iconic

images and slogans. By keeping vivid and ugly images of
Jews before the public eye, for example, Nazi propagandists
shaped the ways the German people thought of Jews. By
keeping images of happy Coca-Cola drinkers before the
public eye, advertisers help shape the way people think about
Coca-Cola.

Tversky and Kahneman's third heuristic is called "anchoring." Anchoring occurs when we make a judgment by beginning with an initial number and making adjustments to that
number. We can get the initial figure in different ways in different contexts. In bargaining contexts, it is the initial offer. In
problem-solving contexts or estimating contexts, it may be suggested by the formulation of a problem or the result of a partial
computation. In one experiment, Tversky and Kahneman
demonstrated that anchoring can influence our judgment even
when we know the anchor has no connection at all to what we
are estimating. They did this by spinning a wheel in the presence of their subjects to randomly select anchoring numbers.
After the numbers were chosen, they asked their subjects
whether the percentage of African nations belonging to the
U.N. was greater or lower than that number, and by how much.
The anchoring numbers strongly affected subjects' estimates.
Groups that began with ten, for example, had a median estimate of twenty-five percent while groups that began with
sixty-five had a median estimate of forty-five percent. In
another experiment, the anchor was set by partial calculations.
Two groups were each given five seconds to estimate the
answer to a multiplication problem. The first group was given
"$8 \times 7 \times 6 \times 5 \times 4 \times 3 \times 2 \times 1$" and the second group "$1 \times 2 \times 3 \times 4
\times 5 \times 6 \times 7 \times 8$." The median estimate for the ascending sequence
was 512 while the median estimate for the descending
sequence was 2,250 (the correct answer is 40,320). Given the

time constraints, the subjects apparently based their estimates on a few initial calculations and adjusted from that anchor.[13]

Anchoring plays a powerful role in evaluations, appraisals, and negotiations. The higher we set the bar of expectation, the better the outcome must be for us to view the outcome favorably. If someone drags us to a movie we expect to be bad, we may be quite pleased if it is any good at all and judge it to be better than we would have had we no expectations at all. On the other hand, if we expect the film to be great, and it is merely good, we will leave the theater disappointed and likely judge it to be worse than we would have had we entered the theater without any expectations. This phenomenon plays an important role in both business and politics. If a C.E.O. can keep expectations of growth or profit low, she or he can maximize the prospects of a "successful" year. If a political party can keep expectations of electoral gains low, it can claim "victory" even if soundly defeated. Evaluation is always a "compared with what" kind of thing, and the anchor establishes the "what." So, to a significant extent, whoever controls the anchor determines the (perceived) success or failure of the enterprise.

Although bargaining is really not the same as accepting beliefs, it's worth mentioning that anchoring is important in bargaining. The asking price of a house or a car, for example, establishes an anchor on the basis of which negotiations proceed. Typically, the seller expects to accept less and sets the anchor at a place that is likely to keep offers at or above what he or she is actually willing to accept. The buyer knows this but also knows that an offer too far below the asking price will seem ridiculous. Most negotiations are like this (e.g. labor–management ones). Interestingly, salesmen may also sometimes set the anchor *below* the price they want to get. A car salesman once asked me if I would pay $15,000 for a car I was looking at. When I asked whether he was offering the car at that price, he said, "No, I just wanted to see whether you'd be willing to pay $15,000 for it." If I had said "Yes," my guess is that he would have tried to sell it to me for $16,000. After all, that's just an increase of one-sixteenth and "my boss just couldn't let it go for $15,000." He probably thought that if he asked $16,000 to begin with, that price would have seemed too high and I might have counter-offered $15,000. By trying to get me to agree to an anchor, he hoped to make the higher price seem reasonable.

Favoring Preexisting Beliefs

As we all know, other people have strong tendencies to ignore or discount evidence that conflicts with what they already believe. Our political opponents do this all the time. So it should come as no surprise to us that the tendency to ignore or discount such evidence has been demonstrated by experiment many times. In one of the most famous, college students read two phony studies on whether the death penalty deterred capital crimes.[14] One study compared the capital crime rates of states that had the death penalty with those of states that didn't. The other compared the capital crime rates in particular states before and after they adopted and/or abandoned the death penalty. One study found that the death penalty did deter capital crimes; the other study found that it did not. When the subjects were asked to evaluate these studies, they tended to identify the one that supported their own preexisting beliefs as "more convincing" and "better conducted" than the one that did not. They also tended to pounce on the flaws of the latter and overlook the flaws in the former (which were enthusiastically exposed by students on the other side). Midway through the process – after reading just one study – they were asked whether their views had changed. If that study supported their own view, their confidence in that view increased (despite the weak methodology). If that study conflicted with their own view, their view was affected very little. Also, after reading both studies, the subjects were more convinced of their own original position than they were before they read either of them.

This could be a case of directional thinking. Instead of seeking the truth, at least some of these students may have just been looking for data that supported their favored conclusion. But other experiments show that we tend to favor preexisting beliefs even when we are after the truth. For one thing, the way we treat information is time sensitive.

In many contexts we are disproportionately influenced by what we read or see first. That's why our mothers tell us that first impressions are so important. Psychologists refer to these phenomena as "primacy effects." We are all familiar with this. If we read or hear something that conflicts with what we "know" – say, that Shakespeare wrote *Titus Andronicus* – often our immediate response is to say, "No, that's not right." We don't wonder why we believe what we believe in the first place, and compare this with the reason given for the conflicting claim. That is, often we don't try to remember where we read the first claim and compare the reliability of that source to the reliability of the source that made the second claim. This tendency to favor the old and established against the new and conflicting is an instance of our more general tendency to discount or explain away evidence that contradicts what we already believe.

Like most psychological phenomena, primacy effects don't occur in all contexts. In fact, there are contexts in which later information receives more weight (for example, in contexts where availability operates). These are called "recency effects." But primacy effects have been observed by psychologists since the mid 1940s. They occur even when the time lapse between earlier and later exposure to information is very small. In a classic study by Solomon Asch subjects were presented with a list of adjectives describing a person and asked to evaluate that person. In one case, the target person was described as intelligent, industrious, impulsive, critical, stubborn, and envious. In another he was described as envious, stubborn, critical, impulsive, industrious, and intelligent. The evaluations were significantly better when the favorable adjectives came first.[15] In another experiment, subjects watched fake test takers solve thirty multiple-choice analogy problems that were described as equally difficult. The problem solvers always got fifteen right. But the ones who got more right at the beginning were judged to be more intelligent than the ones who got more right toward the end. The subjects also later "remembered" that the early solvers had solved more problems than the late solvers, and predicted that the early solvers would do better than the others on a similar test.[16]

In fact, so strong is our tendency to favor preexisting views that we sometimes retain them even after the evidence for them has been completely discredited. It's not clear how extensive this tendency is, but there is good experimental evidence for it in some contexts. In one famous experiment subjects were asked to distinguish between authentic suicide notes and false suicide notes and then given false feedback about their success rates. Later they were told that the feedback was false and were even shown the experimenter's instruction sheet which randomly assigned students different success rates. But even after this debriefing, subjects who "did well" rated both their actual performance and their abilities far higher than subjects who "did average," and subjects who did average rated their performance and ability higher than subjects who "did badly."[17] In another well-known experiment, high school students were tested on problems of reasoning. Half the subjects were given a clear, coherent lecture that gave them techniques for solving the test questions. The other half were given a rambling and unhelpful talk about how to approach them. As expected, the well-taught students did much better than the badly taught students. Later, they were all fully debriefed (each group was even shown the lecture the other had received). Even though the subjects realized that the preparation had made a big difference on the performance in general, their rating of their own abilities continued to be influenced by how well they had done on the rigged test.[18]

Like many experimental results in psychology and social psychology, these are open to alternative explanations. For example, they can be also taken to show the power of first-hand experience in forming beliefs, especially beliefs about one's own abilities. Still, these results suggest that we stick with our preexisting beliefs even after our original reasons for holding them are completely discredited.

If we are interested in truth, this tendency to favor preexisting beliefs may seem like a bad thing. The fact that we acquire a belief earlier rather than later is irrelevant to its truth. The fact that we ignore or discount contrary evidence seems especially bad. People who do that are usually called dogmatic, pigheaded, and closed-minded. They seem to lack our enlightened and sophisticated commitment to the truth and to reject the scientific attitude that every theory should be vulnerable to refutation by conflicting evidence. But these judgments oversimplify our situation.

The problem is that we can always find *some* reason to deny or affirm almost any belief. Even the wildest conspiracy theories have *some* evidence in their favor. Most of us, though, dismiss these theories without considering the evidence. The theories themselves seem too outlandish. For example, a group called "the 9/11 Scholars," consisting mostly of academics, claims to have proof the 9/11 attacks were not actually performed by terrorists but rather by the Bush administration in an attempt to generate an atmosphere of fear. They argue that the Twin Towers would not have collapsed the way they did unless there were explosives planted inside the buildings. Most of us simply refuse to take this seriously. We don't look at their evidence. The conclusion just seems too crazy to warrant serious attention.

Is that dogmatic? Well, science works in a similar way. Scientists don't take seriously certain results that undermine their established theories. Most high school chemistry experiments don't generate the results they are supposed to yield. But no one thinks this is a reason to reconsider the basic principles of chemistry (or to conclude that they hold only some of the time). We discount and explain away these failures by chalking them up to experimental error. Also, as Thomas Kuhn and other historians of science emphasize, working scientists continue to use certain theories even when they conflict with evidence those scientists accept as reliable. They don't ignore the conflict. They regard it as a puzzle, a problem to be solved in a manner consistent with the theory. They tend to do this until some alternative comes along that explains at least most of what the prevailing theory explains, and explains the conflicting evidence as well. Arguably, this is not just what scientists do but (often) what they should do. Established theories are established because they have predictive power. So in many cases it makes sense to keep them until something better comes along.

The situation is even more complicated for individuals. If our general theories of the world are working well for us, we are reluctant to give them up. In fact, we have more reasons for our reluctance than scientists do in relation to scientific theories. After all, in theory at least, the central goal of science is to discover the truth about the natural world. We, on the other hand, have lives. We have relationships, children, jobs, political concerns, things we love to do for their own sake, and the rest. This means we don't have the time and energy to update our beliefs *continually* in response to new evidence. Consider how many beliefs you have about political, social, and environmental issues which are disputed by others. Have you really weighed all their arguments and considered all the angles? Do you really know as much as you would about these things were you willing to spend a few days in the library? Compare what you know with what specialists know. Of course, truth is important to most of us. But to say we are after truth is really just to say that we want as much as we can get *given the time and energy we are willing to commit to the process.* We all take shortcuts. None of us considers *all* the evidence for and against each of our beliefs, and we all refuse to take seriously some theories and beliefs that challenge our own. This is not to say that dogmatism, pig-headedness, and closed-mindedness are good things. It is just to say that what counts as instances of these vices is not as obvious as may at first appear.

Because our preexisting beliefs and theories strongly influence our response to new information and experience, thinking, like observation, is theory dependent. Our most fundamental beliefs about the world structure the way we understand our experience. A Christian fundamentalist may understand that melodious voice in his head as a message from on high (which further confirms his belief that there is a God). The atheist will think it's all just a matter of brain chemistry. Interestingly, though, it doesn't always work this way. We are not theory dependent through and through. Sometimes new evidence and new experience can revolutionize our entire worldview. As a surgeon tries to remove a tumor from a young girl's brain, her apostate/atheist father might find himself praying. If the child survives against all odds, he may return to the Church, rejecting his atheism in the face of this "new" evidence (this actually happened to a friend of mine). As she watches her innocent infant suffer the fatal horrors of Tay Sachs disease, a fundamentalist believer may lose faith. She can no longer believe in a God that cruel. Although both interesting and important, these cases are exceptional. When it comes to business as usual, theory dependence rules.

Our view of the world is theory dependent in another, more profound way too. Our theories provide us with the basic categories in relation to which we understand the world. A contemporary medical doctor may look at my flushed face and dilated pupils and conclude I have an overactive thyroid. An eighteenth-century doctor might have concluded I have an excess of blood (and bleed me). A practitioner of Chinese medicine might conclude I have too much heat in my body (even with no fever) and give me herbs to cool me down. These doctors will understand my condition differently not only because they have different theories of how the body works but also because their theories include different concepts. There is no condition called "excess heat" in contemporary Western medicine (outside fevers). There is no condition called "hyperthyroidism" in Chinese medicine or eighteenth-century European medicine.

The pervasiveness of theory dependence does not imply any specific policies with respect to acquiring, amending, and rejecting beliefs. But it should make us humble, especially in relation to our most basic views about the world. We are all hostages to the systems of theories and concepts of our traditions. Because they have been around so long, they may strike us as eternal truths. But they change. Aristotle's biology, astronomy, and metaphysics dominated European universities for hundreds of years before they were finally rejected. So did Newton's conception of absolute space and time. Very few intellectuals in those periods ever thought those theories and concepts would be replaced. But they were wrong. We can only speculate about which of our theories and concepts will be discarded two hundred years from now.

Confirmation Bias

When information doesn't conflict with our preexisting beliefs, we tend to be surprisingly charitable. If what we read or hear is clear, we tend to look for instances that confirm it. If what we read or hear is vague, we tend to interpret it in a way that makes it plausible or true. This tendency to find the truth in what we read or hear is part of what keeps so many of us believing in psychics and astrologers.

The experimental psychologist Ray Hyman did a lot of interesting work on our understanding of vague sentences. He became interested in this subject after reading palms as a teenager. He did not believe in palm reading when he started, but the more he did it, the more he heard responses like "That's amazing! How could you possibly know that about me!" For a while, these responses got him to think that maybe there was something to palmistry after all. Eventually, though, he realized how it works. The terms we use to describe character traits are vague. Almost everyone is courageous and fearful, sensitive and thick-skinned, sociable and shy in some ways and in some contexts. When we are told by a palmist, astrologer, or psychic reader that we are foolish with money or shy with our friends, most of us can think of contexts in which that is true. And that's exactly what we tend to do. We look for confirming instances in these cases and we almost always are able to find them. We ignore the rest.[19]

Hyman's hypothesis has been tested many times by psychologists who employ what are called "stock spiels." A stock spiel is a very general personality description that is often presented as a profile of a particular individual (for example, as the result of a personality test). Here's an example:

> Some of your aspirations tend to be pretty unrealistic. At times you are extroverted, affable, sociable while at other times you are introverted, wary and reserved. You have found it unwise to be too frank in revealing yourself to others. You pride yourself on being an independent thinker and do not accept others' opinions without satisfactory proof. You prefer a certain amount of change and variety, and become dissatisfied when hemmed in by restrictions and limitations. At times, you have serious doubts as to whether you have made the right decision or done the right thing. Disciplined and controlled on the outside, you tend to be worrisome and insecure on the inside.

This stock spiel was first used by Bertram Forer in a classroom demonstration. He asked his students how accurately the description fit them. On a scale of one to five, his students gave the test an average accuracy rating of 4.26. Sixteen of his thirty-nine students rated it a five (a perfect description of themselves). In another test, the psychologists Synder and Shenkel presented a very similar spiel to two groups of students. One group was told that the sketch is generally true for all people and was asked to say how well it fit them. The other group was told that the description was made specifically for them. The former rated the test between average and good. The latter rated the test midway between good and excellent.[20]

When we are dealing with statements that don't conflict with our established beliefs, we interpret them generously and look for ways in which they are true. Interestingly, Hyman believes that we can learn by treating statements in this manner. If an astrologer tells a generally timid person that they are courageous, that person may think of a way in which they are courageous which may not have occurred to them before. I think this point can be generalized. Since people often make rather general statements with something more particular in mind, our tendency to look for confirming instances helps us to see the truth in what they are saying; or, anyway, it helps us see what they had in mind. If instead we immediately look for disconfirming instances, we might miss their point and lose their insight. Of course, not everyone looks for confirming instances first. Lawyers, philosophers, scientists, and other intellectuals are trained to look for disconfirming instances (and some people are contentious in this way without the benefit of formal training).

In the Hyman cases, the sentences we try to confirm are vague and open to a variety of interpretations. In at least some contexts we also look for confirming rather than disconfirming instances when sentences are clear. Psychologists call this "confirmatory bias" and "biased recruitment of evidence" and have shown experimentally that we do it in a number of contexts.[21] Like so many experimental results in psychology and social psychology, it is hard to know to what extent these results extend beyond the contexts in which they have been tested. There is, however, one famous (though also controversial) experiment that suggests that our tendency to look for confirming instances is quite general. In this experiment – the Wason selection test – subjects are dealt four cards. There are letters on one side of each card and numbers on the other. Two cards are dealt with the number side up and two cards are dealt with the letter side up. In the original version of the experiment the visible letters are "K" and "A" and the visible numbers are "2" and "7." The subjects are asked which cards they need to turn over to tell whether the following sentence is true: "If there is a vowel on one side of the card, there is an even number on the other side." Typically, about four percent of the people given this task get it right. Everyone recognizes that you need to turn over the "A" card to see whether there is an even number on the other side. That is, they look immediately for the case that obviously confirms or disproves the statement. But typically about eighty percent of the people also think you need to turn over the "2." You don't. What's on the other side of that card is irrelevant. The statement would be true whether the latter were a vowel or a consonant. Still, a vowel is a confirming instance and that is why people are drawn to it. The amazing thing is that only ten percent of the subjects looked for (or, anyway, found) a way to disconfirm the hypothesis. You do that by turning over the "7." If there is a vowel on the other side, we know that the target sentence is false. The fact that so few people think of this suggests that our tendency to look for confirming instances is much stronger than our tendency to look for disconfirming instances (for these four cards, the target sentence is true if and only if there is an even number on the other side of the "A" card and a consonant on the other side of the "7").[22]

As I said, this experiment is controversial. Some argue that people may ignore the disconfirming card in this highly abstract context because they simply don't understand the meaning of "if . . . then" sentences in highly abstract contexts. Some experiments in fact suggest that in less abstract cases – where we are not dealing with numbers and letters but sentences that have plausible connections to one another – people make this mistake less often. However that may be, it is clear that confirmation bias exists in a significant range of cases. If we read that a stitch in time saves nine, most of us will think about cases where prompt action is called for. If we are told that haste makes waste, we will think about cases where patience is wise. Again, though, this tendency is limited to cases in which what we read or hear is consistent with our preexisting beliefs. It is also limited to cases in which we do not feel under attack. When we are fighting with our loved ones we don't respond to statements that begin "You always . . ." and "You never . . ." by looking for confirming instances.

The advantage of confirmation bias is that it helps us to see the truth in what someone else says. The disadvantage is that it leads us to ignore what is false. That is dangerous. Almost every generalization, however inaccurate, has some confirming instances. If we think only of those instances, we may find ourselves agreeing with a lot of false and even dangerous propositions. For example, we may find ourselves nodding in agreement to racist stereotypes ("Most Italians have Mafia connections;" "Most young black men are felons;" "Most Muslims support terrorism;" "Most Jews are money hungry;"

etc.). If our tendency is to look for confirming instances, we will almost always be able to find some. This tendency is exploited by demagogues, public relations people, televangelists, advertisers, ordinary politicians, and everyone else schooled in the arts of persuasion. The trick is to support a generality with a vivid confirming instance so that when people hear the generality they think of *that* confirming instance. "You ask me what these homosexuals are like and why they are destroying the American family. Let me tell you about Horace Green . . ."

Anyone who thinks about it for a moment realizes that this is bad reasoning. It invites us to move from a single case or a few cases to a generality (to start with "a few" or "some" and conclude "most" or "all"). Nonetheless, this is a very powerful technique. We may recognize the general point that it is a logical fallacy and still fall for it in a particular case. As noted earlier, iconic representations – vivid confirming instances – can become deeply seated in our imagination and are hard to escape. To immunize ourselves against them, we need to do more than recognize their danger in the abstract. We need to train ourselves to look for disconfirming instances. We need to complement our normal, more charitable ways of understanding each other with the style of thinking characteristic of philosophers and scientists (on the job).

As we've seen, we also learn by interpreting vague and ambiguous sentences in ways that make them true. But this is also dangerous. For example, it can lead us to believe that our personalities and the opportunities and hazards we face each day depend on the alignment of the stars. It can also be exploited in the cause of knavery. Consider biblical interpretation. By assigning specific contemporary references to vague biblical passages, some fringe Christian sects insist that black people are subhuman ("mud people") and Jews are demonic ("spawn of Satan"). By assigning specific contemporary references to passages from the Book of Revelation, a much larger number expect that the Apocalypse is just around the corner. One can only guess how this affects attitudes toward global warming, looming water shortages, and other ecological issues. Since fundamentalist Christians are currently an influential political force in America, their style of biblical prophecy may have worldwide consequences. Somehow it does not occur to them that there were equally plausible "references" for their end-of-the-world passages at almost every period in European history. The Last Days are long overdue.

Cognitive Styles

In his famous essay "The Will to Believe" William James tells us that inquiry is guided by two rules, "Seek truth!" and "Avoid error!" He also suggests that different people honor these separate imperatives in different ways. Some people are error-phobic. They don't like to make mistakes, and therefore need very strong evidence before they are ready to accept a proposition. Other people are more worried about missing the truth, and the benefits of accepting the truth. They are willing to accept a proposition on the basis of weaker evidence. In relation to beliefs that "can't be decided by the intellect alone" – and James thinks there are many – he believes that neither attitude is more rational than the other.[23] The attitudes we adopt simply reflect our personalities.

The ways our personalities express themselves in the realm of belief obviously affects what we believe. So if we are trying to decide which of our beliefs are worth retaining and which are not, it helps to understand them. When we are trying to decide how much weight to give someone else's judgment or advice – especially on topics we don't understand all that well – it helps to know how her personality expresses itself in her beliefs as well. Let's call this her cognitive style. Cognitive styles are not always easy to identify. They differ not only from person to person but from one topic or situation to the next. The careful and judicious accountant or laboratory scientist may make snap judgments about other people, and jump to wild conclusions in romantic situations.

When we weigh someone else's judgment or advice, most of us consider the source. We ask ourselves whether that person is competent in the relevant area, whether they are honest, whether they have a vested interest in the outcome, and so on. But we are less likely to think about aspects of their cognitive style. This is partly because that is often harder to discover. But sometimes we can discover it and when we can it should affect our judgment. Among the questions we might ask are: How strict are their standards of evidence? How strong a case does it take for them to be confident? How thorough are they? Do they pounce on the first plausible idea or theory or do they insist on making a complete inventory of the alternatives before they decide? How open-minded are they? How willing are they to think about arguments and evidence against their views? How stubborn are they? How hard is it for them to change positions and admit they were wrong? How self-confident are they? How willing are they to trust their own judgment even when it's unpopular or conflicts with the consensus of expert opinion? To what extent do they trust their own first-hand experience even when it conflicts with the experience of others? How theory driven are they? To what extent do they try to fit everything into some Big Picture narrative? When considering our own judgments we need to ask the same questions about ourselves.

There is no right answer or wrong policy on these matters. It's possible to do or be too much or too little of any of the above, but what counts as too much or too little depends on the particulars of the situation. Where immediate, decisive action is called for there may not be time to consider all the alternatives or even all the possible arguments against one's proposed course of action (however far-fetched). Cognitive styles that serve us well in some jobs (say, combat officers) may not serve us well in others (say, judges). Still, when we are deciding whether to trust someone's judgment (even our own), it helps to know her cognitive style. And some obvious generalizations can be made. Other things being equal, for example, we should take someone with high standards of evidence more seriously than someone with low standards of evidence, open-minded people more seriously than closed-minded people, and so on. We should also be suspicious of people who seem to be confident about everything. But most of us know this already.

Although philosophers have largely ignored cognitive styles, psychologists have recently started to study this phenomenon under the heading "regulative focus theory." Among other things, they distinguish between people with a "promotion focus" (or "eager judgment strategies") and people with a "prevention focus" (or "vigilant judgment strategies"). The former are primarily motivated by finding "hits" and avoiding "errors of omission" (that is, they want to find *all* the hits). The latter are motivated by making "correct rejections" and "avoiding errors of commission."[24] While this work may someday develop James's thoughts on truth seekers and error avoiders, I have seen little sign of that thus far. In fact, the work I have seen seems plagued by conceptual confusion and a dubious interpretation of the evidence. Readers are, as ever, urged to reach their own conclusions.

Emotion

Obviously, our thinking is affected by our moods and emotions. We tend to be open and optimistic when we are happy, closed-minded and critical when we are angry, oblivious when we are in love, and so on. Many of the connections between thinking and feeling are built into our language. Part of what it *means* to be depressed is to have negative thoughts and part of what it means to be jealous is to be suspicious and distrustful. Plays, novels, poems, songs, and history provide iconic illustrations of these relationships. In fact, they provide us with a lot more insight in these matters than experimental psychologists do. In fact, where it does not elaborate the obvious, much of the research literature here defies common sense, conflicts with the experience of clinical psychologists, and conflicts with itself.

Although the relationship between thought and feeling has been a major topic in experimental psychology, much of the research seems aimed at establishing the obvious. According to one researcher, when we are feeling good

> the evidence indicates that we tend to view others more positively . . . to give more favorable reports about products we have purchased . . . to rate ambiguous slides as more pleasant . . . to have more positive expectations for the future . . . and to give more positive associations situations in which we imagine ourselves . . . In other words, when we are feeling good we tend to behave in a more positive fashion and to perceive the world more favorably than would otherwise be the case.[25]

The ellipses mark places where the author cites studies that establish these startling conclusions. She cites nine of them. She goes on to summarize equally unsurprising findings about bad moods (e.g. that depression seems to lower people's estimates of their future success at a task).

In a more recent work, Leonard Martin and Gerald Clore cite four findings that "seem to show up most consistently in affect–cognition research." They are "mood congruent recall, mood congruent judgment, negative affect leading to more systematic processing and positive affect leading to more creative processing."[26] Since almost all this research focuses on two moods – happiness and sadness – this amounts to saying that when we are happy we tend to (a) remember more positive things, (b) make more positive evaluations, and (c) think more creatively than we do when we are sad; and that when we are sad we tend to think things through more than we do when we are happy. (I'll elaborate a bit more presently.) The first two claims – (a) and (b) – seem obvious. The latter two claims – (c) and the point about thinking things through when we are sad – are intriguing but vague and highly questionable.

They are questionable because the experiments that support them are ridiculously artificial. In most cases moods are induced in experimental subjects by playing happy or sad music or by exposing the subjects to happy or sad pictures or descriptions. It's not at all clear that the short-lived and superficial moods induced in these ways affect us in the same way the longer-lived and deeper moods we experience in our lives do. In elaborating on the claim that people in sad moods think things through more, researcher Herbert Bless writes, "Empirical evidence suggests that information processing in positive affective states is strongly influenced by heuristics, stereotypes or scripts while people in negative affective states seem more likely to be affected by the implications of specific information provided in the situation."[27] But is this really true of people who are genuinely sad, depressed, hopeless, or despairing? Many clinical psychologists, who deal with such people regularly, take the opposite view. Sad, despairing, and depressed people are dominated by their own scripts (or "tapes," as the psychologists sometimes say) and are slaves to their own personal patterns of thought. Happier, healthier people, on the other hand, are more able to assess what is really going on in a situation, and to deal with it. Psychotherapists, especially cognitive therapists, have developed many techniques that are supposed to help sad and depressed people recognize the inaccuracy of their pessimistic assessments and to provide them with tools to think things through better.

The corresponding point holds with respect to happy people being more creative. People who have been induced into a superficially elevated mood may perform certain highly specific tasks in a more creative way than people in a superficially sad mood. They may have a bit more energy or enthusiasm for the task. But it doesn't follow that happy people are more creative than sad (anxious, depressed, or driven) people outside the lab. The stereotype of the tortured genius has a factual basis. Many artists, musicians, novelists, poets, world-class chess players, and creative scientists and mathematicians have been depressed, anxious, or disturbed people. In 2006 the Grand Palais in Paris hosted a show called "Melancholy – Genius and Insanity in the Western World," which included more than three hundred artworks from antiquity to the present. According to the *Scientific American Book of the Brain* (1999),

Increased rates of suicide, depression and manic depression among artists have been established by many separate studies. Artists experience up to eighteen times the rate of suicide as seen in the general population, eight to ten times the rate of depression and ten to twenty times the rate of manic depression in its milder form.

The research, then, leaves us with only the obvious conclusions. People in bad moods think more negatively. People in good moods think more positively. Or, anyway, this is true about most people in relation to most things most of the time.

On the other hand, it may be impossible for experimenters to produce anything more fine-tuned than this. The ways our moods and emotions express themselves vary a lot from person to person and situation to situation. Why expect anything different with respect to how our moods and emotions affect our thinking? Some lovers are more blind than others. Some jealous people are more distrustful, or distrustful about different things. Some furious people can't think straight about anything, while others are coldly and maniacally focused. And, for that matter, some happy people are much more in touch with the depressing state of the world than others, and some sad people are more capable of counting their blessings. These differences create fertile ground for novelists and playwrights but difficult terrain for social scientists.

The relationships between affect and cognition are deep, complex, pervasive, and sometimes very profound. Because these relationships differ from person to person, it is difficult to give more than the obvious advice. First, if you are thinking about something important, pay attention to your moods and emotions. Second, try to be aware of how your moods and emotions affect your thinking, apply that to the present case, and act on it. For example, if you know that anger or jealousy distorts your thinking, don't send that angry or jealous email. Save it as a draft and reread it after you've calmed down. Of course, this is easier said than done.

Clinical psychologists of every school agree that we are not always aware of (or, as they say, in touch with) our feelings. Most of us recognize this about ourselves and others (hence the sitcom cliché, "Don't tell me I'm angry. I know when I'm goddam angry!"). Self-help books by psychotherapists and meditation teachers are filled with techniques to make us more aware of what we feel. My guess is that different techniques work for different people. Some people make good progress in cognitive therapy; some improve simply by keeping a journal; others do well with meditation to develop attentiveness (or mindfulness) of their current states. The more we become aware of our moods and emotions, of course, the better able we will be to investigate their impact on our thinking. This influence is pervasive. It doesn't just apply to thinking about our personal relationships. We are influenced by emotions like fear, loyalty, love, envy, jealousy, and hate in our political thinking, our financial thinking, and our thinking about science (even if we are scientists).

It's one thing to recognize how we feel, and another to understand how that affects our thinking. In order to make progress in freeing ourselves from feeling-based distortions of thinking, we need both to recognize how we feel and to understand how that affects our thought. To do the latter, we need to remember and track judgments we've made in various moods and emotional states. That is, we need to ask questions like: How blind has *my* love been before? How has fear (or pride, guilt, etc.) affected my financial thinking? When I am angry at someone, how self-righteous and accusatory do I become in my thinking? To what extent do my evaluations change when I am feeling very good indeed, thank you? To what extent does my affection for people influence my evaluation of their work? To what extent does my dislike of a colleague influence my choice to agree or disagree with her claims? Few if any of us will ever have a perfect understanding of these matters. But if we make an honest and serious effort, we can make progress; perhaps enough to help us correct or avoid some of our own worst tendencies.

Directional Thinking

That everyone believes what he wants to believe is a cliché of contemporary life. Our speech is peppered with language testifying to our capacity to resist strong evidence in favor of unwelcome conclusions ("You're in denial;" "You're just projecting your fears on to me;" "You're rationalizing"). We all recognize that there are costs and benefits to believing what we do. Our beliefs may be sources of hope, happiness, and inspiration, or shame, depression, and despair. They may help us to fit in or consign us to the lunatic fringe. They may unite us with friends, family, and fellow workers or alienate the affections of those we hold dear. When our beliefs are motivated by these costs and benefits, we engage in what psychologists call "directional thinking." Most research on directional thinking focuses on beliefs that promote comforting beliefs about ourselves and those important to us. Some of it also focuses on beliefs directed at pleasing others in ways that improve our lot in life (e.g. by enhancing our status and by helping us to advance in our careers). The point of all this research is to determine the scope and limits of our capacity to believe what we want to believe. Although there are some interesting results, the research has not gotten very far.

Since few of us realize that our thinking is directional when we are doing it, experimenters can't rely on what we tell them to identify directional thinking and discover how widespread it is. Instead, they test it by asking experimental subjects to evaluate a theory (a study, or a packet of information) that is unwelcome news to some of them and either welcome news or neutral to the others. If the group to whom the results are unwelcome reject or criticize them significantly more often than the group to whom they are welcome, experimenters infer that they are not evaluating what they have read or heard on the basis of the evidence alone (however much they may think they are). That is, they infer that what the subjects want to believe plays an important role in determining what they do believe. If the experimenters can run these experiments with enough variations of belief types, circumstances, and subjects they can determine the extent to which and the conditions under which we believe what we want to believe.

Experimentalists have gotten some suggestive results. In one study, for example, individuals were told that they had tested positive for T.A.A., a fictitious enzyme in the body. Half the people were told that T.A.A. is good for one's health and the other half were told that it is bad for one's health. The latter significantly discounted the test results when they were told that the test had ten percent false positives and were only somewhat more accepting when told that it was highly accurate (0.05% false positives). The former judged the test to be highly accurate in both cases.[28] In another study, subjects read a scientific article according to which caffeine had bad health consequences for women. Women who drank a lot of caffeine found the article less convincing than women who drank just a little.[29] With respect to health issues, at least, these studies suggest that we engage in directional thinking.

Experiments also suggest that this capacity has its limits. When subjects are told that certain personality traits are linked to success, they tend to rate themselves more highly on those traits than they otherwise do. On the other hand, they do not rate themselves as highly as they could. This has prompted some researchers to conclude that directional thinking operates within "reality constraints."[30] In their review of this literature, Moldon and Higgins conclude, "Overall, these results suggest that thinking and reasoning inspired by directional outcomes does not so much lead people to ignore the sometimes disappointing reality they face as it inspires them to exploit the uncertainties that exist in this reality to their favor."[31]

All in all the experimental literature is undeveloped at this point and not very helpful. At its best, it tells us mostly what we already know, viz. sometimes people believe what they want to believe, but they can't believe just anything at all (as much as I would like to believe that I'm as brilliant as Einstein and as sexy as the young Marlon Brando, I can't get myself to believe that). If it is to have important practical implications, the experimental literature needs to be much more fine-tuned than this. It needs to tell us how to recognize directional thinking in ourselves and in others. It also needs to tell us what the so-called "reality constraints" are for different people under different circumstances and to what degree they constrain us. We are obviously a long way from that now.

The experimental literature also conflicts with commonsense observations and the experience of clinical psychologists. Understood straightforwardly, the idea that we use directional thinking "not . . . to ignore the sometimes disappointing reality . . . [but rather] to exploit the uncertainties . . . in this reality" conflicts with what most of us believe about denial. I was once invited to dinner at the house of a friend whose husband had recently been an active alcoholic. When I arrived, he was unconscious and breathing heavily on the living-room floor. His wife told me she had just discovered a large stash of empty beer cans under a tarp in his pick-up truck. Before he "fell asleep" he explained that he was keeping the cans for a friend who was concealing his drinking from *his* wife. He also told her he had worked very hard that day and was very tired (apparently so tired he couldn't make it to the bedroom or even the couch). His wife seemed to believe him (which was consistent with her general approach to the problem). Although the line between "exploiting uncertainties" and "ignoring disappointing realities" is fuzzy, this seems like a case of ignoring a disappointing reality to me. I'm sure most of us can think of cases like this.

There is also a tension between the experimenter's perspective and the perspective of the clinical psychologists. Clinicians of almost every theoretical persuasion are impressed by how often our unrealistic views of ourselves and the world make us miserable, not happy. From Freud on, they have been impressed with how unnecessarily harshly we judge ourselves. This tendency has been and continues to be the focus of much psychotherapy. Many therapists take it to be the central problem of depression. Most depressed people hold unrealistic or disputable views about themselves and the world which make them miserable, hopeless, and despairing. The aim of many therapists is to get them to replace these views with more realistic or optimistic ones that make them happier.

Still, we all know that directional thinking sometimes takes place. We are sometimes in denial, we do rationalize, and we do sometimes ignore arguments and evidence against our beliefs. We obviously have tendencies to believe because it is convenient, popular, ego-enhancing, career-advancing, and self-protective. This is what makes witch hunts, bandwagon effects, and blind partisanship of all kinds possible. The trick is to determine when we (and others) are believing for directional reasons, and when we (and others) are believing on the basis of reasons and evidence. Of course, we usually think it's *them*.

One reason it's hard to say when directional thinking occurs is that it's difficult to come up with a model or theory of how directional thinking happens. That is because directional thinking seems to involve a kind of self-deception, and self-deception is difficult to model. In order to deceive ourselves we must believe that something is true and yet somehow convince ourselves that it is false. It is hard to make sense of this unless we divide ourselves into parts – perhaps an unconscious part that believes something is true and manipulates the conscious part to believe that it's false. But what is this unconscious part and how does it work? What are the mechanisms? We are a long way from answers to these questions. We can't escape the need to find answers to them by adopting a less paradoxical picture of how directional thinking works (for example, that it simply involves ignoring or erroneously evaluating evidence). The question remains: How exactly do we pull this off? What are the processes by which we recognize evidence as relevant so that we may hide it from ourselves? There is currently an enormous literature on this question but nothing close to a consensus. The fact that we don't have a successful theoretical model for self-deception seriously hobbles the scientific study of directional thinking.

Reflections

Our aim to pursue knowledge collectively can succeed only to the extent that we are able to overcome our limitations as individuals. These include our reliance on heuristics to make probability judgments, our tendency to reinforce and protect our preexisting beliefs by ignoring or distorting evidence against them, our tendency to evaluate new beliefs (that don't conflict with our old ones) charitably, and the undue influence of moods, emotions, and personal agendas on our thinking.

Guarding against all this is a tall order, and we don't always succeed. As we've already seen, for example, medical schools do a poor job of immunizing doctors against reliance on the availability heuristic when they diagnose diseases, and a disgraceful job of teaching them to take base rates into account when they evaluate test results. The availability heuristic is so powerful it may be impossible for any training program to eliminate it completely. But everyone who makes judgments about risks needs to understand base rates and learn to consult them. In estimating risks and dangers we all need to pay attention to these numbers.

It's also very difficult to train people not to be affected in their thinking by their moods, emotions, and agendas. Instead of trying to do this by training, many knowledge-pursuing communities do it by promoting an ideal of the objective, disinterested researcher. It's hard to say how successfully that addresses the problem. But knee-jerk cynicism about overcoming the problem, however fashionable, is hardly justified. After all, most scientists very much want their research programs to prosper and their own hypotheses and theories to be true. But they still acknowledge disappointing results, blind alleys, and the strength of opposing arguments. This is partly because one looks like a fool in many cases if one doesn't, and no one wants to look like a fool. In the end, it's hard to say how well protected the scientific community is against emotion and agenda-driven thinking. There are clearly cases in which it isn't very well protected at all. This is especially so in controversies heated by personal animosities and opposing political ideologies. When scientific findings have, or are thought to have, political consequences, discussions can roil, even at customarily tepid professional meetings. Accusations of self-deception, directional thinking, and outright dishonesty may fly like spears in a Stone Age war, and truth is often the first victim.

Knowledge-seeking communities do better at giving up theories when the evidence in their favor has been discredited. Individuals have a hard time doing this partly because we don't keep careful track of the evidential relations between our beliefs. Often, we simply forget why we came to believe something (for example, that Bertrand Russell believed in free love). Knowledge-seeking communities don't have this problem because they keep records. They make connections clear and explicit in books and journal articles. When the justifications for a belief are undermined and discredited, everyone is in a position to recognize that (although, given the information glut in some fields some may be late getting the news, or not get it at all).

As we've seen, both individuals and knowledge-seeking communities may hold on to beliefs even when there is strong evidence against them. But there is an important difference. Individuals tend to do this by discrediting, discounting, or ignoring the evidence. But knowledge-seeking communities have norms against this. Ideally, at least, they make note of the conflicting evidence and treat it as a problem to be solved, a subject for further research. Once again, they can do this because they keep public records of the evidential connections between their beliefs.

Most knowledge-seeking communities also differ from individuals in their attitude toward new beliefs (that is, beliefs that don't threaten preexisting ones). Individuals tend to be charitable. When confronted with a generality, they tend to look for confirmation. In philosophy, the sciences, and certain other knowledge-seeking communities we do the opposite; that is, we look for counter-examples and opposing arguments. The philosopher of science Karl Popper famously argued that the very point of scientific experiments is to disconfirm hypotheses, not to verify them (he thought authentic verification was impossible). Although many have argued that Popper's position is exaggerated, there is some truth in it. Before we are willing to accept new beliefs and theories, we do our best to prove them false. That's why it usually makes sense to trust the conclusions of these communities rather than the opinion of the person on the next barstool (although, as we will soon see, these communities are far short of infallible, and sometimes the person on the next barstool can tell us why).

CHAPTER 3

Flawed Data: Problems of Design from the Brokerage to the Therapist's Office

Chapters 1 and 2 discussed problems of perception and thinking that may distort or obscure our view of the world. To overcome these problems and otherwise transcend our limitations as individuals we pursue knowledge collectively; that is, we organize ourselves in ways that are meant to avoid or correct errors to which we are prone as individuals. On the whole, we have been remarkably successful, especially in areas of science and technology. But even in these areas we have been far from perfect.

The organizations we've developed to overcome our limits and fallibilities as individuals take data from the world as input, produce conclusions from those data as output, and publicize those conclusions. Because this is analogous to taking raw materials from the world and turning them into products,

I've called these organizations "Knowledge Machines." This chapter begins our examination of how Knowledge Machines can go wrong. It focuses on the first stage of that process, data gathering.

Data gathering can go wrong in two ways. First, the methods, techniques, and principles on the basis of which we gather and filter data from the world may be flawed (problems of design). And, second, we may not adhere to those methods, techniques, and principles even when they are in good working order (problems of compliance). Both problems may result in errors of omission and errors of commission. That is, they may lead us to overlook or ignore data that are relevant and important (diagnostic data). And they may lead us to accept and work with data that are flawed (undiagnostic data).

Data may be flawed because it is false or unreliable. This happens, for example, when our methods or equipment are faulty and when we are careless or incompetent. But data may also be flawed because they are misleading or irrelevant to the question at hand. Typically, that happens because we hold false theories. In the mid-nineteenth century, many people thought that phrenologists could read people's character and intellectual abilities from the shapes and sizes of the bumps on their heads. Sometimes these bumps were measured by instruments like calipers. More often, the phrenologists would just run their highly sensitive, highly trained fingers over the client's skull and make inferences from that. Without studies comparing the phrenologists' estimates with the actual measurements, there was no good reason to believe they got them right. For this reason, those data were unreliable. But, of course, they were also misleading and irrelevant. The theory of phrenology is false. Unless bumps are signs of brain injuries, there's no connection between bumps on people's heads and their personalities.

These are errors of commission. Knowledge Machines may make errors of omission for the same reasons. They may overlook or ignore data because their methods or equipment are defective. Or, because their theories are weak, they may simply not recognize diagnostic data as relevant. In addition, Knowledge Machines are vulnerable to both kinds of errors because practitioners are careless, incompetent, or dishonest. They may manufacture data, hide or suppress data or otherwise cook the books to win fame and fortune (to advance their political or ideological agenda, to help their friends and harm their enemies, and so forth). We will examine these problems in Chapter 4. This chapter is about problems that arise because we operate with faulty methods, techniques, or principles or because we are hampered by weak theories. Although we will focus on particular cases, these cases illustrate more general problems.

Before getting down to cases, I need to say something more about the term "data." For our purposes, it is best to think of data as a type of information. More specifically, it is information that we think relevant to answering some question or settling some issue. This means that the same piece of information may be a datum in one context and a conclusion from data in another. For example, we understand the extent to which smoking contributes to lung cancer because we have done studies. That piece of information is a conclusion of those studies (studies in which medical records, for example, are the data). But if our question is the social cost of smoking, that information becomes a datum. To calculate the social cost of smoking we need to know, among other things, the extent to which smoking contributes to lung cancer. As this suggests, data are not pure, unrefined, atomic bits of information. They come in all shapes and sizes. They may be statements about some particular object at some particular time or they may be statistical generalizations about large classes of objects over long periods of time. This description of data leaves some open questions (for example, how to distinguish between data and theories). But it is complete enough for our purposes.

Plausible but False Assumptions: The Case of Eyewitness Testimony

In Chapter 1, we examined two examples of the way plausible but false assumptions about observations introduced bad data into physics and psychology. In one case, the French physicist Blondlot and his colleagues thought they had discovered a relative of the X-ray – the N-ray – on the basis of naked-eye judgments about the comparative brightness of reflective surfaces under different conditions. Since the scientists in Blondlot's lab all agreed on these judgments, they plausibly assumed they were accurate. But, as it turned out, Blondlot and his colleagues saw what they expected to see, not what was actually there. In the second example, facilitated communication, facilitators experienced their own keyboard strokes as responses to the hand movements of people they were assisting. Quite plausibly, they assumed that their subjective experience was an accurate indication of what was going on. But, as we saw, they couldn't tell, on the basis of their subjective experience, that they were leading rather than following. They too were victims of expectancy. These are both examples of Knowledge Machines failing to guard us against mistakes we make as individuals.

The case of eyewitness testimony in the legal system is another example. We assume quite plausibly that witnesses at a crime scene accurately observe and recall what the perpetrator looks like and other details (well, quite plausibly if we are unaware of the research). But too often this is false. The case of eyewitness testimony also shows how Knowledge Machines can resist change even in the face of highly convincing research results produced by other Knowledge Machines.

Excluding prisons and the parole system, we can think of the criminal justice system as a big Knowledge Machine whose purpose is to identify and convict criminals (while protecting the innocent). Its practitioners are police, prosecutors, defense attorneys, judges, and juries. The police identify suspects and witnesses, prosecutors attempt to prove that suspects are guilty (or get them to confess their guilt), defense attorneys try to create reasonable doubt, and juries (and sometimes judges) decide the guilt of the accused on the basis of the evidence. Judges also enforce the rules that are supposed to assure a fair trial. These include rules of evidence. Since these rules exclude certain kinds of testimony and other forms of evidence from trials, we can think of them as data filters.

Eyewitness testimony is the most dramatic and convincing form of courtroom evidence. When a crime victim or a witness to a crime points to the person at the defense table and says, "That's her; I'm completely sure of it," everyone takes notice. But psychologists have been suspicious of eyewitness accounts since the early 1900s. Writing in 1908, Hugo Munsterberg argued that the study of perception "may help clear up the chaos and the confusion which prevail in the observations of witnesses."[1] And, as we saw in Chapter 1, research on perception and memory in general provides reasons to doubt many perceptual reports. In the 1970s, moreover, a number of psychologists initiated programs specifically designed to study eyewitness errors. From 1974 to 1999, psychologists published well over two thousand papers on eyewitness issues in psychology.[2]

Some of these papers describe experiments in which psychologists stage crimes and then interview witnesses to them. In one such experiment, researchers staged an assault on a professor on the campus of California State University at Hayward, to which there were 141 witnesses. The reports of these witnesses differed significantly as to the perpetrator's weight, appearance, and dress and other aspects of the "crime" (witness accuracy averaged twenty-five percent of the maximum possible score). In a similar experiment involving a staged purse snatching, only seven of fifty-two witnesses were able to identify the perpetrator from two videotaped lineups. Ten witnesses made no identification. Thirty-five witnesses identified the wrong man.[3] Psychologists have also conducted numerous studies that explain why eyewitnesses may go wrong. In addition to obvious factors like bad lighting and expectancy, there is a lot of research on the ways that stress, arousal, focus on weapons, and difficulties in cross-race identification may affect both perception and memory.

Despite these reports, in the U.S., at least, little if anything has been done to change the rules of evidence themselves. All forms of eyewitness testimony are still admissible. This is partly mitigated in some cases by allowing defense attorneys to bring in expert witnesses to testify about the reliability of eyewitness testimony in cases that rely on eyewitness testimony alone.[4] But these expert witnesses are also excluded from testifying under a variety of other conditions.[5] In those cases, the court relies on the ordinary forms of cross-examination by defense attorneys to undermine eyewitnesses (and, in some cases, some general instructions by the judge). So, although eyewitness testimony may be very important in these cases, the criminal justice system has done little if anything to respond to research on its limitations.

What happens at trials is just one part of the problem and arguably not the most important one. Eyewitnesses influence criminal investigations from the start. They provide descriptions of the perpetrator and are often asked to identify the perpetrator from a lineup or an array of photographs. As a result of being identified by eyewitnesses, suspects are arrested and indicted. Sometimes they are convinced to plead guilty in exchange for a reduced sentence. They have an incentive to do this because eyewitness identification makes it likely that they will be convicted at a trial and face a stiffer sentence. We don't know how often this happens. But it is not unreasonable for someone, say, to plead guilty and serve six months to avoid a likely conviction at trial that carries a five- to ten-year sentence.

If the suspect does not cop a plea, the eyewitnesses that identify him or her will usually testify at the trial. Often these eyewitnesses identify suspects from photo arrays (mugshots) or pick them out of a lineup. And too often they are mistaken. This is partly because eyewitnesses face the kinds of problem we have already discussed. But it is also partly because of the way police conduct photo arrays and lineups. The police in charge of a lineup know who the primary suspect is and (usually) want the witness to identify him or her. Often they cue the witness (sometimes intentionally and sometimes not). In addition, they may fail to include "fillers" in a lineup or photo array who fit the witnesses' verbal description of the perpetrator.[6] Often, they fail to instruct witnesses that the actual perpetrator may not be in the lineup. When this instruction is given, there is a forty-two percent reduction in mistaken identifications from perpetrator-absent lineups. Finally, they almost always present members of a lineup simultaneously rather than sequentially. When the perpetrator is in the lineup both methods do equally well. But when the perpetrator is absent the rate of misidentification is forty-three percent in the simultaneous case and only seventeen percent in the sequential.[7] All of these problems are described in the psychological literature on eyewitness testimony and all of them are easily avoidable. But the police carry on with business as usual.[8]

Although some of the research on lineups was done in the 1960s and 1970s, it had little impact on the criminal justice system. It was almost entirely ignored until 1999, and the attention it received after that time did not occur because law enforcement officials and judges kept up with the research literature. The issue was forced by events. In 1991 Attorneys Barry Scheck and Peter Neufeld helped found the Innocence Project, which used D.N.A. testing to fight wrongful convictions. During the 1990s sixty-five innocent people were freed, the vast majority of whom were convicted largely on the basis of eyewitness testimony. Some of these cases were highly publicized and difficult to ignore. In 1995 the Justice Department began to review cases of people freed by D.N.A. evidence and concluded that eighty percent of them were convicted on the basis of eyewitness testimony. Attorney General Janet Reno read this report and in early 1997 she met with eyewitness researcher Gary Wells to discuss ways to improve the situation. Shortly after, she established a panel to work on this problem. The final working group – which included a Justice Department official, six eyewitness researchers, six prosecutors, four defense attorneys, and seventeen law enforcement personnel – produced an eight-thousand-word document called *Eyewitness Evidence: A Guide for Law Enforcement*, which was published by the Justice Department (you can download it from www.ncjrs.gov). This booklet recommended changes that responded to some of the problems listed above, but two of the big ones were not addressed. In particular, the working group did not recommend that officers who conduct lineups should not know which person in the lineup is the chief suspect (to prevent cueing of witnesses), and it did not recommend that lineups be conducted sequentially rather than simultaneously. According to Gary Ward, a member of the panel, the resistance to these proposals came mostly from prosecutors.

Although this booklet is better than nothing, it's just one of many documents produced by the Justice Department each year and there are no rewards or penalties for adopting or failing to adopt its recommendations. Until the criminal justice system gets serious about making changes to accommodate the research, we can expect false convictions based on eyewitness testimony to continue. It's hard to know how often such convictions actually occur, but in another document on the Justice Department website researcher A. Daniel Yarmey claims that approximately 4,500 people are falsely convicted in the U.S. and Canada every year.[9]

How Bad Theories Manufacture Flawed Data: "Recovered Memories" of Childhood Sexual Abuse

During the late 1960s and the 1970s, childhood sexual abuse became a major issue in American society. Encouraged by the Second Wave of feminism, many women who had suffered abuse in silence during the 1940s and 1950s began to speak out about it. Many men, myself included, were shocked to find out how many women we knew had been groped, fondled, and even forced to have sex against their will by family friends and relatives. These women remembered their abuse. By the late

1970s some clinical psychologists began to claim that the situation was much worse than anyone had suspected. They claimed that women who remembered their abuse were just the tip of the iceberg. Many other men and women (but mostly women) had also been abused but just didn't remember it. To avoid the pain, they had repressed their memories, exchanging them for other forms of misery and dysfunction. The good news was that these memories could be recovered in therapy, eliminating the misery and dysfunction and otherwise allowing the victims to heal.

This theory was based on a more general theory of memory, depression, and neurosis widely (though not universally) accepted among clinicians. That theory originated with Charcot and Jenet in the late nineteenth century and was endorsed for a time but later rejected by Freud. Roughly, it claimed that we can repress memories of traumatic events to defend ourselves against the pain they would otherwise cause. It also claimed that the price of this repression is neurosis and sometimes depression. Contemporary therapists appended an astonishing array of symptoms of repression to this theory. Not only may repressed memories of traumas make us depressed or anxious; they may also be responsible for drug addiction, sex addiction, gambling addiction, eating disorders, bad dreams, unexplained episodes of intense emotions, and many other conditions (in some books the checklist for abuse symptoms runs to many pages).[10] According to many accounts, some therapists almost immediately considered new patients who arrived with such symptoms to be likely victims of past abuse and candidates for recovered memory therapy. But recovery is not easy. The patient has repressed memories to begin with because she does not want to face them. Ingenious techniques must be employed to finesse these defenses and rescue the patient from her state of denial. Recovery techniques included hypnosis, trance writing, visualizations, attention to bodily sensations, interpretations of dreams, and guided imagery.

The recovered memory movement took the country by storm. By the mid 1980s, stories about recovered memories appeared often in newspapers and magazines, victims made guest appearances on television and radio talk shows, celebrities went public with their own "journeys to recovery," self-help books were bestsellers, survivors groups formed throughout the nation, and there were some very highly publicized legal cases. There's really no telling how many patients took part in recovered memory therapy. Some respected psychologists estimate that at its peak the number exceeded a million a year. This figure is contested – the most conservative say only tens of thousands a year – but no one denies that this diagnosis was made many times every day.

The emotional costs to all involved were staggering. Imagine believing that one or both of your parents sexually molested you. Imagine believing that they did this repeatedly. Imagine that it started in the crib. Imagine that it was part of a Satanic ritual in which babies were sacrificed. (I had a good friend whose "memories" unfolded in just this way, over a period of five years.) Now imagine being accused of this by your child. Or imagine that your parents were accused of it by your sister. Many of us don't need to imagine. Either we went through it ourselves or someone dear to us did (as accused and accusers). Others simply found themselves in a radically altered world in which their cheerful, helpful, normal-seeming neighbors were accused of raping their own children. People who worked with children – day-care workers, teachers, babysitters, and the rest – became objects of suspicion. Many child-friendly adults avoided all contact with children and many parents just didn't feel safe leaving their kids alone with the neighbors any more.

Because the damage was so great and the emotions ran so high, skepticism took courage. To voice doubt was to create doubt that could interfere with recovery. And in a world in which pedophilia seemed epidemic, it seemed to believers that skeptics were asking for the benefit of the doubt for Satan. But every academic psychologist who studied memory had reason to be skeptical and some brave souls were quite vocal about it. Their reasons for skepticism should be clear to readers of Chapter 1. Memory – or what we experience as memory – is highly suggestible. And the techniques used by recovered memory therapists exploit and increase the patient's suscepti- bility to suggestion.

Hypnosis is notorious for that. Under hypnosis, many people can be made to remember past lives, alien abductions, and opening Christmas presents they never received. In addi- tion, as we saw in Chapter 1, it doesn't take anything remotely as powerful as hypnosis to implant memories. Sometimes we can do that simply by asking someone to imagine an event that we later ask them to remember. Sometimes we can do it by describing fictional events we claim their parents or siblings remember and asking for details later. So it isn't surprising that a therapist can do this by repeatedly describing a patient's thoughts, feelings, dreams, and behavior as symptoms of abuse, especially if the therapist also asks her to engage in sug- gestibility-enhancing activities like guided visualizations and trance writing. The point is that even if Charcot and Jenet were correct – even if we do sometimes repress painful memories of trauma – these techniques of recovery can manufacture data. Unless they are supported by corroborative evidence, they are unreliable. Many therapists were not aware of this because they were not familiar with the research literature on memory. As we saw in Chapter 1, a surprising number of even doctoral-level practitioners mistakenly believed that whatever happens to a person is accurately stored in memory and can be retrieved without distortion.

The result of this disconnect was a prolonged conflict pitting academic psychologists against the recovered memory therapists and their allies. The academic psychologists stressed the vulnerability of memory to suggestion. Some of them also argued that the theory of repressed memories in general had no empirical support. The therapists argued that they saw clients recover memories and get better as a result of it. They also attacked the academic research, arguing that lab results were artificial and did not apply to real life situations in general, and to memories of trauma in particular.

Because the stakes were and are so high – because so many lives have been scarred and crippled – the early stages of the controversy were particularly heated and polemical. No therapist welcomed the news that they might have planted false memories in their patients, memories that destroyed families and sent people to prison. That is the very opposite of why therapists choose their profession and show up to work every day. Many researchers, on the other hand, empathized strongly with the patients and the accused, and went after the clinicians with two guns blazing. They had the stronger case, and by the mid 1990s both public and professional opinion began to swing in their direction. By the early 1990s professional organizations began to issue position papers cautioning against accepting recovered memories as evidence of abuse. In 1993 the American Medical Association (A.M.A.) issued a statement concluding that recovered memories are "of uncertain authenticity which should be subject to external verification. The use of recovered memories is fraught with problems of potential misapplication." And the American Psychiatric Association stated that it is impossible to distinguish accurately between true and false recovered memories. In 1994, the Council on Scientific Affairs of the A.M.A. recommended "that the AMA recognize that few cases in which adults make accusations of childhood sexual abuse based on recovered memories can be proved or disproved and it is not yet known how to distinguish true memories from imagined events in these cases." As the decade progressed, professional opinion shifted further to the side of the researchers. In 1997 the Royal College of Psychiatrists in England issued a statement that, among other things, advised psychiatrists "to avoid engaging in any 'memory recovery techniques' which are based upon the expectation of past sexual abuse of which the patient has no memory."[11]

By the mid 1990s the media also began to turn against the recovered memory movement. According to sociologist Katherine Becker, eighty percent of the articles on repressed memories that appeared in *Time*, *Newsweek*, *US News and World Report*, and *People Magazine* in 1991 were weighted in favor of the therapists. These stories simply accepted the memory reports of the alleged survivors almost entirely without question. By 1994, however, eighty percent of the articles focused on false accusations of abuse and false memories. There were many such stories. Some ex-patients successfully sued their therapists for negligence. In some cases, there was indisputable medical proof that the remembered abuse never occurred.

Now that the dust has settled, more nuanced positions are emerging. Many therapists and academic researchers now agree that memories of traumatic events can be repressed and recovered (including memories of sexual abuse) and claim to have strong corroborative evidence of that in many cases. A website at Brown University (www.RecoveredMemory.org) lists and partly describes 110 allegedly confirmed cases. Although some research psychologists continue to deny the very possibility of repression and recovery, even some who were among the strongest critics of the recovered memory movement now acknowledge that there may be a few genuine cases. On the other hand, there is now also widespread agreement among therapists that recovered memories can be implanted and that there is no reliable method for distinguishing between the accurate and inaccurate ones.

This story, then, has a better outcome than the story of eyewitness testimony. Nonetheless, it took nearly twenty years of conflict for most recovered memory therapists to acknowledge the problems with their techniques. In the meantime, hundreds of thousands (perhaps millions) of lives were seriously damaged. And the conflict has not entirely ended. Some therapists – we don't know how many – continue to do recovered memory therapy.

Bad Data Born of Bad Theory Born of Desperation: Professional Ethicists and "Our" Ethical Intuitions

To repeat an earlier point, expert status is not always bestowed on the basis of proven successes. Sometimes we bestow it just because we need people to bless us and protect us from life's contingencies and to help us recover from life's catastrophes. Enter the omen readers and medieval court physicians.

Many of the uncertainties of our time and place are moral and ethical. We've lived through a century of vast and fast political, economic, demographic, ecological, and technical changes. We also face new problems: ecological disasters, terrorist attacks, and pandemics. These changes challenge traditional values and raise new ethical questions. As our societies become more culturally and religiously diverse, we can't rely on traditional religious leaders for solutions. We need thinkers who can speak to and for us all. It is natural to look to philosophers. Philosophers have been thinking about ethics since Socrates (if not before). Over the last thirty years or so, many have assumed the title "professional ethicist."

Philosophers were happy to have their fifteen minutes of fame and also thought they had a lot to offer. Public discussion of policy issues is a rich source of silly slogans, bad analogies, empty rhetoric, logical errors, ambiguities, and sloppy distinctions. Professional philosophers live on such prey. So, over the last thirty years, many of them (myself included) have contributed to public discussions of abortion, capital punishment, euthanasia, economic justice, bribery, affirmative action, terrorism, humanitarian intervention, and other issues. In addition, specialists on ethics have surfaced in schools of business, education, law, and medicine. Many of them appear regularly on television with the title "ethicist" under their name. Much of this has been a good thing. Philosophers in particular are good at spotting drivel, clarifying issues, making key distinctions, presenting arguments in their strongest form, and so forth. But in what way do they arrive at their own positive conclusion about what's right and what's wrong? What is their method? What data stand behind their conclusions?

Well, not surprisingly, philosophers disagree a lot about methods and data. But one strong tendency stands out, a tendency that is embarrassing to confess to people who do serious intellectual work. That is, many philosophers (and other ethicists) reach their conclusions about abortion, euthanasia, justice, and the rest partly or entirely by consulting their "ethical intuitions." Basically, one's "ethical intuitions" are one's moral responses. Or, rather, these responses count as intuitions after we've thought them over in a cool state of mind and from an impartial point of view (John Rawls, the leading American moral philosopher in the second half of the twentieth century, called these judgments "considered moral judgments" and used them – along with other considerations – to justify his highly influential theory of justice). We may have intuitions about moral principles (for example, that it's wrong to torture babies for the fun of it) and about what is right or wrong to do in a particular situation (for example, it's wrong for Jane to rob Peter to pay Paul, given her circumstances, her relation to Peter and Paul, and so forth). Since we disagree about principles precisely because we have different intuitions about them, intuitionism about principles doesn't get us very far. The usual strategy is to justify principles by appealing to intuitions about cases. Either way, intuitions are data from which most ethical philosophers arrive at their ethical conclusions. According to many ethicists, they are also our glimpses into an objective moral order.

To get a better sense of how this works, consider a famous example. In a paper that appeared in the prestigious *New England Journal of Medicine*, James Rachels argues that voluntary active euthanasia (assisted suicide for the terminally ill) is morally acceptable whenever voluntary passive euthanasia is (pulling the plug, discontinuing feeding, etc.).[12] He believes the active case (for example, lethal injection) is killing and the passive case is letting someone die. But he also believes that there is no morally relevant difference between killing someone and letting someone die, all other things being equal. That is, all other things being equal, it is morally permissible to kill someone whenever it is morally permissible to let them die. He defends this moral equivalence by appealing to his (and, he hopes, our) intuitions about cases. That is, he describes two cases in which everything is the same except that one is a case of killing and the other is a case of letting someone die. His intuitions tell him that there is no difference between these cases. He concludes from this that, in general, there is no moral difference between killing per se and letting someone die per se.

Here, briefly, are his cases. A man, who stands to gain an inheritance at the death of his young nephew, is bathing the tot. In case A, the tot slips, hits his head on the tub, and drowns as the uncle looks on and does nothing. In case B, the uncle holds the unconscious tot under water until he drowns. According to Rachels's ethical intuitions, there is no morally relevant difference between what the uncle does in these two cases. Since the only difference between them is that one is a case of killing and the other a case of letting someone die, he concludes that this difference doesn't make a difference morally. Since it doesn't make a difference morally here, he concludes that it doesn't make a difference morally anywhere. Since it doesn't make a difference morally anywhere, he concludes that it doesn't make a difference morally when it comes to euthanasia. This means that whenever it's morally permitted to pull the plug, it's also morally permitted to give a lethal injection.

Many ethicists on both sides of the assisted suicide issue use a similar method of argument. In fact, it's now the method of choice for dealing with ethical issues in influential political circles. Dr. Leon Kass, the chair of President Bush's President's Commission on Bioethics has introduced appeals to intuition into public hearings intended to guide legislation on biomedical issues. In essence, Kass argues (well, claims) that the fact that a practice seems morally repellent is evidence that it is morally wrong (he calls this "the yuck factor"). Kass's own responses of moral repugnance has moved him to oppose many forms of reproductive technology.[13]

The problem with this "method" is immediately obvious to almost every undergraduate in a beginning ethics course. Not only do "intuitions" vary widely from one culture and historical epoch to the next; they vary widely between individuals of the same time and place. That's why we argue about these issues in the first place. In fact, they vary in particular individuals as they move from, say, labor to management, single to married, "closeted" to "out," young to old, etc. And they are obviously heavily influenced by our upbringing, our tendency to hold grudges, our capacity for empathy, and other contingencies of personality. How, then, could I possibly say my intuitions are evidence of moral truth but not yours (unless they agree with mine)? How do I explain to myself and to you how I managed to get so lucky?

Being philosophers, many intuitionists (as they are called) devise ingenious responses to this obvious objection. Anyone seriously interested in this controversy should check them out. They should also check out Chapter 1 of my book *Between Universalism and Skepticism: Ethics as Social Artifact*[14] for a detailed to the point of tedious exposition and critique of these responses (and a discussion of how ethical discussions should be conducted). Because I think the obvious objection against intuitionism is so strong, my view is that intuitionism is essentially an expression of desperation. Philosophers accept it because it seems to them the only game in town. Unless we can trust our intuitions, they think, there is no way to justify our moral positions *at all*, and morality dissolves into social convention or personal taste. That skeptical view of morality may be tolerable in dorm room discussions, but few of us live like that or can live like that. We take our moral stances seriously.

It's not just that we *prefer* not to be cheated, raped, and murdered and *prefer* not to cheat, rape, and murder others. We morally condemn people who do these things because we think they are *wrong, evil, depraved*, and maybe even *rotten to the core*. But the philosophers in question don't see how we can justify such judgments unless we rely on our intuitions as evidence. What other kind of evidence can there be?

I think this sense of desperation is unnecessary because I think there really are ways to justify moral positions. But that is not the point of this section. The point is to illustrate the way Knowledge Machines and those who rely on them are willing to accept very questionable data because it is just too hard to live without any answers at all to certain questions.

Ignorance, Iffy Data, and Economic Interests: Brokers, Economists, and Random Walks

Another area in which expertise seems to be bestowed independently of proven competence is stock market investment. I say "seems" because like most readers I really don't have the technical competence to evaluate all the arguments about this directly and I am unwilling to spend any additional years in school to get it. So I make peace with my ignorance and rely on the kinds of arguments that follow, recognizing their limits. I include this section because we all swim in these waters so much of the time.

Many stockbrokers and traders do what is called "technical trading." This involves looking for patterns in the fluctuations of the price of a stock and trying to trade in ways that exploit those patterns. To take a simplistic example, if a stock has tended to bounce back after it hits a certain low over the last significant time period, technical traders buy it when it hits that low. Of course, the actual models are more complicated. Often they are developed by applied mathematicians, who are heavily recruited by brokerage firms. Still, despite the advanced degrees, elaborate graphs, and fancy formulae, many economists believe that this kind of data is basically useless. These economists believe that the market price of a stock fluctuates *randomly* around the actual value of that stock. This hypothesis, called the Random Walk Theory (or the Efficient Capital Market Hypothesis), takes several forms.[15] But they all imply that technical traders rely on nondiagnostic (useless) data and some of them imply that data about "fundamentals" – for example, price/earning ratios – are useless as well.

Many economists support the Random Walk Theory because it follows from certain basic assumptions of economic theory. In fact, if the stock market fit their definition of an efficient market, it would be true by definition (roughly speaking, an efficient market is defined as one in which the price of everything fluctuates around its true value). But, besides that, the theory has empirical support. There have been a lot of studies comparing portfolios selected by throwing darts and other chance methods with portfolios selected by respected brokers and brokerage firms, and the randomly selected portfolios do as well.[16] How then do we explain all those hotshots who appear on television shows or get interviewed by magazines because they beat the market that week? If we take the Random Walk Theory seriously, and we assume that brokers are using different investment strategies, some of them will always do much better than others in a given week (month, year). The television investment shows and the investment publications are (intentionally or unintentionally) cooperating with the brokers to promote the illusion of expertise. No one would read these magazines, watch these shows, or even hire a broker if he thought that picking stocks involves no more skill than playing the lottery.

Critics of the Random Walk Theory point out that the stock market is not in fact an efficient market. This is because in efficient markets every player has the same information, makes more or less the same inferences from that information, and behaves rationally (that is, tries to maximize her gains). But stock market investors do not all have the same information. Insider traders make billions investing on the basis of information unavailable to the rest of us. They also arrive at different conclusions based on information they share with the rest of us (especially in relation to future technological and social trends that have economic impacts). And investors certainly don't act rationally. Fear and mania are often in the driver's seat, generating bear and bull markets, and leading to bubbles and crashes. Furthermore, some people know how to take advantage of this. Warren Buffet attributes part of his own long-term success at beating the market to his ability to identify areas and times in which the market is not efficient.

This means that people with insider information and/or a sound understanding of market psychology have an edge, especially if they are also good at predicting future trends with economic impact. But brokers don't have insider information (usually), and it's not clear that they are better than the rest of us at predicting future trends with economic impact. Also, the fact that the market is inefficient in the ways noted does nothing to vindicate technical traders who try to pick stocks based on patterns in the numbers themselves. So, while it may be that some brokers are better at understanding the psychology of the market than the rest of us, it's not clear how to pick out their voices from the chorus of equally confident ones. We have very limited access to their long-term track records.

Standing Pat: Lie Detection and the Criminal Justice System

In addition to letting bad data in, Knowledge Machines may keep good data out. In particular, they may be slow to accept data from other sources. This is especially true when they can't explain the data in terms of their own theories or, worse, when the data challenge their methods and theories. We will begin with another example from the criminal justice system, and go on to consider examples from medicine and psychology. In our first example, data from other sources are ignored out of sheer inertia.

The average person is not very good at detecting lies. The average rate of accuracy, established by twenty years of testing, is little better than chance (estimates range from fifty to sixty percent).[17] Still, the outcome of many trials depends on judges' or jurors' ability to tell when someone is lying. Despite the research, no one in the court system seems to worry about their ability to do that. And few people in the system seem motivated to try to find a better way. If they were motivated, they could find one. It's already out there.

Psychologist Paul Ekman developed the tools we need. Inspired by Darwin's work on the expression of emotion in animals, by his own anthropological observations of cross-cultural similarities in human emotional expression, and by a former teacher, Silvan Tomkins, who had an uncanny ability to read emotions in faces, Ekman made a comprehensive study of the way human faces express emotions. In collaboration with his colleague Wallace Friesen, he carefully identified every

muscle in the face, determined that they can produce forty-
three individual movements (called "action units"), and determined that these units can combine to produce three thousand
emotionally meaningful expressions. In 1978, after seven years'
work, Ekman and Friesen published their results as the Facial
Action Coding System (F.A.C.S.).[18]

As they were developing this system, Ekman and Friesen
made another important discovery. Ekman was asked by colleagues in the Psychiatry Department at the University of
California at San Francisco to help develop a method to tell
whether suicidal patients were lying about their suicidal tendencies. Early in his career, Ekman had filmed psychiatric
interviews of forty patients, including one of a woman (Mary)
convincing her doctors that she felt well enough to spend a
weekend with her family. In fact, Mary planned to kill herself
(which she confessed just before she was scheduled to leave the
hospital). Ekman and Friesen played the film of this interview
over and over in slow motion for dozens of hours, looking for
clues that she was lying. Eventually, they found what they
were looking for. When Mary's doctor asked about her plans
for the future, a look of complete despair momentarily flashed
across her face, and was quickly replaced by a more optimistic
look. The expression of despair was almost too fast to see in real
time, even after Ekman and Friesen knew it was there. Ekman
and Friesen hypothesized that when we feel an emotion, a
corresponding message is sent to the muscles in the face. The
involuntary expressions produced – "microexpressions" as
they called them – reveal what we are actually feeling. If we
want to conceal our emotions, to show the world another face,
these microexpressions can be replaced in a fraction of a second.
But these phony replacements use different muscles than
genuine expressions do and genuine expressions are almost

impossible to fake. If we smile spontaneously, in response to genuine pleasure, for example, we tighten the muscles that encircle the eye. It is almost impossible to do this on demand.

Although there is no single microexpression that says "I'm lying" – no equivalent to Pinocchio's nose – microexpressions can be very good indications of lying. Some people, for example, smirk for a fraction of a second before they lie (an expression Ekman calls "duping delight"). In other cases, Mary's for example, people's microexpressions conflict with the content of what they are saying. Their microexpressions may express anxiety, for example, when their words and social faces express calm. Ekman has a collection of film clips illustrating this in some well-known people (for example, Bill Clinton denying he had sex with Monica Lewinsky, and spy Kim Philby denying his espionage activities under oath). When he plays these films in slow motion, the microexpressions are easy to see. Because he studied under the legendary face reader Silvan Tompkins, Ekman realized from the start that some people can see microexpressions in real time. Maureen O'Sullivan, another colleague and collaborator of Ekman's, has tested more than twelve thousand people for this ability, especially as it applies to truth telling. As of late 2003, she had found twenty-nine who could correctly distinguish lying from truth telling at least eighty percent of the time in three tests (using film clips). She also discovered that most people can get much better at this in a matter of weeks. As of 2002, more than five hundred people had been trained and certified to use F.A.C.S. for research. These people not only learn to identify microexpressions on film, in slow motion, but also in real time. In addition, Ekman developed a thirty-five-minute training tape. Before people view his tape, he says, they can't see any of the microexpressions. When they finish, they can see them all.

Ekman's work has received a lot of attention. It has been used by animators at DreamWorks (*Shrek*) and Pixar (*Toy Story*) to create realistic facial expressions. It is also widely used in law enforcement. In conjunction with former U.S. Alcohol, Tobacco, and Firearms agent J. J. Newberry, Ekman put together a program for educating law enforcement people around the world in techniques of lie detection. He has also assisted the C.I.A., F.B.I., and U.S. Department of Defense in counter-terrorism training. But although Ekman's work has been used in police work and spying, it has not been incorporated into the courtroom. This seems ridiculous, since the average juror's ability to tell when someone is lying is not much better than a coin flip.

There are many ways Ekman's work could be used to make jurors' decisions more accurate. For example, we could train jurors with Ekman's thirty-five-minute training tape, video-tape witnesses on the stand, and let the jurors play back the recordings in slow motion, looking for telltale microexpressions. If there are questions, disputes, or other problems, jurors could email the relevant bits of tape to F.A.C.S. certified experts. We could move to this system in a matter of weeks and at very little cost.

Microexpressions are highly diagnostic data. It is a testimony to the power of tradition and institutional inertia that the justice system has not even started to think of ways they could be incorporated into the process.

Rejecting What Does Not Fit: Acupuncture and the A.M.A.

Knowledge Machines are also reluctant to accept data that can't be explained by their theories. Up to a point, this is reasonable. There are a lot of crank claims out there and it would be a waste of time, money, and talent to investigate them all. The trick is to achieve the right balance of skepticism and open-mindedness. The history of acupuncture in America illustrates this problem nicely.

Among other things, practitioners of traditional Chinese medicine believe that something called "chi" energy runs through channels in the body called "meridians" and that the blockage of this energy is the cause of many health problems. They also believe that they can detect these blockages by feeling pulses and by examining a patient's tongue and that they can release these blockages by inserting acupuncture needles in the right places. Among other things, they believe they can use these needles to energize, anaesthetize, diminish chronic pain, relieve muscle spasms, kill viruses, and address organ-related problems. Western medicine does not recognize the existence of chi energy or meridians and can provide no explanation of how these needles work. So until very recently, the Western medical establishment regarded acupuncture as crank and kooky medicine, despite many testimonials of its successes by reliable and respectable witnesses. This testimony was simply ignored, explained away (placebo effect), or dismissed as merely anecdotal.

The change came from below. Although acupuncture was practiced in the U.S. as early as the 1830s, it did not become popular in America until after President Nixon's visit to China opened China to American tourism. During the 1970s many visitors to China returned with amazing stories of operations performed on patients anaesthetized by acupuncture alone. Some of these visitors – including some adventuresome British and American medical doctors with impressive credentials – learned how to do acupuncture and set up practices in their home countries. People began to go to acupuncturists for health problems and report that they had been successfully treated. These testimonial data were not taken seriously by the medical profession for the reasons mentioned for nearly twenty years. But word spread.

By the 1990s so many people were seeing acupuncturists that the medical establishment was forced to confront the practice and test its claims. In response to studies conducted earlier in that decade, a research panel of the National Institute of Health in America issued a consensus statement in 1997 concluding that "there is sufficient evidence of acupuncture's value to expand its use into conventional medicine and to encourage further studies of its physiology and clinical value." The panel also claimed that there is clear evidence that acupuncture is effective for treating adult postoperative and chemotherapy-related nausea and vomiting and for treating postoperative dental pain. It concluded that "promising results" have emerged suggesting that acupuncture "may be useful as an adjunct treatment or an acceptable alternative or be included in a comprehensive management program for addiction, stroke rehabilitation, headache, menstrual cramps, tennis elbow, fibromyalgia, myofascial pain, osteoarthritis, low back pain, carpal tunnel syndrome and asthma." Finally, it asserted that "further research is likely to uncover additional areas where acupuncture interventions will be useful."[19] Acupuncturists continue to insist that there are many more such areas. We needn't review the more recent research findings here. But, despite later favorable studies (and on the basis of a few unfavorable ones), many doctors continue to think of acupuncture as quack medicine and acupuncture continues to be classified as an alternative health care remedy by most American Health Maintenance Organizaions (H.M.O.'s) and insurance companies (which means it's not covered or it's covered at a lesser rate than normal medical treatments).

Did the medical establishment cast too narrow a net for too long in relation to acupuncture? Did it also fail to publicize its favorable test results enough to undermine the skepticism of many working physicians and H.M.O.'s? These questions are hard to answer. The history of medicine is filled with faddish "cures" that spread by word of mouth, catch on for a while, and then disappear. Medical researchers can't investigate all of them and it seems reasonable to ignore the ones that make no sense according to scientific theories of how the body works. Or anyway it makes sense to ignore them for a time. It is hard to say just how long that time is.

But while Knowledge Machines have reason to be conservative in this way, individuals don't. The rate at which the medical profession accepts evidence that acupuncture works isn't necessarily the rate at which individuals should. The fact that a friend tells us that acupuncture helped relieve her back pain or increased her energy level may be reason enough for some of us to try it. We have only the price of a visit and a little time to lose (there is no evidence that acupuncture is dangerous). More generally, Knowledge Machines may need to cast more narrow data nets for their purposes than we need to cast for ours.

Protecting Our Theories: The Willful Ignorance of Behaviorism

This is a cautionary tale. Since there are very few behaviorists left in the world, it is not a warning against an ongoing movement or practice. I have chosen it because it is much easier to argue that a retired research program sustained itself by ignoring data that undermined its theories than to show the same for an ongoing one. Critiquing an ongoing research program is always complicated. Resistance is fierce. Arguments and assumptions that seem plausible to practitioners in the heyday of a movement often seem unreasonable and even silly when the dust settles and there's a new sheriff in town. Illustrating this transformation in relation to a retired program – especially a recent and highly influential one – helps open our minds to the possibility that current programs may have the same problems.

Behaviorism originated with the work of psychologist John B. Watson at the beginning of the twentieth century. Although it developed in a number of different ways, its most famous exponent was the Harvard psychologist B. F. Skinner, probably the most influential American psychologist in the last century. Following Watson, Skinner rejected the idea that the purpose of psychology was to study the human mind or human consciousness. Since other people's minds and consciousness were unobservable, he argued, they were not the proper object of scientific study. What we can study, though, is human behavior. According to Skinner, all human and animal behavior is a conditioned response to stimuli. That is, it is a response that is determined by prior patterns of rewards and punishments. The job of the psychologist is to discover which patterns of rewards and punishments cause which kinds of behavior. To determine this we need only consider inputs (rewards and punishments) and outputs (behavior). Again, we don't need to consider anything that happens inside the head. The brain (sometimes called "the black box") is irrelevant to understanding and predicting behavior. Under Skinner's influence, large armies of psychologists sacrificed millions of lab mice to determine which patterns of rewards and punishment most effectively produced or deterred which kinds of behavior. This movement grew throughout the 1930s and dominated American psychology departments from the 1940s through most of the 1960s.

What is truly astonishing about behaviorism is the degree to which it was able to protect itself against data that challenged its central assumption, viz. that all behavior is a conditioned response to stimuli. There was so much evidence to the contrary. First, behaviorism was in direct conflict with common experience and common sense. It denied what seemed obvious to everyone, namely that our inner lives – our thoughts, our conscious feelings, and our emotions – affect how we act. This departure from the ordinary ways we understand ourselves and each other did not worry the behaviorists. In fact, they often seemed proud of it. They were scientists and science was often at odds with ordinary experience and common sense (after all, if we trusted ordinary experience we would believe the sun moves around the earth).

Second, and more troublesome, the basic premise of behaviorism was inconsistent with the ways governments and corporations were coming to understand and successfully manipulate human behavior. Ironically, the rise of behaviorism in academic psychology coincided with the rise of modern public relations, advertising, and propaganda. Practitioners of these dark arts operated with a very different take on the genesis of human desire and action. In particular, they recognized how public opinion and consumer choice can be shaped by *images and association* (for example, by sexually suggestive words and images and celebrity testimonials). The father of modern public relations and advertising, Edward Bernays, was both a biological nephew and nephew-in-law of Sigmund Freud. Although not an orthodox Freudian, he was deeply influenced by his uncle's ideas. In particular, he recognized the extent to which behavior could be manipulated by words and images appealing to deeply seated fears and desires. Joseph Goebbels had the same idea. Behaviorists tried to understand these forms of behavior manipulation in terms of behavioral theory – a formidable and Procrustean task – or they simply ignored them. They also ignored (or derided) the work of clinical psychologists interested in how these forms of manipulation work.

A still more serious problem is that the fundamental principle of behaviorism conflicted with much established biological science. Evolutionary theory, for example, does not apply only to physical traits. It also explains, for example, the behavior associated with flocking birds flocking and herding animals herding. These tendencies are not produced by schedules of reinforcement, patterns of rewards and punishments. They are inborn. These animals are genetically programmed to behave in ways that promote successful flocking and herding. Many other behaviors are like this as well. Among others, these include displays of dominance and submission, the marking of territories, suckling, and imprinting. Imprinting is particularly interesting. Normally, geese and other fowl form strong attachments to their mothers right out of the egg, and these attachments result in many familiar behaviors. In the 1930s ethologist Konrad Lorenz discovered that fowl imprint on whatever appears in the right place at the right time, even if it's a human being. As a result of his experiments on imprinting, Lorenz was often seen bicycling down country roads followed by flocks of birds that had imprinted on him. These birds didn't learn this behavior through patterns of rewards and punishments. They were simply genetically primed to imprint on whatever appeared at the right place and the right time and to behave accordingly. Since no pattern of reward or punishment is involved, behaviorism can't explain this.

Biology also undermined behaviorism in ways that had nothing to do with the nature/nurture issue. For example, behaviorism cannot explain the impact of hormones on behavior. The discipline that studies this – behavioral endocrinology – began in earnest in the late 1930s with investigations of the role of hormones on mating behavior. By the 1950s there was a large research literature on the ways hormones affect behavior, especially the impact of sexual hormones on mating behavior and aggression. But behaviorists did not take this to be a challenge to their basic theory. They couldn't afford to. Hormones are just one specific instance of the way that brain chemistry affects behavior. Once we begin looking at the way brain chemistry affects behavior, it's all over for behaviorism. Schedules of reinforcement might explain some changes in brain chemistry, but many of these changes are produced by changes in glands and organs and by the interaction between the organism and the world. Our moods and behavior are influenced by a lot of sensory stimuli: fragrances, chanting, another's touch, strobe lights, cold water, and the smoke of burning plants. Behaviorism largely ignored this just as it ignored the ways in which drugs and alcohol can influence behavior (independently of schedules of reinforcement).

In fairness, behaviorists did pay some attention to drugs. In fact, they helped develop the field of behavioral pharmacology, which investigates the ways in which various drugs affect behavior that has been generated by different reinforcement schedules. It did not occur to them, though, that this was the tip of the camel's nose. The fact that drugs and alcohol can reduce or extinguish behavior that is produced by reinforcement is clear testimony to the power of brain chemistry. Again, once we begin to explain behavior in terms of brain chemistry, behaviorism is doomed.

Despite all this and more, behaviorism ruled academic psychology and strongly influenced other social sciences for well over a quarter of a century. This is partly because these programs seemed consistent with the dominant philosophy of science of the day, developed by logical positivists. Although logical positivism was virtually dead in philosophy by the mid 1960s it lived on in the social sciences for many years after. The careers of many methodologists in those fields were linked to it. Still, it did not go unnoticed that by the late 1960s the most influential positivists had recanted publicly and in print and that the work of Thomas Kuhn was attracting a lot of philosophical interest. This weakened the behaviorists' grip. But the most powerful blow against behaviorism did not come from Kuhn or from positivists in recovery. It came from Noam Chomsky, a linguist. In a scathing review of B. F. Skinner's book *Verbal Behavior*, Chomsky argued very forcefully that behaviorism cannot explain language learning or linguistic behavior.[20] It was hard to ignore this direct and penetrating critique, especially since it was accompanied by a new and exciting theory of how languages are learned. Although there's still a tattered remnant of very old behaviorists even today, that was the beginning of the end.

Behaviorist programs cast a narrow net by excluding data that would have contributed and eventually did contribute to our understanding of human behavior. That happened because these data challenged the fundamental assumption of behaviorism itself. This problem is not restricted to behaviorism. Very powerful research programs can monopolize a field for a long time. We will examine how they can do this when we examine organizational and political dimensions of Knowledge Machines in Chapter 6.

Reflections

I began this chapter by stressing that knowledge is social. Not only do we rely on others for what we know, we rely on the coordinated efforts and actions of others, and on the various social organizations and institutions that make their cooperation possible. Still, in the end, society is us. All social institutions and organizations bring together individual people with all the limitations that that entails. Those limitations include all the various problems of perception, memory, and thinking discussed in Chapters 1 and 2. Well-designed Knowledge Machines transcend these limitations. They include mechanisms for avoiding or correcting the mistakes to which they give rise. But they aren't always successful.

Most of the cases discussed in this chapter are examples of those failures. This is obvious in the case of eyewitness testimony. The criminal justice system has simply not taken seriously what psychologists know about perception and memory. The result is a lot of wrongful convictions. It is also clear in the case of recovered memories of childhood sexual abuse. Here many clinical psychologists failed to guard against well-known ways in which memories can be implanted or altered by suggestion. These and other cases suggest a general guideline:

When evaluating a source – a Knowledge Machine – consider the extent to which it has effective mechanisms for guarding against the problems of perception, memory, and thinking that afflict us as individuals.

Problems of thinking are especially difficult to eliminate. As we saw in Chapter 2, those problems include a tendency to discount data or arguments that conflict with our own strongly held views. If anything, this tendency is strengthened – not weakened or corrected for – in many Knowledge Machines. That is because practitioners in most Knowledge Machines have a lot invested in defending the theories and assumptions on which their work is based. No one wants to believe that her life's work is flawed, especially if that work has had a lot of impact on the lives of other people. There is also a tendency for practitioners in a Knowledge Machine (or research program) to circle the wagons, reinforce each other's commitment, and otherwise egg each other on (as, for example, intuitionists in ethics do). Despite all the brave and noble words about the importance of skepticism that get trotted out on ritual occasions, doubters are rarely welcome in the house of faith. But, as the examples in this chapter suggest, most Knowledge Machines do *eventually* correct or abandon old theories and assumptions in the light of powerful new evidence. It's just that these adjustments take time. Often, outsiders see the writing on the wall before insiders do.

This suggests two corollaries to the general guideline stated above. The first is: *ignore practitioner confidence*. Most practitioners in every field will speak with great confidence (remember the omen readers). Even the most honest and sincere practitioners may be invested in what they are doing (and have done), and may ignore data that undermine their basic theories and assumptions (however fast such data may be mounting). This was true of most therapists in the recovered memory movement and of most doctors who condemned acupuncture as quack medicine.

The second corollary is this: *do not easily abandon common sense*. Knowledge Machines are rarely constrained by it. Behaviorism denied that conscious states, genetic predispositions, and brain chemistry affected behavior. At the lab, many of them denied that nonhuman animals had inner lives (and then went home to stroke their purring cats). The recovered memory movement insisted that childhood sexual abuse was epidemic and there was a lot we didn't know and would never ever guess about the shadow side of our friends and neighbors. The fact that common sense was vindicated in these cases doesn't mean that common sense is always right. New knowledge often defeats common sense. Medieval common sense notwithstanding, the world is round, the earth revolves around the sun, etc. But many once-respected scientific theories and principles also now rust in the junkyard of abandoned research programs. And, like the soothsayers and court physicians of yore, experts always speak with great confidence. So I suggest that the burden of proof be shifted to the new knowledge. Before we are willing to surrender common sense, we should demand strong evidence (again, practitioner confidence does not count as evidence). As we have seen, we don't always need to be specialists to see that the evidence is weak or, in fact, little more than aspiration. In these cases, I advise erring on the side of common sense.

Finally, because we rely on Knowledge Machines to deliver the truth, they need to be more careful than we are. Scientists, for example, must insist on scientific proof (or what passes for that in their field). The rest of us are not so constrained. We might quite legitimately believe something based on less. For example, we might believe that acupuncture works because it worked for us and a few friends. This suggests another guideline: *the fact that there is not enough evidence for a Knowledge Machine to accept a claim does not mean that there is not enough evidence for the rest of us.*

CHAPTER 4

Flawed Data: Incompetence, Subjectivity, and Cooking the Books

No matter how well designed a Knowledge Machine is – no matter how powerful and accurate its methods and theories – it's only as reliable as its human components. To the extent that practitioners don't carefully, competently, and honestly do their jobs, the results will be unreliable. Carelessness and incompetence are inevitable. We are fallible beings. We get distracted, confused, lazy, and sloppy. As a result, test samples are contaminated or mislabeled, slides are misread, public figures are misquoted, clever forgeries pass muster, and so forth. We could reduce much of this by new technologies, double-checking certain results, and other costly methods, and in some cases we should. But there is no way completely to eliminate human error. As my friend Hugo du Coudray once said, "Nothing is foolproof because fools are so ingenious." And, though even the most competent people make some mistakes, incompetent people make more. Knowledge Machines try to assure competence by at least some of the following methods: certified training programs, licensing requirements, mandatory continuing education, and enforced standards of practice. Too often, though, these are ineffective.

In addition to their varying levels of competence – remember, fifty percent of all doctors finish in the bottom half of their class – some practitioners are truer to their art or craft than others. We are not just fallible beings, but beings with agendas. We want to impress our peers, advance our careers, help our friends and families, promote our causes, and end up on the winning side of the factional wars that arise within all structures of power and prestige. All this can move us to take short-cuts, spin the truth, and even outright lie and cheat. Knowledge Machines have safeguards in effect to prevent this sort of thing, but too often these safeguards are just a little more effective than an honor system would be.

Finally, few knowledge workers are self-employed these days. Some are more or less safely ensconced in universities but many work for the private sector. This includes scientists, especially scientists who do biomedical research. These people are sometimes under serious pressure not to honor their own standards of practice. Each of the cases I describe in this chapter illustrates at least two of these problems. Several illustrate more.

Bad Training and Cost Cutting: Survey Research

We are all curious about how other people live and think. That's one reason we read so many novels, biographies, and

autobiographies and see so many films. Of course, we also recognize that these works can mislead as well as inform. They are
made by a single person or small groups of people and unusual
people at that. The pictures of reality they give us are colored by
their authors' sensibilities, perspectives, and agendas (including, in many cases, their desire to make money). Furthermore,
they can't possibly answer many of the specific questions we
may have about groups of people. For example, how many
upper class women get cosmetic surgery? How many upper
class people cheat on their taxes? At what age do working class
kids become sexually active? How many high school students
smoke marijuana at least once a week? How many high school
graduates have had at least one pregnancy? What news sources
do African Americans trust? What is the rate of alcoholism
among Hispanics, illiteracy among the Irish, drug addiction
among Jews, mental illness in families of C.E.O.'s, or child
abuse among evangelical Christians? Some of these questions
may interest us for purely personal reasons. But some of them
are also important for shaping public policy. In these cases
especially we want reliable information. That means we need
solid evidence about what people do behind closed doors and
how their real attitudes and actions relate to their professed
attitudes and self-descriptions. For this we turn to the social
sciences.

The job of discovering how other people live and think is formidable, especially in diverse societies like the United States.
Often, social scientists need to figure out ways to get intimate
details about the lives of people with whom they have had
little or no contact, people who live in different regions, or
belong to different social classes, or are members of different
ethnic and religious groups. Also, since they want their results
to have *some* claim to being scientific, they can't rely on

biographies, autobiographies, movies, and other literary works the way the rest of us do (for better or worse). How can one possibly do this?

Well, one could move in and live with the people, as anthropologists do. But, as the history of anthropology and recent controversies in that field dramatize, that has its own set of problems. How much do the "natives" reveal to the outsider? Also, however effective (or ineffective) anthropologists are in describing various aspects of a culture, they don't and can't come home with the kind of *statistical* information described above. Barring systematic bugging and spying, the only way to get *that* kind of information seems to be asking. Of course, one can't just ask a few people about such things and it's too costly to ask them all. We need to ask a representative sample of the relevant population. To this end, social scientists have developed statistical techniques to identify representative samples, complete with margins of error for various sample sizes and compositions. Polls and surveys that use these techniques acquire a scientific patina. For fifty years or more social psychologists, sociologists, political scientists, businesses, health care researchers, and others have relied on such "scientific" surveys and polls to gather data about everything from lingerie preferences to religious beliefs. As we will see, there are many problems with their methods. Some problems are unavoidable. Even the best-conducted surveys can't fully escape them. Others, though avoidable, are often not avoided. Either surveyors are unaware of the problems (bad training), or they are aware of them but unwilling to take the often time-consuming and costly measures to eliminate or reduce them.

The big assumption behind all polls and surveys is that people will tell the truth to pollsters or surveyors or, if they lie, the lies will balance out. This may seem reasonable. Most people are honest and cooperative, unless they have reason to be otherwise. So why wouldn't one cooperate with a pollster at the door? As it turns out, though, this assumption is often false. People interviewed by total strangers about highly personal issues do not always tell the truth. This has been consistently demonstrated in many contexts for many years. Techniques have been developed to detect lying, but they are time consuming and expensive and often ignored. Also, despite the research, many poll takers and surveyors seem unaware of the problem.

The Tucson Garbage Project is typical of the research demonstrating the problem of lying to pollsters (or "response bias," as it is called). Pollsters asked people how much beer they consumed in a week, and compared this with what they found in their trash. They discovered that subjects greatly underreported their consumption. In one tract, for example, eighty-six percent of responders claimed they drank no beer at all and none of the sixty people interviewed claimed they drank more than eight cans a week. But investigators found beer in the trash of seventy-seven percent of the households and found more than eight cans in fifty-four percent of them (this fifty-four percent averaged fifteen cans).[1] Response bias is especially acute when white, middle class pollsters collect survey data in poor minority neighborhoods. But it is always a problem. Studies show that people under-report not only alcohol consumption, but also drug use, psychiatric histories, being H.I.V. positive (and other medical conditions), arrest records, declaring bankruptcy, being charged with drunk driving, and being a victim of childhood sexual abuse.[2] Some of these studies are not careful to separate out cases of response bias from simple failures of memory. But if our concern is the reliability of survey data, that doesn't much matter, since failure of memory also yields mistaken results. In any case, no one who studies survey accuracy denies that response bias is a problem and some researchers have developed elaborate techniques to minimize it.

Despite the extensive literature on response bias, many polls and surveys are conducted as if response bias doesn't exist. For example, our information about the extent of mental illness in the population is based mostly on surveys. But a recent review of three major psychiatric journals for the year 1998 showed that such interviews rarely mention the possibility of response bias and almost never take measures to reduce it.[3] The same goes for surveys and interviews about how satisfied people are with their Health Maintenance Organizations. A recent study of these surveys concluded that response bias "may significantly impact the results of patient satisfaction surveys, leading to overestimation of the level of satisfaction in the patient population overall . . . [and] may be most inflated for providers with the least satisfied patients."[4] Still another study shows the significant impact of response bias on a group of studies related to ethical behavior in the accounting profession (also based on interviews and self-reports).[5] These are just a few examples of a very widespread phenomenon.

Another common problem with many polls and surveys, especially those done by mail or email, is "nonresponse bias." In this case, the responders may be telling the truth. The problem is that many people don't respond and nonresponders may well have produced different answers to questions than responders. People with good news to report, for example, may have more incentive to respond than people with bad news. Despite the fact that this problem is well studied, it too is often ignored.

Response bias and nonresponse bias are just two of many problems in survey research. Another serious problem is that respondents often don't understand questions in the way investigators intend them. In one study designed to illustrate this problem, people were asked, "Do you think children suffer any ill effects from watching programs with violence in them, other than ordinary westerns?" This seems like a straightforward question, but only eight percent understood it more or less as intended. More than fifty percent *included* westerns in their understanding despite the clause at the end of the question. There were also lots of differences in how respondents understood "children." In another study respondents were asked, "Do you think any programmes have a bad effect on young people by teaching them slang?" In this case, twenty percent of the respondents understood the question as the investigators intended it. There were lots of differences in how they understood "young people" (the age range went from five to more than twenty). There were also big differences in how they understood "slang" (some thought it meant or included bad grammar, poor pronunciation, swearing, and "bad talk").[6] In still another study respondents understood the expression "energy crisis" in nine distinct ways.[7]

The wording of a question affects answers in other ways too. For one thing, people may answer logically equivalent questions differently depending on how they are worded. In one study, respondents were asked:

1. Do you think the United States should forbid public speeches against democracy?

and:

2. Do you think the United States should allow public speeches against democracy?

These are really logically equivalent questions, since "not allow" means "forbid" and "not forbid" means "allow." But fifty-four percent of the respondents answered "yes" to the first question and seventy-five percent of them answered "no" to the second.[8] Students of survey research methods will theorize about why this is so. But it certainly should make us wonder about survey answers to questions with the words like "allow" and "forbid." The same may apply to questions involving related oppositions such as legal and illegal, reasonable and unreasonable, required and optional, and so forth. It's really not clear just how far our suspicion should extend. But it is clear that survey takers need to ask these kinds of questions in more than one way to check for disparities, and need to tell us about the disparities when they publicize their results. Too often they don't, either because they are unaware of the problem (i.e. incompetent) or because the techniques required to uncover these disparities and to get someone's "real opinions" are too time consuming and hence costly. These techniques are also open to suspicion. If people produce different answers to logically equivalent questions, how can we make a confident judgment about what they *really* believe (and, hence, how they will act)?

People also answer questions differently when they have the option of saying, "I don't know" or "I don't have enough information to say." In one study interviewers asked respondents, "In general, do you think the courts in your area deal too harshly with criminals or not harshly enough?" Given these two options, 5.6% answered "too harshly" and 77.8% answered "not harshly enough." The remaining respondents volunteered answers, 9.7% answering "about right" and 6.8% answering "I don't know." When "I don't have enough information to say" was added to the options, the answers were significantly different. In that case 4.6% answered "too harshly," 60.3% answered "not harshly enough," and 29% said they didn't have enough information to say (6.1% volunteering "just about right"). This is a good reason to be suspicious of any survey that does not give people an option to say, "I don't know."[9]

Also, the order in which items are presented on a survey appears to affect the way people respond to them. In 1960 the Institute of Practitioners in Advertising in the U.K. commissioned a National Readership Survey to discover what the British population reads. In the first stage respondents received the following instruction: "I want you to go through this booklet with me, and tell me, for each paper, whether you happen to have looked at any copy of it in the past three months, it doesn't matter where." The booklet consisted of a set of mastheads or logos for each of ninety-one publications. They included dailies, monthlies, weeklies, and Sunday papers. The booklet grouped these publication types together (for example, all the dailies were in one place), but different interviewers presented them in different orders (in some dailies came first, in others weeklies, etc.). An analysis of the data showed that in every case the responses differed depending on the order in which the publication types were presented. In some cases, the differences were relatively small. But in some cases they were quite dramatic. For example, more people said "yes" to monthlies when shown monthlies first. When monthlies were in the second position the "yes" responses dropped by seventeen percent; when monthlies were in the third position they dropped by thirty-three percent. In contrast, the "yes" response to dailies was highest in the second position, at 107% of the first, then dropped to 102% in the third position, and rose to 103% in the third.[10] "Order effects," as they are called, are also common in surveys in which one is asked to rate or rank a group of items. Items presented first tend to be endorsed more strongly than the same items presented last.[11]

The order in which *questions* are asked may also make a significant difference. In one survey conducted during the Cold War respondents were asked the following two questions: (1) Do you think the United States should let communist newspaper reporters come in here and send back to their papers the news as they see it? and (2) Do you think a communist country like Russia should let American newspaper reporters come in and send back to America the news as they see it? When (1) was asked first, thirty-six percent answered "yes." When the order was reversed, seventy-three percent answered "yes." When (2) was asked first, ninety percent answered "yes." When (2) was asked second, only sixty-six percent did.[12] The most plausible explanation is that the ordering suggested a kind of argument to the respondents. The overwhelming majority initially believed that the communist countries should give American reporters access. So that is what ninety percent of them said when (2) was asked first. Once they took that position, though, some were moved by fairness to say that America should give Russian communist reporters access to America as well. This phenomenon is called a "consistency effect" and is common in surveys.

Many surveys are about past problems, past behaviors, and the like. Answers to these questions are only as accurate as people's memories. But, as we saw in Chapter 1, memory is not always reliable. In one study high school students were asked to report drug use during the last year and during the last month. The monthly report was three times as high as one would expect given the yearly report.[13] This result is consistent with other studies that show that reports of past events decrease as they recede into the past. The best-documented cases are doctors' visits, hospitalizations, and other health events that can be checked against medical records. These are consistently under-reported on standard questionnaires. For intervals longer than six months the under-reporting can exceed fifty percent. As it turns out, much of the under-reporting of these and other events can be eliminated through special interview techniques that enhance memories. However, these techniques are quite time consuming and therefore expensive and are not used in ordinary surveys.[14] As a result, these surveys have limited accuracy. Some researchers think that future research will tell us how fast memories for different types of events fade and will calculate the actual incidence of events in that way. But given all the various possible categories of events in question, I'd advise against holding your breath.

Finally, some survey questions are not diagnostic. That is, the answers to them don't settle the issue they are supposed to settle. In 1990 the American Association of University Women (A.A.U.W.) commissioned a survey intended to measure and compare the development of self-esteem in boys and girls from elementary school to high school. The results of that survey were widely reported and taken as evidence of a national crisis. The education system was systematically short-changing the girls. According to the A.A.U.W.'s summary of the survey, "In a crucial measure of self-esteem, 60 percent of elementary school girls and 69 percent of elementary school boys say they are 'happy the way I am.' But by high school, girls' self-esteem falls 31 points to only 29 percent, while boys' self-esteem falls only 23 points to 46 percent."[15]

This widely quoted piece of the summary is misleading, since it only reports the percentage of boys and girls who answered "always true" to the question, "Are you happy the way you are?" (There were actually five possible answers: "always true," "sort of true," "sometimes true/sometimes false," "sort of false," and "always false.") But the main problem is the question itself. As many critics have pointed out, high school girls tend to be a lot more thoughtful and reflective than high school boys. They are also more realistic and more willing to admit their weaknesses and imperfections. This means they are going to have a stronger tendency to find and acknowledge things about themselves they would rather change than their relatively less reflective male counterparts ("It's all good, dude!"). So one can't *assume* that answering this question "always true" indicates high self-esteem – at least if high self-esteem is supposed to be a good thing. It could also indicate a simple lack of reflection. It could be that the girls have simply become more reflective and more realistic than the boys. Anyway, this is a possibility one would need to consider before declaring that there is a national crisis involving the short-changing of girls.

Fame, Fortune, and Licking the Hand that Feeds You: Scientific Fraud

Over the last thirty years the image of science has been tarnished by a number of high-profile cases of fraud. Most recently, the Korean scientist Hwang Woo Suk published two papers in *Science* falsely claiming that he had created stem cell lines from cloned human embryos. Both papers contained fabricated data. Responding to this case, Donald Kennedy, editor-in-chief of that journal and past president of Stanford University, said, "Scientific fraud is not new and it is not rare. Luckily it's not common either."[16] It's not clear exactly what he meant by "rare" and "common" – compared with what? – or how he knows how often scientific fraud occurs. It really is hard to tell how often. According to Linda Miller, the U.S. executive editor of *Nature*, "If the fraud is clever enough, it is likely that referees and editors will not notice it."[17] The problem is especially acute in biomedical research. The scientific community traditionally relies on replication to assure the accuracy of test results, but biomedical trials are often expensive. As Drummond Rennie, deputy editor of the *Journal of the American Medical Association*, says, "When a single trial costs $150 million, how is anyone ever going to replicate it?" According to Jules Hallum, director of the National Institute of Health's Office of Scientific Integrity, "Nobody gets funding to do replications, so science is not the self-cleansing apparatus it once was."[18]

One reason that it's hard to know how often scientific fraud occurs is that it's so hard to detect. Some people who were finally caught got away with it for years. John Hendrik Schon, a researcher at Bell Labs, had published more than one hundred papers on superconductivity, molecular crystals, and molecular electronics before it was discovered that there were at least sixteen incidences of fraud. Some of these papers appeared in the most prestigious journals, including *Science*, *Nature*, *Physical Review*, and *Applied Physics Letters*.[19] Robert Slutsky, a radiologist at the University of California at San Diego, had published 137 papers (seventy-seven valid, forty-eight questionable, and twelve proven fraudulent).[20] Stephen Breuning, who fabricated data on the effects of psychotropic drugs on the mentally retarded, was responsible for thirty-four percent of the papers on that subject between 1979 and 1983.[21] John Darsee, a researcher in labs at Emory and then Harvard, published more than a hundred papers on the use of drugs and other interventions in recovery from heart attacks. After his fraud was discovered, seventy papers or abstracts in which he manipulated data were withdrawn.[22] Some cases of very bad fraud are detected earlier. In a case that attracted a lot of media attention in the mid 1970s, William Summerlin, a skin cancer researcher at Sloan Kettering, claimed to his boss that he had successfully transplanted skin from a mouse to a genetically unrelated mouse by keeping that skin in an organ culture for four to six weeks. His evidence, two white mice with apparently black skin patches, was faked. A lab technician discovered that the dark patches had been drawn on the white mice with a felt-tipped pen. The technician was able to remove the "patches" with alcohol. Needless to say, this fake never made it into a medical journal.[23]

These cases are just suggestive anecdotes; it's impossible to tell from them just how deep the problem is. But scientists themselves have been worried about it for quite some time. In November 1991 the American Association for the Advancement of Science was concerned enough to sponsor a survey on the extent of this problem. Of the fifteen hundred scientists polled, more than twenty-five percent said they had personally witnessed faking, falsifying, or outright theft of research in the past decade. Since theft does not necessarily result in suspect data, this doesn't say anything definitive about types of fraud that pollute the data pool. But many scientists seem quite worried. According to Walter Stewart, a National Institute of Health staff scientist who has participated in several fraud investigations, "There is no hard evidence but my gut feeling is the problem has gotten much worse in the past five years. There has been a collapse of the professional consensus that you have to behave correctly."[24]

This is also suggestive but still well short of hard data. In the end, how much fraud we think there is will depend on the extent to which we think scientists can withstand the pressures and temptations that come with their positions. Some of these temptations are born of the long and troubled marriage between science and commerce. A good recent example of this is way the tobacco companies have used doctors and scientists. From the early twentieth century tobacco companies hired doctors and scientists to sell the public the health benefits of smoking – a campaign that lasted well into the 1960s. More recently, they have employed scientists and doctors to lobby against regulating second-hand smoke. According to a study by researchers at the University of California at San Francisco, that campaign started in 1987 and included the recruitment and management of more than sixty scientific and medical experts. These paid representatives of the tobacco industry attended conferences, presented papers and lobbied government officials, all the while concealing their connection to the tobacco industry. In one case, representatives of the tobacco industry made up the entire organizing committee of an international conference on air quality.[25] Of course, we're talking about a very tiny percentage of doctors and scientists. We don't know how many doctors and scientists the tobacco companies wanted to hire for this job, and how many people turned them down for ethical reasons. But the tobacco companies were able to recruit a cadre of doctors and scientists to distribute their propaganda.

There is also chicanery in pharmaceutical research. The evidence suggests that either researchers employed by drug companies report negative results less often than their colleagues with other employers, or they simply cook the books. According to the *British Journal of Medicine*, for example, drug tests by pharmaceutical company scientists are four times as likely to produce positive results than drug tests backed by other sponsors. In an interview with the *New Scientist*, Joel Lexchin, the leader of this study, is quoted as saying, "What we found was that in almost all cases there was a bias – a rather heavy bias – in favor [of a drug] when the study was industry funded."[26] There are also known cases of out and out fraud. In December 2005, for example, the prestigious *New England Journal of Medicine* reported that its five-year-old report on Vioxx contained "inaccuracies" due to incomplete data on potential side effects. In January 2006, the same journal issued "an expression of concern" that two cancer research studies it had published in 2001 and 2004 contained misleading evidence. A few days earlier the prestigious British journal *The Lancet* announced that a 2005 study from the same research team included fabricated data. These corrections notwithstanding, the misuse of science by commerce is aided and abetted by the editors of scientific journals.[27] Journals treat papers by industry-affiliated scientists in the same way they treat papers produced by other scientists. Until very recently, journals did not require that authors employed by drug companies (or doing research financed by drug companies) even note that affiliation in their published papers. Although that practice is changing, it still operates in many journals.

But service to commerce is not the only cause of scientific fraud. Many scientists are simply ambitious. They want to win the respect and acclaim of their colleagues, move to better universities, earn higher salaries, and join the jet-setting scientific elite at exclusive conferences at posh resorts in exotic places. Or they may simply want to attract grant money to keep their labs running and their families fed. None of this is easy. Science, especially Big Science, is highly competitive. If one's research program flags – if one's results are disappointing – funding agencies will dispense their largesse elsewhere. So there is a big incentive for all serious researchers to produce promising numbers. Again, it's almost impossible to tell how many cheat. But the power of temptation always rises as the chances of getting caught falls. In the case of science, policing is weak.

I have already mentioned that many results – especially results of very expensive projects – are no longer replicated. In addition, although many scientific research projects are collective efforts involving lots of people, there is often not much oversight of any particular scientist's work. Often, project supervisors just assume that their coworkers are honest and know their business, and simply accept what they come up with. If someone in a lab is paying attention to someone else's numbers, they have little incentive to report suspected fraud to their supervisor. As a rule, whistle-blowers are treated badly. In a very high-profile case involving a paper co-authored by Nobel Laureate David Baltimore, a post-doctoral researcher Margot O'Toole accused Baltimore's co-author Theresa Imanishi-Kari of fabricating data. Since this project involved large federal funds, it was investigated by the Office of Research Integrity (then part of Health and Human Services) and was also the topic of a congressional investigation. O'Toole blew the whistle in the face of considerable pressure and discouragement from important scientists. She did this because she could not duplicate Imanishi-Kari's results and Imanishi-Kari could not produce notes that vindicated her data. The Office of Research Integrity decided that Imanishi-Kari had fabricated data. Its decision was overturned on appeal five years later by its successor agency, the Office of Scientific Integrity, which found Imanishi-Kari guilty of sloppy research instead. Meanwhile, Margot O'Toole was effectively black-balled by the scientific community for her efforts. Despite her doctorate, her promise as a scientist, and her integrity, and despite the fact that she alerted the scientific community to a piece of bad research, her later jobs included answering the telephone for a moving company.[28] Hers is not an isolated case.

Not even universities have a vested interest in protecting us against fraud. On the contrary, Robert Bell, an economics professor at Brooklyn College who has done considerable research on this topic, writes,

> Like the Pentagon's defense contractors, the scientific community has evolved into another patronage system which enriches those at the top. Universities have a vested interested in not finding anyone guilty of fraud. Because if they do, they may have to return the delinquent researcher's grants. When someone blows the whistle, universities set up investigatory panels, which are almost inevitably kangaroo courts that cover up abuses.[29]

The last line of defense against fraudulent data are scientific journals. But journal editors just don't try very hard to detect fraud. They rely on a traditional but very weak peer review system. Papers submitted are sent to experts in the relevant field. These reviewers – or "referees," as they are called – are unpaid and anonymous. Since their names are not associated with the papers they evaluate – there is no "reviewed by Dr. Adrian Richardson" – they do not vouch publicly for the papers they approve. They are generally busy scientists with big research projects of their own and little free time. It takes a lot of time and energy to investigate cooked data and other fraud and, right or wrong, one doesn't make a lot of friends questioning the integrity of one's colleagues. Reviewers have nothing but their own self-respect to gain by doing a good job and, if they suspect fraud, they risk a lot by making an issue of it. So, to repeat an earlier quote from Linda Miller, "If the fraud is clever enough, it is likely that referees and editors will not notice it."

Accounting Fraud: Money, Power, and Politics

When people have a lot to win or lose by providing information about themselves, it is a good idea to check the truth of what they say. We don't let criminal suspects off the hook because they *tell us* they didn't do the crime and we don't let students into universities because they tell us they finished first in their class. We investigate crimes and ask students for transcripts. Before 1933, though, no independent check was required on the balance sheets produced by publicly traded companies to describe their own financial health. Investors relied on that data to make investment decisions and those decisions made a big difference to companies and their executives. The more money invested in a company, the more valuable the company becomes. The more valuable the company becomes, the better its executives do. Executives are generally big stockholders and get raises as their company's market value increases. Yet before 1933 these very same executives – C.E.O.'s and C.F.O.'s (chief financial officers) – were in charge of generating their own numbers. It was as if college applicants could make up their own transcripts and S.A.T. (Scholastic Aptitude Test) scores.

This ended soon after the stock market crashed in 1929. The crash occurred partly because companies had misrepresented themselves. That created widespread public distrust of both corporations and the stock market. To help restore trust, Congress passed the Securities Act of 1933 and the Securities

Exchange Act of 1934. In effect, these laws created the Security and Exchange Commission and required that publicly traded firms file financial reports with that organization. It also required that these forms be reviewed and approved by independent auditors. The reason for an independent audit was obvious. Since the stock market value of a corporation and the careers of its executives depend on its financial performance, we can't trust those same executives to tell us how well their company is doing.

It's not clear how well this system ever worked. But it is very clear that it has not worked well recently. One problem is that independent auditors do not prepare their own, independent balance sheets. Instead, they are supposed to verify that *a company's own accountants* prepared its balance sheets in accordance with accepted accounting principles. They do not, for example, check most figures the company provides against the original records (for example, billings and receipts). Instead, they simply sample transactions. They may ask for documentation of suspicious numbers in the transactions they do check, but these represent a small sample of the transactions in which a company actually engages. So even if their audits were truly honest and independent, a lot could slip past them.

Also, corporate bookkeeping is a highly complicated and specialized enterprise. Even without fraud, accountants make discretionary choices that affect our perception of a company's financial health. Fraudulent transactions can be concealed by highly skilled accountants (in some cases, accountants who have themselves been auditors). Like Cendant, companies may claim revenues that have not yet been earned to boost revenues. Like Lucent, they may also set aside funds for some purpose (e.g. restructuring) at one point and then pull funds from that account as income at another point to enhance their outlook. Like Enron, they may hide debt by creating "special purpose entities" to assume them (Enron created more than three thousand). Like Freddie Mac, they may hide earnings from one quarter and bring them back as needed so that executives can make their bonuses in a later quarter (a practice called "slush fund accounting"). Like many firms, they may inflate their sales numbers shortly before their balance sheet comes out by recording sales they anticipate making at a later date. There are many clever ways to conceal and to falsify numbers.[30]

To make matters much worse, auditors are not really independent. There are many reasons for this. First, auditing firms are hired and fired by the companies that they audit. If the C.E.O. or C.F.O. of a company is in fact cheating, this is like letting a criminal suspect hire and fire the police who investigate him. Not surprisingly, the chances that a client will fire an auditing firm increases after a critical audit report and, of course, this reduces the auditor's desire to file such a report.[31] It is sometimes replied that the major accounting firms are so large that losing a client or two is no big deal. But it is a big deal to the person in charge of the audit. His career depends on his success with clients. A second reason for this lack of independence is that auditing firms make a lot of money selling non-auditing services to their clients. Before the passage of the Sarbanes–Oxley Bill in 2002, they made most of their money from these services. In 1999 nearly two-thirds of the revenue of the major accounting firms and seventy percent of their profits were tied to these services.[32] This gives auditing firms still another reason to lick the hands that feed them. Also, since these non-auditing services are supposed to improve a company's performance, an evaluation of that company's performance by the auditing firm is also an evaluation of its own non-auditing services. If the company does well, consultants from the auditing firm get some of the credit. Third, just as many former congress-men and -women become lobbyists, many auditors take jobs at the firms they audit. So they have a reason to be chummy with clients, which discourages asking hard questions or any other acts suggestive of suspicion. Finally, auditors spend a lot of time with clients over a number of years and it's common to become friendly with the people one works with. This also makes it difficult to ask the hard questions.

The result of all this is very unreliable numbers. In 2002, an especially bad year for scandals, the list of American companies caught up in major accounting fraud included the following: A.O.L., Adelphia, Bristol-Myers Squibb, C.M.S. Energy, Computer Associates, Duke Energy, Dynegy, El Paso Corporation, Enron, Freddie Mac, Global Crossing, Halliburton, Harken Energy, HealthSouth, Homestore.com, ImClone Systems, Kmart, Lucent Technologies, Merck & Co., Merrill Lynch, Mirant, Nicor Energy, L.L.C., Peregrine Systems, Qwest Communications, Radiant Energy, Tyco International, Waste Management, Inc., and Worldcom.[33]

Most of the so-called independent auditing in the United States (and worldwide) is now conducted by four major accounting firms – Deloitte & Touche, Ernst & Young, K.P.M.G., and PricewaterhouseCoopers. These firms audit more than seventy-eight percent of publicly traded U.S. companies (and more than ninety-nine percent of public company sales). In 2002 there were five firms. Arthur Andersen, the Enron auditor, folded as a result of the Enron scandal. When most Americans think of accounting fraud, they think of Arthur Andersen and Enron. But the firms involved in these scandals were not all clients of Arthur Andersen. In fact, every one of the major accounting firms – firms that continue to audit more than seventy-eight percent of publicly traded companies – has been implicated in multiple scandals in recent years.

Here is a selection of companies involved in major accounting scandals which were audited by these firms. *Deloitte & Touche* audited Adelphia, A.E.S., Duke Energy, El Paso, Merrill Lynch, Reliant Energy, Rite Aid, and Pharmalat. *Ernst & Young* audited A.O.L. Time Warner, Dollar General, P.N.C. Bank, and Cedant. *K.P.M.G.* audited Citigroup, Computer Associates, General Electric, ImClone, Peregrine, and Xerox. *PricewaterhouseCoopers* audited Bristol Meyers, H.P.L., J. P. Morgan Chase, Kmart, Lucent, MicroStrategy, Network Associates, N.K.F.S., and Tyco. And, before it folded, *Arthur Andersen* audited C.M.S., Cornell, Dynegy, Enron, Global Crossing, Halliburton, Omnimedia, Merck, Peregrine, Qwest, Sunbeam, Waste Management, Inc., and Worldcom.[34]

These are major scandals involving hundreds of millions and sometimes billions of dollars in fraud, fines, and/or losses to investors. To take just the first six firms on the 2002 list in alphabetical order:

Adelphia, went bankrupt after it was discovered that it had $2.3 billion in off-balance-sheet (i.e. concealed) debt.

A.O.L. Time Warner misrepresented hundreds of millions of dollars in ad revenues to inflate the market value of A.O.L. (they settled their case by paying $510 million in fines).

Bristol Myers Squibb illegally claimed $1.5 billion of revenue from sales to wholesalers and agreed to pay $150 million in fines and perform numerous remedial tasks.

C.M.S. Energy overstated its revenue by $4.4 billion from 2000 to 2001 by reporting trades that, according to the U.S. Securities and Exchange Commission (S.E.C.), "lack economic substance";

Computer Associates was charged with prematurely recognizing $2.2 billion in 2000–1 and $1.1 billion in earlier quarters (in 2004 it reached a deal with the S.E.C. to pay $225 million to shareholders victimized by its criminal conduct). *Duke Energy* was charged with falsifying trades that added $1 billion to revenues over three years.[35]

These scandals, of course, are small potatoes compared with the mega-scandals at Enron, Worldcom, and Cendant. From 1999 to 2002, Worldcom committed more than $7 billion in accounting errors in its favor. The company filed for bankruptcy in 2002. In 2003 Cendant agreed to pay $3.2 billion to investors who had lost $14 billion in one day after the company disclosed accounting problems. The company's accountant, Ernst & Young, also paid $325 million to Cendant investors.[36]

The point of all this detail – just the very tip of the iceberg – is to emphasize just how seriously inadequate so-called independent auditing has turned out to be. Time after time these independent auditors have falsely assured us that the numbers – the data – are reliable when they were not. The results have been bankruptcies, lost pensions, lost jobs, lost tax revenues, and huge losses to investors. From 1996 to 2007, more than 2,600 class action lawsuits were filed in response to these frauds.[37]

Given the cozy relationship between auditing firms and crooked corporate officers, the reader might wonder why so much fraud has been exposed. Well, in most cases they were not exposed by auditors. According to the major study of fraud exposure, auditors were responsible for discovering just nine percent of the major accounting frauds from 1995 to 2004. Before the Enron scandal that number was a mere five percent. After the Enron scandal, and the collapse of Arthur Andersen, it grew to fourteen percent. In roughly thirty-five percent of the cases, the fraud was revealed by the company itself or by its board of directors. This sometimes happened after a change in management and sometimes after a severe downturn or other bad news that cried out for explanation. Nearly another twenty-five percent of the scandals were uncovered by business analysts and newspapers. Employees of the firm and other stakeholders blew the whistle in nineteen percent of the cases and regulators uncovered fraud in fourteen percent of them (the S.E.C. accounted for just two percent). The average time it took to detect a fraud was two years.[38]

In 2002 Congress passed the Sarbanes–Oxley Act to address the problem of accounting fraud. Most importantly, Sarbanes–Oxley was supposed to make accounting fraud harder by eliminating conflicts of interest between auditors and the firms they audit. For one thing, it requires auditing firms to rotate audit partners – the people in charge of the audit – every five years. For another, it puts restrictions on the revolving employment door between auditors and their clients. Finally, it limits the non-auditing services a firm may offer its clients.

But the provisions of Sarbanes–Oxley are quite weak. First, although it probably does some good to rotate audit partners, this does not get rid of the most important conflict of interest between the company being audited and the auditing firm. If the auditing team does not please the corporate client, it still risks being fired and the auditing partner still gets a black eye for that reason. Second, the restrictions on the revolving door are laughable. They do nothing to prevent companies from hiring members of the auditing team. Instead, they regulate traffic moving in the other, less dangerous direction. That is, they impose limits on the hiring of executives at client companies by auditing firms. And they don't do much of that either. The restrictions apply only to C.E.O.'s, C.F.O.'s, and the controller or chief accounting officer at the client firm, and prohibit them only from auditing their former company for one year. Finally, although Sarbane–Oxley restricts some of the non-audit services auditing firms may offer clients, it continues to allow others, including lucrative tax services. It also allows the Public Company Accounting Oversight Board to make exceptions to these prohibitions on a case-by-case basis. Arthur Levitt, then chairman of the S.E.C., originally proposed much more stringent requirements, but the accounting industry lobbied hard against him (Levitt said that he was the target of an "intensive and venal lobbying campaign" and he later expressed regret to caving in to pressure from the large accounting firms).[39] In fairness, Sarbanes–Oxley does mandate some important changes in the way audits are conducted. In particular, auditors are required to devote more attention to evaluating a company's own "internal controls" for detecting and preventing fraud. But it leaves the biggest problems unaddressed.

Has Sarbanes–Oxley done any good? It's hard to tell. For what it's worth, sixty-five percent of respondents to a November 2005 survey conducted by Oversight Systems, Inc. reported believing that Sarbanes–Oxley had been "somewhat effective" or "very effective" in helping identify fraud. Nonetheless, sixty-seven percent of the respondents said that institutional fraud was more prevalent at the time than it was five years earlier, before the passage of Sarbanes–Oxley, and only seven percent said it was less prevalent. Furthermore, only seventeen percent of the respondents predicted that business leaders would do more to prevent fraud in the future.[40] Of course, stories of accounting fraud continue to proliferate. According to Forbes.com, for example, as of November 6, 2006, 150 companies were either embroiled in internal probes or being investigated by the S.E.C. for potential stock option back-dating abuses. The deluge is growing "with a fresh batch of companies announcing stock option accounting problems with each passing day."[41]

What is clear is that we need much stronger reforms than Sarbanes–Oxley if we are to trust the data corporations produce about themselves. But the chances of getting such reforms are slim to zero. The major accounting firms will resist them just as they resisted the stronger recommendations of Arthur Levitt. What is a conflict of interest from the standpoint of public policy is a cash cow for them. Sarbanes–Oxley passed in the first place because corporate America feared that the scandals of 2002 would reduce investor confidence in the stock market. For reasons noted, that would lead to lower share values and a loss of personal wealth among C.E.O.'s, C.F.O.'s, and other corporate officers. But despite all the scandals investor confidence is high. Maybe the minor reforms of Sarbanes–Oxley have contributed to this. Or maybe people just need someplace to put their money. The stock market has always been risky but it has usually paid well. The fact that we can't tell whose books are cooked and by how much just spreads the risk across the range of investment options.

Media Misrepresentations: Training, Ideology, Careerism, Politics, and Organization

However much we bemoan it, we rely on the news media for almost all our knowledge of the contemporary social, political, and economic worlds. Without newspapers, magazines, radio, television, and the internet we would have very little access to current events and conditions. And, some media critics

notwithstanding, the overwhelming majority of fact-based stories in the mainstream media are accurate. As reported, the
Democrats did win control of both houses of Congress in the
2006 U.S. election, Tony Blair did support George Bush's policy
in Iraq, Enron executives were convicted of fraud and sen-
tenced to prison, and (as I write this) Arab militias are mas-
sacring black Africans in Darfur. That said, it is also true that
the media – the practice of journalism – suffer from every one of
the various problems of compliance mentioned at the beginning of this chapter. Before elaborating on that, though, I need
to say a bit more about what journalists do.

During the 1950s and early 1960s, American journalism students were taught that the reporter's job was to report the facts
and nothing but the facts. The basic facts – who, what, where,
when, how, and sometimes why – were supposed to appear in
the first paragraph of a story and be elaborated in the sequel.
The journalist was not supposed to be influenced in any way by
their own attitudes, emotions, theories about the world, or ideological slants. The practice of journalism was supposed to be
objective through and through. The journalist's job was to mine
data from the world and accurately represent that data in their
story. It was up to the public to interpret or otherwise make
sense of "the facts."

Almost every working journalist now realizes that this picture is hopelessly simplistic. Journalists don't just randomly
gather facts and write them up. They cover what they – or,
more often, their editors and publishers – think is important to
cover, and these judgments reflect beliefs about what the world
is like and about what sells papers (or attracts viewers). The
New York Times's slogan – "All the news that is fit to print" – is
about as helpful as St. Thomas Aquinas's declaration that we
should do good and avoid evil. Just as we may disagree about

what actions are good and evil, so may we disagree about which events are newsworthy and what makes them fit or unfit to print. Editors and reporters who believe that accounting scandals are anomalies – just the result of a few bad eggs – will cover them one way. Editors and reporters who believe accounting scandals are deep, systemic problems of corporate capitalism will cover them in another. What seems newsworthy to a socialist may not seem newsworthy to a free market capitalist and what seems newsworthy to a Christian conservative may not seem newsworthy to a secular humanist.

The range of political, economic, and social theories that shape the news in a country generally reflects the ideological range of that country's major political parties. That range is much greater in Europe and South America than it is in the U.S. Many major European and South American countries have socialist newspapers that are fundamentally suspicious of and even hostile to multinational corporations. Even on the editorial pages, the range of opinion in Italy and Brazil is far wider than it is in American newspapers. The more limited ideological gamut in the U.S. influences which stories get covered there and how those stories are written. European, South American, and some American intellectuals consistently complain that American news coverage is one-sided. Most American journalists don't worry about this. Like most Americans, they fall somewhere on the political continuum whose end points are the "extremes" of America's own major political parties, and it seems to them that there is plenty of room for differences within that range. Although there may be nothing that qualifies as a left perspective in the U.S. by European standards, Fox News's coverage of American politics, the war in Iraq, global warming, reproductive rights, the separation of church and state, and many other issues is much different than that of the *New York Times*.

In principle, one could have theories about how the world works without caring what happens or who wins. But outside the classroom and the café, few of us adopt this detached perspective. Usually our theories and assumptions about how the social, political, and economic worlds work are parts of a larger narrative organized around themes of justice and injustice, freedom and oppression, saved and sinner, purity and corruption, and so on. We don't simply nod in recognition at a world divided into hostile camps, each fuelled by a sense of its own righteousness. We take sides. We become partisans. We develop loyalties. We identify our own good with the success of certain causes or principles. We adopt ideologies. And, if we are journalists, this influences our writing.

Because one needs theories and assumptions about how the world works to choose the news that's fit to print, all news reporting is shaped by them. If Objectivity requires a God's-eye view – what Thomas Nagel calls "the view from nowhere" – Objectivity is impossible. Still, despite their loyalties and allegiances, journalists can and should aspire to a weaker form of objectivity. This kind of objectivity is about fair and even-handed coverage. Most importantly, it means that stories should be written without concern about their political consequences. One should cover them without spinning them. Allegations helpful or hurtful to one's own causes should be treated with the same skepticism as allegations helpful or hurtful to the other side. Sources on one's own side of an issue should be investigated just as thoroughly as sources on the other side. One should cover everything in a story which a reasonable person would judge relevant, whatever their ideology (for example, that Al Gore won the popular vote in the U.S.

presidential election of 2000, that there were allegations of voter fraud in Bush's favor in Florida, that had Gore won Florida he would have won the election, etc.).

These are very demanding standards and few people if any can satisfy them completely. But, just as therapists should try not to let their personal feelings influence their treatment of patients, and jurors should try not to let their personal feelings affect their verdicts, so journalists should strive not to let their political allegiances and partisan sentiments affect their stories. Again, the data-gathering and -filtering standards of the profession demand equal skepticism toward sources and allegations that help and hurt one's favored causes.

Of course, journalists often fail to comply with these standards. A very dramatic example of this was (arguably) the CBS news report on George W. Bush's National Guard service on September 8, 2004. In that report, Dan Rather claimed to have documents proving that President Bush had received special treatment as a member of the Texas Air National Guard. But CBS News did little to authenticate the documents before the broadcast. As it turned out, many experts judged them to be forgeries. CBS convened an independent investigation of the incident which unearthed ten serious mistakes in the handling of the story. CBS subsequently apologized for the story, fired the producer of the *Evening News* program, and demanded the resignation of five top executives in the news department.[42] Why was CBS so sloppy? Although it is impossible to be sure, the best explanation is that the political allegiances of key players at CBS News made them less skeptical than they should have been. The fact that CBS took this breach of practice so seriously, however, shows that it supports the kind of objectivity to which journalists should be committed.

A less dramatic but perhaps more typical example occurred in an October 21, 2004 airing of Fox News Channel's *Special Report with Britt Hume*. Major Garrett, a general assignment reporter for that show, broadcast a report on Republican allegations of voter fraud in Philadelphia which concluded with the following statement:

> There's been a phenomenon going on that the Republicans have found quite curious. For example, in 2000, Philadelphia had an astonishing rate of registration among adults: 99 percent, one of the highest rates in the country. And, Republicans note, in Philadelphia the number of registered voters keep rising even though the population in that city keeps declining.[43]

Had Garrett investigated a little further he would have discovered why the number of registered voters had increased while the population had declined. The explanation is simple. In 1993 Congress passed the National Voter Registration Act (commonly known as "Motor Voter"). This act makes it difficult to remove people who did not vote in recent elections from the voter rolls. So-called "inactive voters" must remain on the rolls for two-and-a-half to three-and-a-half years after receiving that designation. In addition, although more people have been leaving Philadelphia than moving in, thousands of new people arrive every year and many of them register to vote.[44] If the number of registered voters is updated more frequently than the census records – which seems likely and worth investigating – this too will skew the percentages. Of course, ninety-nine percent is a very high number and it's not clear how much that figure would diminish if one took the effects of Motor Voter and new residents into account. But it is clear that a responsible journalist should check that out and that in this case Garrett was simply uncritically parroting what Republicans were saying.

Ironically, failures to investigate may also occur because journalists try too hard to *appear* objective. According to some, this is partly responsible for a series of stories in the *New York Times* during the run-up to the invasion of Iraq. These stories basically supported the Bush administration's claims that Saddam Hussein had weapons of mass destruction and had strong ties to al-Qaeda. As the *Times* later acknowledged in an editorial mea culpa on May 26, 2004, these stories were based significantly on information from "a circle of Iraqi informants, defectors and exiles bent on 'regime change' in Iraq, people whose credibility has come under increasing public debate in recent weeks." At the center of this circle was Ahmad Chalabi, "an occasional source in *Times* articles since 1991 . . . and a favorite of hard-liners within the Bush administration and a paid broker of information from Iraqi exiles, until his payments were cut off last week." According to the *Times*'s self-critical editorial, "Editors at several levels who should have been challenging reporters and pressing for more skepticism were perhaps too intent on rushing scoops into the paper. Accounts of Iraqi defectors were not always weighed against their strong desire to have Saddam Hussein ousted." Well, maybe. An article on these incidents that appears in *New York Magazine*, however, tells a different story. Most of the *Times* articles about Iraq were written by reporter Judith Miller under the editorial supervision of Howell Raines. Miller had close connections with neo-conservative hawks in the Bush administration. According to one former editor at the *Times*, Raines "wanted to throw off his liberal credentials and demonstrate that he was fair-minded about the Bush administration. This meant that he bent over backwards to back them often." According to another (or perhaps the same) former editor (it's not clear in the article), "In the months before the war, Raines consistently objected to articles that questioned the administration's claims about Iraq's links to al-Qaeda and September 11 while never raising a doubt about Miller's more dubiously sourced pieces about the presence of weapons of mass destruction." [45]

Ideological sentiments are not the only source of bad data gathering and filtering. Journalists may get their facts wrong or may leave out something important simply because they are not competent enough to write about a particularly complex or difficult topic. This is a problem of training. Although many journalism schools now allow students to specialize in certain subject areas – for example, science, economics, or religion – they do not generally require their students to have or get a deep understanding of those subjects. For example, most graduating M.A.'s in science journalism programs take many fewer biology and physics courses than undergraduate biology and physics majors. The Center for Science and Medical Journalism at Boston University offers prospective applicants this bit of advice: "If you are a professional with no science coursework in your background, we encourage you to take some adult-education science classes." Once admitted to this three-semester program, students are not required to take any science courses at all. They are allowed four electives, which may (or may not) include graduate science classes. Although some programs are more demanding, this is not unusual. [46]

The problem is not limited to science journalism. According to Richard Lee Colvin (director of the Hechinger Institute on Education and the Media at Teachers College of Columbia University), "it is rare for education writers to have formally studied education. And as far as I've been able to determine, no journalism schools today have classes that deal specifically in all you'd have to know to write in-depth stories about teaching and learning or other central components of schooling."[47] Or, to take another example, many foreign correspondents often have little or no training in the history or culture of the areas they report on. In many cases, they don't even speak the languages and need to rely on local interpreters.

This need for specialized training in specialized subject areas is now widely recognized. A 2005 report by the Carnegie Corporation, based on extensive interviews with deans of journalism programs at five major research institutions, listed the following as one of its three recommendations: "Help reporters build specialized expertise to enhance their coverage of complex beats from medicine to economics and help them to acquire first-hand knowledge of the societies, languages, religions and cultures of other parts of the world."[48] But only one major U.S. school of journalism has made really serious moves in this direction. In addition to its ordinary M.S. in journalism, the Columbia's School of Journalism now offers an M.A. that allows students to focus in one of four subject areas (politics, art and culture, business and economics, and science). This program, initiated in 2005, is regarded as groundbreaking.

Mistakes are one thing. Flat-out misrepresentation is another. Motivated by career ambition and the pressure to produce interesting stories, some journalists manufacture sources, characters in stories, or even events. It is impossible to tell how often this happens. But it is clear that the fact-checking practices of many prestigious publications – their editorial data filters – are weaker than they should be. *Wikipedia* details fifty American scandals since 1998 (and that list is incomplete).[49] There have been many recent high-profile scandals involving journalists who became famous and won prestigious awards on the strength of wholly or partly manufactured stories. In 2005 Diana Griego Erwin resigned from the *Sacramento Bee* while under investigation for manufacturing sources over a period of *twelve years*. The newspaper could not verify forty-three of her sources. Erwin worked on a project that won a Pulitzer Prize at the *Denver Post*. She also won a George Polk award, and the 1990 commentary prize from the American Society of Newspaper Editors.[50] In 2003 Jayson Blair was fired from the *New York Times* for fabricating sources and manufacturing quotes from unattributed sources.[51] In 2002 Christopher Newton was fired from the Associated Press (A.P.). After reviewing hundreds of Newton's stories, the A.P. found quotations in forty pieces from sources that could not be located.[52] In the same year, Michael Finkel, once a contributing editor for the *New York Times Magazine*, made up the principal character in a feature he wrote for that publication.[53]

Perhaps the biggest journalistic scandals of all involved Janet Cooke of the *Washington Post* and Stephen Glass, who wrote for the *New Republic* and several other major publications. Janet Cooke won a Pulitzer Prize for a series of stories about an eight-year-old heroin addict in Washington, D.C. who aspired to be a heroin dealer when he grew up. There was no such person.[54] Stephen Glass published perhaps thirty stories that were wholly or partly fabricated. Most of these appeared in the *New Republic* but some also in *Harpers, Policy Review*, and *George*. The amazing thing about some of Glass's fabrications is how wild his stories were. Had they been presented as fiction, many would be considered satires (for example, a story about a political memorabilia convention featuring Monica Lewinsky condoms and a story about an evangelical church that worshipped George Herbert Bush). None of Glass's stories was questioned by his editors or adequately vetted by fact checkers on the magazine staffs. What fact checking there was consisted mostly of reviewing Glass's (fake) notes (though Glass also covered his tracks by creating phony voicemails, business cards, and newsletters). What brought him down was not the data-filtering processes in place at the magazines for which he wrote but the fact that another magazine – *Forbes On-line* – tried to do a follow-up on a story Glass had written about a convention of computer hackers and they could not verify a single fact. While that was under investigation, Glass actually created a false webpage to support his story, but it was too late.[55]

Reflections

Knowledge Machines are reliable only if they adjust for and avoid the mistakes in perception, memory, and thinking to which we are prone as individuals. Given the research described in Chapters 1 and 2, we have a pretty good idea of what some of these mistakes are. So we can look at the data-gathering methods of a Knowledge Machine – the standards of practice – and get some sense of how well designed they are to guard against those mistakes. Our job is made easier by the fact that the methods of a Knowledge Machine are often public.

Unlike problems of design, however, problems of compli-ance are often concealed. This is obviously true of noncompli-ance born of dishonesty and fraud. But it is sometimes also true of incompetence and of error born of carelessness, laziness, sloppiness, and mistakes that have no real explanation (like simple mistakes in arithmetic). Often, people try to hide their negligence, incompetence, and even honest errors as well as their dishonesty and fraud. This makes it hard to tell how much there is. Our guesses are based on cases in which perpetrators get caught. But we can't really infer frequency from these cases because we have no idea of the ratio of successful to unsuccessful concealment.

It is almost impossible to know how often practitioners make errors because they are negligent or simply make honest mistakes. With a few exceptions, nobody really keeps track of these things. Sometimes we become aware of errors because they affect us in ways that are obvious. A good deal of medical error is like this. In this case, there are statistics and they are frightening. According to a 1999 report by the Institute of Medicine (of the American National Academy of Science), five to ten percent of people admitted to U.S. hospitals are victims of serious medical errors. And forty-four to ninety-eight thousand of these people *die* in U.S. hospitals each year. There have been some reforms since that report came out but it's not clear to what extent the problem has diminished.[56] If you need to be admitted to a U.S. hospital, it's a good idea to have friends and family around who are familiar with your condition. I managed to prevent medical errors on several occasions for friends and family, and I have friends who have done the same (in one case, a friend prevented a nurse from adjusting his wife's bed in a way that would have almost certainly paralyzed her). Usually, though, we know much less about how often honest or careless mistakes are made and we are less prepared to guard against them.

We are in a slightly better (but still not very good) position to estimate the frequency of dishonesty and fraud. In most cases, our estimates will depend on our judgments about five factors: (1) the strength of the temptations practitioners face; (2) the strength of the mechanisms in place to detect fraud; (3) the seriousness of the penalties for fraud; (4) the strength of the professional norm against fraud; and (5) the psychology and character of the practitioners. Some of these are easier to judge than others. Take scientific fraud, for example. The culture of science strongly stresses truth seeking and cooperation. Scientists who commit fraud not only violate these norms but also make the life of other scientists more difficult by polluting the waters of knowledge. These are deterrents. On the other hand, the mechanisms for detecting fraud are weak. Intelligent fraud is difficult to detect and the scientific community has not made fraud detection a priority. To make matters worse, the penalties for fraud in science are mild compared with the penalties in other professions. Reputations are tarnished and people are sometimes barred from receiving federal grant money for a period of time but almost no one goes to jail for fraud or gets sued for it (as they would in law or medicine). There is not even the equivalent of losing one's license. Sometimes people don't even get fired. So it all comes down to the character and personalities of the scientists. How many scientists have internalized the norm against fraud and how deep does that go? And how risk averse are the ones who haven't taken these norms to heart? Note that if a scientist needs to fake numbers to keep his job, to get tenure, or to continue to attract funding, *not* faking the numbers has some of the same bad consequences for him as faking the numbers and getting caught. In both cases he is out of a job (well, usually; as noted, sometimes people caught cheating keep their jobs). In any case, given the weaknesses of policing and penalties, those who think scientists are no more honest than auditors or C.E.O.'s will expect a lot of fraud where the temptations to cheat are strong. Those who think scientists really are more honest than auditors or C.E.O.'s will expect less.

This way of thinking about fraud gives us a general idea of how much to expect in a field but it doesn't help us identify fraud in any particular case. Unless one becomes a full-time investigator, it's very unlikely one will uncover fraud in a particular case. For that, unfortunately, we need to rely on the mechanisms for detecting fraud in place in various Knowledge Machines. As we've seen, these mechanisms can be very weak. In many fields it's just very hard to detect fraud.

In the case of incompetence we have a bit more to go on. Fraud is private, concealed, and results from weaknesses of character. But the factors that create incompetence are sometimes a matter of public record. We can all find out what medical schools, journalism schools, business schools, etc. teach and don't teach. Their training, licensing, and continuing education requirements are not secret. This can give us some idea of the sorts of errors to which practitioners are prone. In some cases, there are also studies about the errors practitioners make. These not only help us estimate the level of incompetence in a certain field – or the level of incompetence dealing with a specific kind of issue – they may also help us to identify particular cases of incompetence. As we saw in Chapter 2, for example, most doctors can not correctly calculate the probability that someone has a disease on the basis of a test result for that disease (they ignore base rates). This is because medical schools don't teach doctors how to avoid common mistakes in calculating probabilities. Knowing this, we can and should check whether our doctor has miscalculated in our own case. We can do this by asking for the rate of false positives, the rate of the false negatives, and the base rate (the percentage of people tested who have the disease). Given these numbers, we can calculate accurately following the method described in Chapter 2. If the doctor doesn't know the base rate, we can be sure the doctor has miscalculated.

Of course, we usually don't have this kind of clear evidence of bad training and widespread incompetence. And it isn't always this easy to detect and correct incompetence in particular cases. Often detecting incompetence takes specialist knowledge or facts to which we lack access (for example, what happens in jury deliberations). But we are not as helpless as we may think. Sometimes a little research is all we need. Since fifty percent of all doctors finish in the bottom half of their class, we know that some doctors are more competent than others. If you are diagnosed with a serious condition, it's a good idea to check your doctor's diagnosis and treatment plan by researching it on the internet (there are plenty of good webpages). One can also go to another doctor for a second opinion. Or, to take another example, because you now know how science journalists are trained, you realize that science journalists don't always get complicated and technical matters right. Also, because journalists like big stories, they may misrepresent a finding by inflating its importance. This gives us a general reason for suspicion when it comes to stories about the Next Big Thing in plagues, pandemics, nutrition, aging research, immunology, superconductivity, etc. If we're worried about the accuracy of a particular story, we have resources to find out how accurate it is. With a little effort, we can locate a scientist in the relevant field and ask about the accuracy of the story by phone or email. When I do this, I get about a fifty percent response rate.

CHAPTER 5

From Data to Conclusions: Values, Assumptions, and Politics

As we have seen, what counts as data for Knowledge Machines depends on its theories of how the world works. These theories also guide the movement from data to conclusions. We can diagnose certain diseases from what we see under a microscope because we have theories about viruses and bacteria and about what they do in our bodies. As we will see, though, the move from data to conclusions may also depend on certain more general assumptions about the subject matter and our methods of knowing it. In some cases, that move depends on hidden value judgments as well.

Often a Knowledge Machine's theories of how the world works are too technical for nonspecialists to evaluate. But sometimes they aren't. We've already looked at examples. Any intelligent person willing to do a bit of reading would have understood the objections to the central theory of behaviorism and to the theory of memory underlying recovered memory therapy. The same goes for many trendy theories that light up academic disciplines and the business world for ten to twenty years and then burn out. Often the objections that finally extinguish them were just common sense and there from the start. Since we have already discussed examples of theory gone wrong, this chapter will focus on how value assumptions and general assumptions about subject matters guide the move from data to conclusions.

Knowledge Machines are social organizations and the move from data to conclusions is a social process. Key players must be convinced and/or a consensus must be mobilized. This process may be structured in ways that make its results more or less reliable. If it is to succeed, it must be designed to guard against the many common sources of human fallibility and dishonesty. These include results generated by personal ambition, power struggles, greed, and political ideologies. In addition, Knowledge Machines need to be free of information black holes and bottlenecks that prevent productive discussion and create imbalances of knowledge and influence. These are the subjects of the second part of this chapter.

Almost all Knowledge Machines have journals, newsletters, conferences, and other means of publicizing their results internally. Often, they rely significantly on outsiders to get their results to the general public. For example, most of us learn of the latest scientific developments from magazines, newspapers, popularizing books, and television shows. If we are interested in having a reasonable view of the world, we also need to understand how reliable these vehicles are. In the last part of this chapter we will consider this in relation to science.

Value Judgments

Value judgments are like mushrooms. Once you begin to notice them, they appear in all kinds of unexpected places. A few examples should help sharpen the reader's awareness. Let's begin with something straightforward. Government regulatory agencies enforce laws and implement policies. Among other things, they investigate circumstances to which the laws are supposed to apply, and take action to assure that they do. This sounds like a straightforward fact-finding, rule-applying mission. But often it involves value judgments. For example, some regulatory agencies are supposed to protect us against products and activities that are *unsafe*. To that end, they investigate the risks and damages associated with those practices and activities. But it's one thing to say that some activity or product creates a certain level of risk or damage and another to say that it's unsafe. Everything we do poses *some* risk. To call a product or activity *unsafe* in regulatory contexts is to say the risk or damage is excessive and calls for action. Since risk reduction and prevention are costly, that amounts to deciding that the price is worth paying, which is clearly a value judgment.

We often think of medicine as a kind of value-free applied biology (or bioengineering). But value judgments pervade medicine. For one thing, doctors often help patients to decide what benefits are worth what risks. In emergencies they make these decisions for the patient. For another, we make value judgments as a society when we decide how to use biomedical technology and who should pay for various uses. Doctors do a lot of things that have nothing to do with preventing or curing illnesses, diseases, and injuries. Unwanted pregnancies are not illnesses. Neither are ugly birthmarks or smaller-than-preferred breasts. Doctors address these problems because we have decided that they are proper uses of medical technology. We have also decided *against* certain uses of medical technology (e.g. cloning humans and administering performance-enhancing drugs in sports). These are obviously value choices.

More surprisingly, medical diagnosis itself involves value judgments. That's because the ideas of health, illness, disease, and injury themselves have strong value components. We all have different levels of energy, endurance, and strength. How low do we have to be on these scales before we become unhealthy? Well, that depends. A sixty-year-old Bangladeshi considered healthy in his own country might not be considered healthy by British and American standards. This is partly because the norm is different in the First World (life expectancies are higher, etc.). But it is also partly because First World countries have the resources and the will to treat as *medical problems* certain conditions that might be regarded as normal aspects of aging in less wealthy places (for example, menopausal symptoms). Our standards of health and illness depend significantly on what capacities and levels of comfort we believe people *should have* at certain stages of their lives. And these are value judgments.

The value component of medicine is even more pronounced in psychiatry. Brain science is a glamour discipline of our new century and it is easy to think of mental health and mental illness as simply matters of brain chemistry (or structure). But these diagnoses are almost completely based on value judgments. We diagnose mental health and mental illness (neuroses, psychoses, etc.) on the basis of thoughts, feelings, and behavior. If there are no problems in those areas, there is no "mental condition" regardless of what someone's brain chemistry or brain structure is like. But exactly what problems with thought, feelings, and behavior count? How much and what kind of anxiety

does someone need to have? How much and what kinds of sadness, numbness, purposelessness, self-hatred, delusional thinking, addiction, sexual obsession, anger, or aggressiveness?
These are not biological questions. We don't answer them by
looking at someone's brain. Among other things, we decide
them by assessing the impact of a person's thoughts, feelings,
and behavior on their life and the lives of others, and making
value judgments about that. Can they function effectively
enough, are they *intolerably* miserable, is their behavior *intolera-*
bly disruptive, are they a *big enough* danger to themself and
others? What we are really deciding is how badly off someone
must be in these respects to warrant treatment and/or to
be deprived of the rights and liberties (and be absolved of the
responsibilities) that come with the labels "psychotic" or "mentally ill." How much does it take, for example, to justify locking
them up, drugging them, and/or subjecting them to electric
shocks? The answers obviously depend on our values.

This value component is strong even in the area that seems
most straightforwardly factual, viz. delusional thinking. We're
all delusional in some ways (unreasonably optimistic or pessimistic, suspicious or trusting, fearful or crazy brave, etc.).
Many of us believe things that are completely outlandish (e.g.
that the world is run by a secret cadre of Jews, that the world is
four thousand years old, that lizard-like aliens disguised as
humans now hold key political and economic positions, that
we are all under constant surveillance by someone who knows
everything we think and do, etc.). Some of these delusions are
multimedia. A college acquaintance of mine, who graduated
with honors in history, told me he took after-dinner walks with
Jesus every night (for those of you who are curious, Jesus
appeared to him in a body that was about six feet tall and had
blond hair and blue eyes – I asked). But no one is locked up and

drugged for taking nightly walks with Jesus or noticing incompletely transformed lizard skin on the neck of a banker. Again, these decisions have nothing to do with brain chemistry. Some delusions are not dangerous enough and/or fall well enough into the protected categories of religious and political beliefs and/or are simply too widely shared to be written off as crazy. Some religious beliefs are exempt even if they make one a serious danger to oneself or others. Whatever we think about suicide bombers and self-flagellators, we don't label them mentally ill. This is because, for better or worse, we are vigilant about protecting religious freedom (though, of course, there are limits). This is obviously a value choice.

Value judgments can even shape our thought in what we take to be purely theoretical matters. The field of economics is a good example. Economists often describe themselves as social scientists, suggesting that they investigate economic activity from a detached, theoretical perspective (for example, that they develop theories that predict how economies will behave under various circumstances). But fundamental to this discipline is a concept of economic well-being (or "welfare," as they call it) which, like any conception of well-being, is a value judgment. That measure is called "utility." The modern economic concept of utility has its roots in the philosophical concept of utility developed by Jeremy Bentham. According to Bentham, utility is another name for "good." Since Bentham thought that pleasure is the only intrinsic good and pain is the only intrinsic evil, he defined utility in terms of the intensity and duration of pleasure and pain. Despite Bentham's talk about a "hedonistic calculus," though, neither he nor his successors were able to devise an effective way to measure pleasures and pains. But some of his successors believed that we could rank and/or measure our preferences for these sensations or feelings. In the end, it was decided that our preferences don't even need to be restricted to feelings and sensations All that matters is preference satisfaction per se. According to mainstream welfare economics, preference satisfaction is the good and we are well off to the extent that we are able to maximize the satisfaction of our preferences over our lifetime. According to the theory, that's what every rational person strives to do.

But preferences come in many shapes and sizes. I prefer having love in my life to living without love, and I prefer this lover to that one, either in general or right now. I also prefer Pepsi to Coke right now but Coke to Pepsi more often. These variations in types of preferences are too complicated to be worth sorting out here. Suffice it to say that we can distinguish between types of preferences in ways relevant to our well-being along five dimensions, which leaves us with thirty-two preference types.[1] Most economists address this problem by ignoring desires for global states of affairs (like being happy) and limiting themselves to preferences that are revealed by our economic choices (for example, the consumer goods we buy and the terms at which we sell our labor). These are sometimes called "revealed preferences." But if we understand preference satisfaction in relation to revealed preferences, the view that preference satisfaction is the good is a highly debatable value judgment. One can maximize one's satisfaction of consumer preferences and even job preferences over a lifetime and still be miserably unhappy.

It might be replied that preference satisfaction is not a measure of good per se, but only of economic good, and that it is an open question to what degree economic good contributes to our good per se (just as, for example, the proper use of semicolons is a good of punctuation but it is an open question to what degree goods of punctuation contribute to good per se).

But this response is disingenuous for two reasons. First, welfare economists rely on the assumption that economic good is a good (perhaps the most important good) per se when they argue that market economies make us better off than economies of other kinds. In particular they argue that in efficient markets (where all players are fully informed) every trade makes all parties better off. The reasoning is simple. If you didn't value my corn more than the price I'm asking for it, you wouldn't buy my corn. If I didn't value the money you offer me for my corn more than my corn, I wouldn't sell it to you. So we both satisfy our preferences in this transaction and in every other transaction (in an efficient market). This applies even in cases where I agree to slave away under miserable conditions at a subsistence wage (if I didn't prefer the arrangement to the available alternatives, I wouldn't take it). If preference satisfaction were not a powerful good in and of itself, this argument for a market economy would be quite unconvincing. Without that assumption, it's hard to see how a market economy makes workers better off by allowing them to satisfy their preference for work at starvation wages to starvation itself (although, of course, economists have other arguments to support market economies as well). Second, both economists and policymakers treat economic good as an important good; in fact, they often treat it as the most important public policy priority.

This brings us to another, closely related value judgment. Economists and governments measure the health of an economy in terms of its gross national product or gross domestic product. These are regarded as at least rough measures of total utility or preference satisfaction. This means that, all other things being equal, the higher the rates of production and consumption in an economy, the healthier an economy is. Whether one agrees with this or not, it is clearly a value judgment. It rejects the idea that small is beautiful (that the simpler, low-consumption life is better than the more harried, high-consumption life). It is *indifferent* to the types of goods that are produced and consumed (bombs are equal to food and each Hummers is worth a thousand bicycles). It does not take the distribution of consumption patterns into account (two economies may be equally healthy even if one has a huge gap between the rich and the poor and the other does not). And it ignores externalities (e.g. polluted air and water and toxic waste dumps). One could argue that all of this should be taken into consideration when we judge the health of an economy. Of course, that is also a value judgment. But that's the point. In the last analysis any account of what makes us better off economically which is intended to guide policy necessarily rests on assumptions about what makes life worth living.

These cases by no means exhaust the list of value judgments disguised as factual judgment. My hope is that these examples will help the readers identify other cases.

Big Picture Assumptions

Roughly speaking, when we set out to investigate some aspect of the world we make two assumptions: (1) that the subject matter admits of understanding; and (2) that we have the intellectual resources to understand it. More exactly, we assume that our chances of understanding *that* subject matter with *these* tools are good enough to make the effort worth our while. Sometimes these assumptions are more reasonable than others.

To repeat, it is a remarkable fact about our species that almost every human society has had its own story about how the world/universe began. We are so familiar with these stories that their ambition rarely even seems strange to us. On reflection, we might marvel at the audacity of the stories told by the Sumerians, the ancient Greeks, and countless Stone Age tribes. But in a way, our own current story is the strangest of all. We know (or think we know) how unthinkably old and unthinkably large the universe is. And we identify ourselves as recent descendents of apes who share 99.9% of our D.N.A. with chimpanzees.

The specifics are daunting. We live on a planet that is approximately 24,900 miles in circumference. We have been around for perhaps 100,000 years (there is some debate) and have had telescopes less than five hundred. The universe, on the other hand, is somewhere between ten and twenty *billion* years old (with most estimates around 13.7 billion). And it is 1,000,000,000,000,000,000,000,000 miles across. Yet our theory tells us what happened in the first 10^{-43} of a second of its existence (that's 0.0000000000000000000000000000000000000000001 *of a second*). How is this possible?

Our first assumption is that nature is uniform. The laws of nature that hold here hold everywhere and have held everywhere for all time. Our second assumption is that we can discover what those laws are from what we can observe here, in our own unimaginably small fraction of a space-time drop in the cosmic sea. We believe that our process is expansive and self-correcting. We formulate laws based on what we see locally. We build instruments based on these laws that enable us to see more. We revise and expand our theories on the bases of those observations. We construct additional instruments based on *those* theories, and so forth. Eventually, our instruments will allow us to observe aspects of the universe that are billions of years old. But how believable is that really?

Suppose the universe were like a river. Rivers have calm spots and rapids, eddies and whirlpools, backwaters and back currents, bends and falls. In the spring they are high and fast; in the summer slow and dry; in the winter partly frozen. Suppose that the universe had areas that were as different from one another as the parts of a river and that it goes through cycles in the same way that rivers do. In that case, inhabitants of any given area might develop a science that explained how the universe behaved in their own tiny particular sector over some miniscule time interval. Given those theories, they might develop instruments for "observing" what happens in other areas of the river and revise their theories on the bases of those observations. They might develop new instruments on the bases of those revised theories and make still newer observations, and so on. But it's hard to see how this process can escape the limitations of its starting point. Scientific traditions that endure for the equivalent of a second or two on a spring day on a rock in the rapids will almost certainly generate different results than scientific traditions that endure for the equivalent of a second or two on a summer day on a rock in a backwater, or scientific traditions that endure for a second or two on a winter day on a tiny rise in the ice. If the beings concerned are like us, they will all think their instruments enable them to see the space-time origins of the river. But how likely is that?

This does not imply that our first assumption is false. Nature may be uniform. There are, after all, general laws governing the behavior of rivers – laws in relation to which we can explain the bends, rapids, falls, whirlpools, and back currents and so forth. The question is whether our short-lived, spatially constrained river dwellers have the intellectual resources to discover them. Our own theories suggest that we are very like the river dwellers. Things do seem to behave in unexpected ways in different areas of the universe.

If our own theories were stable and consistent we would be entitled to greater confidence. But our current cosmologically related theories are unstable, full of uncertainty, plagued by controversy, and open to revision. To begin with, the universe contains much less matter than is required to explain various gravitational effects, including its rate of expansion. To explain these effects, cosmologists have simply asserted the existence of dark matter and dark energy. Dark matter is defined negatively, i.e. it is matter not made from quarks (protons or neutrons). It emits no light and no radiation. It can't be detected by our instruments. In fact, we know almost nothing about it at all. Yet, according to some estimates, it makes up ninety to ninety-five percent of the matter in the universe (others put the figure at eighty to eighty-five percent). Furthermore, according to a team of astrophysicists at Cambridge University, *galaxies* contain four hundred times as much dark matter as matter.[2] In few other areas of science do we allow ourselves so grand a theory-saving gesture. If our observations of the bloodstream produced only fifteen percent of the white blood cells our theories predicted, we would not save our theories by positing dark white blood cells.

To make matters worse, estimates of the amount of dark matter vary in part because they are related to estimates of the age of the universe (which, as we have seen, also vary). Both of these estimates are related to the expansion rate of the universe (the Hubble constant). According to one of the two major studies, the rate is fifty kilometers per second per megaparsec; according to the other it is one hundred kilometers per second per megaparsec. Despite this uncertainty about the age and expansion rate of the universe, and despite the recognition that our theories fail unless we posit something about which we know nothing, we claim to know what happened in the first 10^{-43} second of the existence of the universe.

This doesn't necessarily imply we should stop trying. Whether it's worth our while to continue investing so much time and money in cosmology is a value question that raises a lot of issues. But, for the reasons noted, it does seem highly unlikely that we will produce results we can trust. Some mysteries of the universe are, well, mysterious.

Other deep mysteries to which we think we're rapidly approaching solutions are associated with what philosophers call the mind–body problem. First, there is the mystery of consciousness itself. How do we explain the capacity of beings like ourselves to consciously experience the world (the tastes, the feels, the colors, the fragrances, etc.)? Among other things, an answer to this question will tell us how beings with consciousness differ from objects that detect and respond to the same aspects of the world but without consciousness (for example, motion detectors and thermostats). That is, it will explain what sorts of beings are capable of consciousness and why. The typical answer to this is that beings with consciousness have brains. But what exactly are brains? Where do they appear in our evolutionary history? Do spiders and ants have them? Do spiders and ants feel pain or heat, or experience fragrances (as opposed to merely detecting certain kinds of molecules)? The fact that we can't answer these questions – that we can't even imagine experiments that will settle them – should give us pause. Perhaps we don't now have the intellectual tools to understand the mystery of consciousness.

This is not a popular stance among philosophers of mind and neurologists. They are enormously impressed with advances in brain science that appear to promise explanations of all

brain-related phenomena not far in the future. They are especially impressed with work on the human brain. There are two
reasons for skepticism about work on *the* brain solving the
problem of consciousness, even for human beings. First, there
is no such thing as *the* brain. Human brains are not identical to
each other in the way that iMacs of the same vintage are. Most
obviously, they are all wired differently. Our neurons begin
connecting to one another as soon as we begin to experience
and learn, and, since we experience and learn different things
at different rates, we each have different patterns of connection. There are also big structural/functional differences. In
normal right-handed people, the left side of the brain is supposed to perform linguistic and analytic tasks, and the right
brain is supposed do imaginative, synthetic, and artistic tasks.
In about half the left-handed people, this specialization is
reversed. In the other half, hemispheric specialization disap-
pears entirely and the so-called left brain and right brain tasks
are distributed through both hemispheres. In addition, some
brains are so anomalous in their structures that it makes no
sense to talk about hemispheric specialization at all. Some
people have only one cerebral hemisphere (typically as a result
of surgery). Others have no hemispheres at all. The British
neurologist John Lorber did C.A.T. (computerized axial
tomography) scans of six hundred hydrocephalics (people
with an excess of cerebral spinal fluid). In nearly sixty of them,
ninety-five percent of the cranial cavity was filled with fluid.
Half this group were severely retarded. The remaining half
had I.Q.'s of more than a hundred. Lorber also discovered a
young man with an I.Q. of 126 and a first class honors degree in
mathematics who had almost no brain at all. That subject's
brain tissue – about a millimeter thick – was spread across the
inside of his skull.[3]

This makes it difficult even to imagine a brain-based explanation of particular conscious states, given the intellectual resources of the moment. According to the kinds of explanations we now employ all conscious states are produced by neurons firing. We have the experience of yellow, for example, because certain neurons fire in a certain order in our brain. But if this is intended as an explanation of the experience of yellow in the brain, it requires that the same neurons fire in the same order in every brain (or, at least, that we can state some general feature of neuron firings common to all experiences of yellow). It's not at all clear how we can do that. Since everyone's brain is wired differently, it's hard to say what makes a set of neurons in one brain the same as a set of neurons in another. That's like trying to say which connections on the motherboard of an iMac are the same as the connections on the motherboard of a P.C. We could perhaps identify them as the same in relation to their function (that is, what they make happen). But, obviously, if we try that in the present case, the theory that we see yellow because certain neurons fire in a certain order becomes true by definition. Either that, or the theory reduces to the claim that we experience yellow because some neurons or other are firing in our brains. There is a remote possibility that we could identify some feature common to all the sets of neuron firings that produce our experience of yellow. But we don't at this point have the remotest idea of what that feature would be.

Even if we could identify the neurological activity that causes our experience of yellow, we would not have a satisfying explanation of how the brain produces that bit of consciousness. Of course, whether an explanation is satisfying depends on what we want an explanation for. If we're interested in the mystery of consciousness, though, we need more than an account of which brain states cause what experiences. That's a start, but it's not enough. To explain the mystery of consciousness – for example, to help us eventually understand what kinds of creatures are capable of it – we need more. In particular we need to know why a given brain activity produces the experience it does. Why yellow rather than red or, for that matter, why a color experience instead of an itch or a thought? It will take a conceptual revolution in brain science before we can answer questions like that. Our current brain science currently has no concepts that provide bridges between experiences and neuron firings (or any other brain activity) in this way.

The same kinds of difficulties face our attempts to understand how *the* brain produces thoughts, perceptions, emotions, and the rest. Again, since there is no such thing as *the* brain, different brains produce them differently. This problem is further complicated by the fact that we are not the only thinking, perceiving, and feeling beings in the world. Other animals also do these things, perhaps even ants and bees. We will have a fully satisfying understanding of these processes when we have a principled basis for saying what creatures are capable of doing them and what are not. At present we don't even have a *principled* basis for limiting them to carbon-based life forms. That is, we don't have a principled basis for saying that we could not build a creature that thinks and feels out of silicon chips. Of course, the only thinking and feeling beings we know are living, carbon-based creatures. But we won't solve the mystery of how material systems think, perceive, and feel until we have principled scientific arguments to show that it must be this way. (There's a great old *New Yorker* cartoon in which two aliens in a spaceship are looking at images from earth and one says to the other, incredulously, "They think with meat??!! What do you mean they think with meat?")

This is not to deny the value of brain research. Many dramatic, interesting, and important discoveries have been made. But they do not take us far in the direction of solving the mysteries of consciousness and thought. That will require a conceptual revolution.

It might be objected that this asks too much. After all, the objector claims, we now know which of the traditional answers to the mind–body problem is true, namely, materialism (or, as it is sometimes called, physicalism). Materialism, the objection continues, is a methodological assumption of science and is vindicated by the successes of science. Science took off when it adopted the assumption that everything in the universe is material (or physical) and can be explained in material terms. This response raises an interesting issue but it misses the point. It misses the point because we don't explain the mystery of thought and consciousness by simply asserting that the universe is material or physical through and through. We would still want to understand how a universe that is material through and through produces consciousness and thought.

The interesting issue is the role that materialism plays in science. It might be thought that materialism is one of those big assumptions about the subject matter which guides inquiry. But this is misleading. Materialism is a philosophical theory and an unstable one at that. It has not guided science. If anything, the shoe is on the other foot. That is, science has to provide materialism with its meaning and content. That is because the idea of matter itself has gone through big changes during its history. Mass and energy are relatively recent arrivals. Thomas Hobbes was a materialist but his idea of matter had no place for mass or energy. Neither did Descartes's. Furthermore, our ideas of mass and energy have themselves changed significantly. In the interim between Newton and Einstein they were separate phenomena. Einstein brought them together (in the Law of the Conservation of Matter and Energy). Many physicists now describe matter as a "lumpy" form of energy. According to Newton, every bit of matter occupied some position in absolute space. Since Einstein, all positions in space are relative. Since quantum mechanics, with its Uncertainty Principle and probability waves, the relation between particles and space has become more complicated and problematic. According to quantum physics, the very existence of a particle may depend on the presence of an observer. Today, some physicists are seriously suggesting that particles can move backwards in time and that every possible universe is an actual universe (ours just happens to be the one we occupy). Given the rapid rate of change in theoretical physics, chances are that our current concepts of mass, matter, and energy will change again soon. In fact, given all the blanks to be filled in with respect to dark matter and dark energy, and given the major effort now underway to understand gravity in a manner consistent with quantum mechanics, we can probably expect major changes soon. It's impossible to predict what these changes will be and therefore impossible to say what the materialism of tomorrow will actually assert. So, again, it's not as if materialism guides physics. Physicists have always shown an admirable willingness to let the philosophical chips fall where they may.

This is not to say that materialism plays no role at all in science. At any given period in the history of science, the materialism of the day has limited inquiry (for example, by eliminating gods, ghosts, faith healers, witches, magicians, clairvoyants, and a nonmaterial mind as respectable explanatory concepts). But, since the materialism of the day really just confines science to the world described by physics, it is really physics that is constraining the rest of science, not some philosophical theory. Furthermore, it's not clear that all the banished phenomena will be banished for ever. According to some physicists, quantum mechanics itself calls for a new understanding of the relation between mind and matter in which mind has pride of place (since the presence of an observer reduces a probability wave to an actuality). This shows how loose and changeable the constraints of materialism are. In the thought of some physicists, they are loose enough to put consciousness in the very center of things.

Organization and Politics

Thus far we've looked at intellectual factors that affect the move from data to conclusions. We turn now to organizational factors. Although Knowledge Machines allow some differences of opinion within their ranks, there is generally a core set of principles and propositions on which they speak with one voice (or almost one voice). Some of them have formal mechanisms in place for producing definitive conclusions. Juries reach verdicts; regulatory bodies issue official rulings. Others have mechanisms for arriving at a nearly universal consensus. Although there is no one official body issuing proclamations binding on all physicists, chemists, biologists, etc., there are social mechanisms for assuring consensus on many issues. Whether formal or informal, the convergence of belief is a social process that typically involves the circulation of information and discussion. To succeed – to converge on accurate beliefs, or the best one can do at the time – these processes must negotiate a range of obstacles and hazards with which we are now familiar. I will begin by mentioning some problems that face them all, and then go on to discuss problems specific to types of organizational structures.

First, Knowledge Machines need to guard against personal agendas. Nearly every actor in a knowledge-seeking community has one. They want to get more money or get more status, get more power or more fame, help their friends or advance their causes (or ideologies), make their jobs more relaxing and please their coworkers, and so on. People with any of these agendas may skew or attenuate the flow of information and discussion. They may even intentionally argue for conclusions they do not think are justified by the data. It is hard to fight this kind of dishonesty. The world is richly endowed with rhetorical devices and a reasonably intelligent person can usually make arguments of both sides of a complicated issue.

Knowledge Machines are also vulnerable to other common dynamics that affect social groups. Perhaps the most dangerous of these are the tendencies to follow the leader and to go along to get along (to bow to peer pressure and to spout the party line to win friends and allies). These tendencies are partly responsible for the fads and bandwagon effects that periodically sweep through many Knowledge Machines. They are also responsible for very bad decision-making in particular cases. According to many commentators, for example, the pressure to produce "good news" is a pervasive feature of the Bush White House and, among other things, is responsible for the "failed intelligence" on which Bush now blames his decision to invade Iraq (and his approach to the occupation). That "failed intelligence" was a direct consequence of pressure from above. According to these commentators, senior officials in the Bush White House made it clear to the heads of intelligence agencies that they wanted information that supported the case for invasion (even after the decision to invade had been made). To some extent, the heads of these agencies complied. For example, they passed along information supplied by Iraqi exile groups they correctly suspected of being self-serving.

All Knowledge Machines also operate under constraints of time and money. No matter how they are structured, they are willing to spend only so much to safeguard accuracy and reliability. Although there are sometimes significant differences between what pathologists see in a biopsy sample, there is often only one pathologist for each case. Although criminal defendants are innocent until proven guilty beyond a reasonable doubt, many of them can't afford to hire detectives, fly in expert witnesses, or hire top attorneys. The criminal justice system will provide lawyers but there is a big difference between well-funded and minimally funded defenses and we are not willing to spend the money to give every defendant the best defense. As we have already seen, newspapers, magazines, and scientific journals are only willing to devote so many resources to checking facts and investigating fraud. All Knowledge Machines set these kinds of limits. The question is always whether they are willing to spend enough to achieve a tolerable level of reliability.

But certain problems that plague Knowledge Machines are rooted in their specific organizational structure. Although theorists categorize knowledge-producing structures in a variety of ways, it makes most sense for our purposes to organize them along two continua.[4] The first continuum runs from free-standing to embedded. A Knowledge Machine is embedded to the extent that it's part of a wider organization – say, a corporation or a government – that has purposes of its own, or to the extent that it depends on such an organization for its funding. It is free-standing to the extent that it is not embedded.

Free-standing Knowledge Machines can develop and operate by their own internal methods and principles. The disciplines of philosophy and literary studies are relatively free-standing. They are not completely so because they are mostly supported by universities and they are affected by that. For example, in order to win tenure junior faculty are under pressure to write papers that might not otherwise have been written to fill journals that might not otherwise exist. The sciences are less free-standing. Many scientists work directly for governments and corporations and most rely on government, corporations, and big foundations to fund their research. This seriously influences the direction of their research and sometimes affects its reliability (recall the cases of scientific fraud in Chapter 4).

The pursuit of knowledge is rarely a pure thing. Much of it is sponsored by or happens within organizations that are not interested in truth or knowledge for their own sake (corporations, branches of government, advocacy groups, etc.). These organizations have their own goals, purposes, and interests and pursue knowledge to promote those objectives. When truth gets in the way, truth is often the casualty. Researchers may be pressured to abandon, spin, or even fake results, or to remain silent as their work is misrepresented by others. They may also do these things even without pressure simply to please their sponsors and employers. Or they may want to feel like part of the team.

The pressure to produce "positive results" is usually subtle, but sometimes quite explicit. One chilling example of this occurred the evening before N.A.S.A.'s disastrous launch of the Space Shuttle *Challenger* on the morning of January 28, 1986. The engineers and management from Morton Thiokol who worked on the Shuttle were on the phone with N.A.S.A. officials in charge of the launch. The engineers wanted to postpone the launch. A certain set of seals in the booster rocket – O-rings – lost too much resiliency at temperatures below fifty-three degrees (Fahrenheit), and the overnight low at the launch site (the Kennedy Space Center) was predicted to be eighteen degrees. The engineers explained that if the seals failed the Shuttle could explode. The N.A.S.A. brass were initially sympathetic. Joe Kilminster (the Vice President of Space Booster Programs at N.A.S.A.) favored postponement as did a second senior official, George Hardy. But a third senior N.A.S.A. official, Larry Mulloy, maintained that the engineers' arguments were inconclusive. After Mulloy had spoken, Joe Kilminster asked for a five-minute off-line caucus to re-evaluate the data (*five minutes!*). According to an engineer at Thiokol (Roger Boisjoly), as soon as the mute button was pushed the general manager at Thiokol (Jerry Mason) announced, "We have to make a management decision." At that point the four Thiokol senior executives in the room moved to one end of the table and began discussing the matter among themselves. When Boisjoly and another engineer tried to join the discussion to restate their case they were rebuffed. After the managers had completed their discussion, Mason turned to Bob Lund, the Vice President of Engineering, and told him "to take off his engineering hat and put on his management hat" (in effect, to lie about the real danger). When the conversation with N.A.S.A. resumed, the Thiokol management recommended launching on schedule and the recommendation was accepted by N.A.S.A. without any probing discussion. The engineers at Thiokol remained silent. As you may remember, the *Challenger* disintegrated seventy-three seconds after takeoff due to a failure in the O-rings, killing seven astronauts.[5]

In addition to producing false conclusions and bad decisions, embeddedness obviously affects the direction of scientific research. Governments and corporations hire scientists and sponsor their research to get results of interest to governments and corporations. In the case of governments, these are very often war related. Of course, much scientific research sponsored by governments and corporations has been highly successful and useful. It's led to important discoveries and opened up new fields of research. But it's hard not to wonder what science would be like if the scientific community had complete freedom to pursue its own research interests (that is, if science were a pure process of inquiry). In addition to the probable differences in concepts and theories, the world would almost certainly be a safer place.

The second organizational continuum runs from democracy to dictatorship. Knowledge Machines are democratic to the extent that all players are equal and decision-making is unaffected by differences in official positions, status, and prestige. Juries, special investigative commissions, and American town hall meetings approach this ideal. They don't realize it completely because they have chairpersons who can influence the direction of discussions, and because their deliberations are often affected by differences in status and prestige. Probably the closest we get to this end of the continuum is a Quaker meeting. As we move toward the dictatorial end, decision-making is increasingly dominated by official position, status, and prestige. In the limiting case, one person makes all the decisions. No organization realizes this ideal completely either. Even the most hierarchical structures – armies, for example – allow lower-level personnel to make some decisions. Most academic disciplines fall somewhere in the middle of this continuum. Prestigious professors, departments, journals, and think-tanks exert disproportionate influence. Professional organizations sometimes take positions on issues. But no one is officially designated to speak for the group and people are rarely drummed out of the corps for heresy. It is very difficult to fire tenured professors for holding unorthodox views. When it comes to producing knowledge and making good decisions, both hierarchies and democracies have serious problems.

Hierarchies have three main problems. First, there are pure problems of design. The success of any coordinated knowledge-gathering or decision-making process depends on how well the parts work together. Information must flow to the people who need it when they need it. It cannot disappear into black holes or end up in dead letter boxes. Bottlenecks must also be avoided. Bureaucratic structures are often plagued by such problems. Even when people do their jobs effectively, the flow of information may be circuitous or even blocked. Second, there are problems of personal politics. These plague all Knowledge Machines, but hierarchical structures are particularly vulnerable to them, since they have so many gatekeepers and potentates. These are all points at which information and discussion can be skewed or altered as a result of jealousy, competition, resentment, and so forth. Finally, there are problems related to protecting one's position and covering one's back. All managers and department heads want to be bearers of good news and otherwise look good to their superiors. So they may block, spin, or even alter bad news. As a result, important information from lower levels may not make it to the top.

The *Challenger* tragedy provides a good example of how the flow of information can be blocked. According to N.A.S.A.'s official estimate, the risk that the Space Shuttle *Challenger* would fail was one in 100,000. After examining the data available to N.A.S.A. management, Richard Feynman, a Nobel Prize winner in physics and a member of the commission investigating the disaster, estimated the chances at one in fifty.

Feynman's estimate was close to that of N.A.S.A.'s own engineers (and also that of an independent engineering consultant hired by N.A.S.A.). All the estimates were based on test runs revealing problems with components in the solid rocket booster and the rocket engine. Feynman and the engineers were disturbed by the fact that things weren't working as expected. For example, O-rings in the rocket booster weren't supposed to erode at all, but in a test run they eroded to one-third their radius. Management concluded that this was in fact good news. Since they eroded only one-third of their radius, there was "a safety factor of three." Feynman likens this way of dealing with unknown dangers to Russian roulette. But management wanted to assure Congress and the public that things were going well, so they ignored what their engineers were saying. A similar thing happened with respect to estimates that the main engine would fail. N.A.S.A. engineers at the Marshall Space Center put the estimate at one in three hundred. Again, N.A.S.A.'s management estimate was one in 100,000 (for the booster and the main engine combined). This is all in Feynman's Appendix to the Roger's Commission Report.[6]

Democratic structures also have their problems. Since all parties are equal, there is no way to enforce standards of practice. Consider elections (which we might think of as democratically structured processes to identify the best candidates and policy options). The process is so compromised that people don't even pretend to be deciding what's best for the whole any more. Despite occasional high-minded rhetoric, most people unabashedly vote to advance their interests (financial, regional, ethnic, religious, gender, etc.). Political parties and candidates encourage this. Furthermore, most of the individuals and organizations that bombard voters with information and arguments – political parties, advocacy groups, ideologically driven media outlets – have absolutely no interest in fair and balanced discussion. Truth and reason are victimized many times every hour and mourned only in merely ritual orgies of self-recrimination. Strong personalities and effective speaking styles also exert great influence in democratic decision-making. They can sway a jury and win the hearts and minds of an electorate (for better or for worse). We regard this as business as usual. Perhaps we just can't see how to avoid it. The only defense of democracy is Winston Churchill's: anything else is even worse.

Most democratic decision-making also has trouble making effective use of expertise. Partisans are always skeptical of experts bearing bad news. The response is to look for someone – anyone – with credentials who brings good tidings (however few or mercenary they may be). Since most of the electorate cannot evaluate disputes between specialists (or don't think they can), this often does the trick. This is how George Bush and his cronies were able to convince so many Americans for so many years that human-generated global warming was not a serious problem. Since each side had its "experts" and much of the electorate could not (or thought it could not) follow the scientific argument, the latter took the matter to be undecided. That lasted until the tide of expert opinion was all but universally on the other side.

The same phenomenon occurs on a smaller scale when jurors hear the testimony of expert witnesses. The issues are often complex and technical, so attorneys urge the experts to rely on colorful language, memorable phrases, and analogies (there are workshops and conferences to teach these skills). The contest between competing experts becomes one of rhetoric and self-presentation. Knowing they can't rely on their own technical competence, jurors rely on (what they take to be) signs of intelligence, sincerity, and competence in the witness. A relaxed, smooth, self-confident presentation goes a long way. The triumph of rhetoric over argument and expertise is an old story. In Plato's dialog *The Gorgias*, the Sophist Gorgias brags that he can be more persuasive than any doctor at the bed of a sick person despite knowing nothing about medicine.

But not all democratic decision structures have these problems. Democratic structures can make use of expert knowledge in two ways. First, the decision-makers may themselves be experts. Special government commissions established to investigate specific issues or events may consist of experts organized more or less democratically. Second, special provisions can be implemented to assure that decision-makers understand the issues. This can be done even in elections. The Jefferson Center in the U.S., for example, has developed a very helpful citizen jury process that does this well. Citizen juries are assembled to make public policy decisions. Jurors begin by reading a lot of material on both sides of an issue. They then invite experts to come before them, explain difficult concepts, and answer their questions. After discussing matters among themselves, the jurors may recall witnesses for further clarification. The proceedings of citizen juries can be (and have been) televised and their reports have been published. On many issues, jurors move from considerable disagreement at the start to considerable agreement at the finish. Getting the facts straight makes a big difference. So do prolonged and serious discussions. The more the electorate pays attention to the proceedings and conclusions of citizen juries – as opposed to political ads and sound bites – the better its decisions will be. Citizen juries are not a uniquely American phenomenon. According to the Jefferson Center webpage, a similar movement developed in Germany in the 1970s (Planungzelle). Both of these models were introduced in the U.K. in the mid 1990s by the Institute for Public Policy Research in London. The good news is that this movement is spreading. The bad news is that it is spreading slowly.[7]

Democratic decision-making does have advantages in some cases. In his bestselling book, *The Wisdom of Crowds*, James Surowiecki suggests that in many cases democratic decision-making is actually better than expert decision-making. Surowiecki is impressed by a series of experiments in which the aggregate judgment of large groups of people is more accurate than the judgment of nearly every individual within that group. Most of these experiments involve estimating the size or amount of something or solving a particular kind of problem (like finding the best way to move through a maze). In one experiment fifty-six subjects were asked to estimate the number of jelly beans in a jar and only one of them beat the average of the group estimate. In another experiment, two hundred subjects were asked to rank objects by weight and only five of them beat the average estimate. Reflecting on these experiments, Surowiecki argues that crowds – democratically structured groups – make better decisions than most individuals on a variety of topics provided four conditions are met: (1) there must be diversity of opinion; (2) there must be independence (people's opinions are not determined by others around them); (3) there must be decentralization (people are able to draw on local knowledge instead of getting all their information from a central place); and (4) there must be some means for turning private judgments into collective decisions.[8]

Surowiecki does not try to define the range of cases in which crowds do better than experts. Obviously, many problems require more expertise than estimating the numbers of jelly beans in glass jars. But most decision-making processes can benefit by meeting the conditions he cites. Taken together, these conditions protect us from false consensus, groupthink, and one-source stories. In many cases, communities of investigators who satisfy these conditions will probably solve problems better than any individual within them in a wide range of cases (at least if the method for turning private judgments into collective decisions is reliable). It's worth investigating the range of cases in which this is true.

Academic disciplines and certain other Knowledge Machines fall somewhere in the middle of the democratic–dictatorial continuum. They lack official positions from which occupants may speak for the group, and have very weak mechanisms for disciplining mavericks and dissenters. But there are big differences in status and prestige among investigators, institutions, conferences, and journals and there are professional organizations that issue position papers and declarations on some issues. So some players have much more decision-making influence than others. And there is also informal pressure on lesser lights to remain within the boundaries of respectable opinion.

But structures of this kind are more vulnerable to fads, fashions, and bandwagon effects than structures at the ends of the continuum. Dictatorial organizations are only as faddish as the people at the top. They have mechanisms for quashing new ideas and enforcing orthodoxies. Often, their organizational cultures discourage change. Genuinely democratic structures, on the other hand, have weaker mechanisms for getting everyone on board. (To the extent that a society or a structure can be manipulated from the top – e.g. by propaganda – it's not genuinely democratic.) Structures in the middle are more vulnerable. Although they lack mechanisms for compelling belief, they do have ways to encourage it. It's always exciting for researchers to ride the crest of the Next Big Thing. It can be a big boost to their egos and their careers. And the faster that one moves into a new territory to stake one's claim the better. With the help of conferences and journals, doctrines can be publicized and promulgated in relatively little time. The first ones in win the glory. There is a bit of the Oklahoma Land Rush feeling about the whole thing. It is no wonder that movements come and go so fast in some fields. During the last fifty years in English (literary studies), for example, New Criticism gave way to structuralism, which gave way to post-structuralism, which gave way to post-modernism and deconstructionism, which has now given way to something more diffuse and eclectic called "cultural theory."

These rapid turnovers are possible because there are often good arguments *both for and against* prevailing orthodoxies and their challengers in many academic disciplines and other fields. This is even true in the sciences. Newtonian physics ruled Europe for more than two hundred years. But Leibniz, a contemporary of Newton's, made powerful arguments against Newton's theories of absolute space and time. Some of these arguments anticipated Einstein. A century later Kant also made a powerful attack on these Newtonian concepts. But, since Newtonian physics was so well established at that time, these arguments were largely ignored (they were also ignored because, unlike Einstein, neither Leibniz nor Kant had an alternative that could be the basis of a new physics). The point is that reason, evidence, and argument are not always compelling, even when they seem to be to most specialists. And, when they are not, the fate of a movement or doctrine is a hostage to social and psychological factors. In some cases, those factors dominate, and movements gain currency on a slim evidential basis (for example, promising preliminary results).

This is not to say that just any movement or theory can become influential. There must be *some* evidential support. And there must be other sources of appeal. The source of a theory can make it hot. It may be the latest thing from someone with a big reputation and/or a powerful, charismatic personality. The success of behaviorism in psychology, for example, was due partly to the zealous and tireless advocacy of John B. Watson, a true believer with a strong personal presence. The rise of Ordinary Language Analysis in philosophy in the 1950s and 1960s is attributable almost entirely to the charisma of Ludwig Wittgenstein (and perhaps a few other colorful personalities associated with that movement).

In addition, paradigms may appeal because they fit the mood of the times. The popularity of Freudian ideas has much to do with the intellectual climate of the 1920s, which was a response to the madness of World War I (e.g. the protracted trench warfare in which millions were slaughtered as they charged impregnable positions). The 1920s generated many movements that were impressed by the irrational side of human nature. It was also a time of widespread sexual experimentation. Or, to take a more recent example, post-modernism thrived in an atmosphere created by identity politics. The movement appealed to many leftist academics because they thought it was a good way to combat injustices of race, class, and gender in their research, and also because it provided a justification for transforming the curriculum to address these injustices.

Finally, intellectual movements may be appealing because of their successes elsewhere. In the 1930s and 1940s, logical positivism dominated the philosophy of science. Its successes in philosophy made it attractive to methodologists in the social sciences (who aspired to make their disciplines more scientific). As a result, the positivist conception of science dominated the social sciences for many years. This did much to strengthen behaviorism both in psychology and elsewhere. In the 1970s, most of the methodologists rejected positivism in favor of an outlook inspired by Thomas Kuhn. Still more recently, many of them converted to post-modernism and appropriated the work of French philosophers like Derrida and Foucault. Philosophy also borrows. Most recently, work in the philosophy of mind has been strongly influenced by work in cognitive science and neuroscience.

Whatever the sources of their appeal, as new movements and paradigms achieve popularity, they solidify their position and increase their power by capturing influential positions. Their leaders become journal editors, conference planners, and heads of large and prestigious graduate departments. This enables them to shape the contemporary discussion and also to replicate themselves in the next generation. Behaviorism was spectacularly successful in this regard. For several decades, behaviorists edited the top journals, ran the most prestigious psychology departments, and organized the most high-profile conferences. If a student wanted a career in psychology, the obvious move was to become a behaviorist. Many students who were not attracted to running rats through mazes dropped out of psychology. Those who continued on to graduate school had fewer career options than their more behavioristically inclined fellow graduate students. Because behaviorism enjoyed this sort of self-replicating hegemony, it retained its dominance for nearly five decades despite the compelling objections we examined earlier. Dissenters were professionally marginalized.

This is not to say that the success of a movement or paradigm is all about politics. It's important to remember all our genuine intellectual advances. But history prescribes a healthy dose of skepticism. It's very easy to be swept up in the Next Big Thing. To resist is to swim against the tide (even to stay in one place). It helps to remember how many Next Big Things have come and gone. Who knows what physicists will think about string theory fifty years from now? Of course, it's always much easier to separate the wheat from the chaff in retrospect.

Publication

There are many different kinds of Knowledge Machines and they publish their findings in different ways. In most cases, little or nothing is distorted in the publication process itself. Errors that appear in print are consequences of errors earlier in the process (that is, bad data gathering or reasoning). But there are also cases in which the publication process is at least partly responsible for misinformation. We have already discussed some of these in relation to fraud. In those cases, the publication process did not have adequate fact checking and other safeguards. In this section, we will discuss three additional problems: incompetence, market forces, and the false idea of balance that has entered the culture of journalism.

Most Knowledge Machines publish their results in books and journals written by practitioners for practitioners. These writings tend to be crammed with jargon and otherwise written in stiff and unnecessarily complicated prose. In the course of writing this book, I frequently waded through pages of stilted technical prose I could condense into a few sentences of ordinary English with very little loss of meaning. It wasn't pleasant. Because specialist literatures are so forbidding, there are "translators." Translators fall into three groups: specialists who can write for a general audience, nonspecialists who educate themselves in a specialist literature, and journalists. Not surprisingly, we trust the specialists most because we know they have mastered their subject matter and we're confident that they appreciate its complexities, subtleties, and nuances. Since popularizers are looked at with suspicion in most fields, these translators also have a strong incentive to be accurate and not to dumb down. Some specialists are also excellent writers (for example, Freud and Einstein). But this literature does have two hazards. First, specialists sometimes take positions on controversial issues in their field without giving the other side a fair hearing (in some cases, without even much acknowledging the controversy). Second, specialists may sometimes write about matters in which they are not particularly competent. This most often happens when they take work in their field to have implications for work in another field, and spend some time discussing those implications. This sometimes happens when evolutionary biologists speak to issues in sociology and anthropology.

The second class of translators – professional writers who educate themselves in a specialist literature – are sometimes excellent. They tend to write well and have a sense of what a general audience might find interesting about a subject matter. And often they know their stuff. But those of us who know little about a subject matter can't always be sure about this (although we can sometimes find reviews of their books by specialists). Also, because sales are a major concern, books and articles of this kind may sensationalize, oversimplify, omit qualifications, and ignore complexities to boost readership.

The third class of translators are journalists. They are lowest on the reliability scale. Ben Goldacre, who writes a weekly column in the *Guardian* exposing bad science and bad science journalism, begins a 2005 column with the question, "Why is science in the media so often pointless, simplistic, boring or just plain wrong?"[9] His disappointment is not unique. Daniel Kestenbaum, an American National Public Radio science reporter (with a degree in high energy physics from Harvard), compares reading newspaper stories about science he knows well to hearing a piece of familiar music on a piano that is out of tune.[10] Working scientists also tend to be unhappy with science journalism. According to a 1997 survey, a majority of working scientists believed that reporters don't understand statistics well enough to explain new scientific findings, don't understand the nature of science and technology, and are more interested in sensationalism than in scientific truth.[11] This harsh judgment is not groundless. It is supported by analyses of science stories. In 1990, for example, Eleanor Singer compared news reports from a variety of media with the original research reports by scientists in the literature (on the subject of hazards). She found that only 7.1% of the science articles were entirely free of "inaccuracies." Since common errors included omission of qualifying statements (sixty percent), a change of emphasis (forty-five percent), and overstatement of generalizability (thirty-six percent), she probably should have said "misleading statements" instead of "inaccuracies" but that is cold comfort.[12] In general the biggest complaints of working scientists against science journalists are that their stories are incomplete, sensationalized, and not properly contextualized. That means the stories do not provide the public with a reliable indication of what is happening in the sciences.

Again, one reason for this is incompetence. Many science news stories are not even written by science journalists, especially stories about political or social controversies that are or might be generated by a new scientific breakthrough or technology. And science journalists themselves are often out of their depth. As we saw earlier, it doesn't take a lot of training in the sciences to become a science journalist. Also, science journalists may be assigned to cover developments in many different areas of science and have little or no knowledge of some of them.

As suggested, market forces also play a role. Newspapers and television news shows need stories that hold the attention of their audience, and typically treat their audiences as if they had the attention span of a poodle. As a result, they give reporters too little space and time to provide the background needed to understand the nature and significance of many scientific breakthroughs. How much molecular biology can one really teach in a few paragraphs? Sara Robinson, a well-known science journalist, reports that when she was an intern at the *New York Times* her mentor, John Markoff, told her that the goal of scientific reporting on technical matters was to provide the reader with "the illusion of understanding."[13] According to Ben Goldacre, there are three kinds of science stories: wacky stories, scare stories, and breakthrough stories. Here's what he says of scare stories: "Based on minimal evidence and expanded with poor understanding of its significance, they help perform the most crucial function for the media, which is selling you, the reader, to their advertisers." He also describes amusing cases of breakthrough stories based on little more than a press release from a scientific lab (no published paper, no data, and not even a clear report of the finding itself).[14] In February 2004, for example, two British newspapers reported that cod liver oil was a new wonder drug. According to one, the *Independent*, "They're not yet saying it can enable you to stop a bullet or leap tall buildings, but it's not far short of that." The source was a press release from Cardiff University which, in Goldacre's words, "described a study looking at the effect of cod liver oil on some enzymes – no idea which – that have something to do with cartilage – no idea what." Goldacre reports that seventeen months after the appearance of this story there was still no published paper.[15]

The final problem is grounded in the culture of journalism. Like most journalists, science journalists are expected to provide balanced coverage. As a result they look for and dignify dissenting viewpoints in a way that masks a prevailing scientific consensus. Maxwell and Jules Boykoff analyzed stories on climate change in four major newspapers between 1998 and 2002 (*New York Times*, *Washington Post*, *Wall Street Journal*, and *Los Angeles Times*). Using a random sample of 636 articles, the Bokoffs found that 52.7% gave "roughly equal attention" to the scientific consensus that humans contribute to climate change and to the energy-industry-supported claim that the warming is caused by natural fluctuations in climate. Only 35.3% emphasized the scientific consensus view while presenting the other side in a subordinate fashion.[16]

Reflections

Knowledge Machines never rest. They are continually making new discoveries and producing new theories. Few of us have the time, energy, capacity, or desire to keep up with it all. Many experts and specialists are challenged to keep up with their own fields. At best, most of us are willing to look carefully at research we have some personal reason to care about. If we get cancer, we will look carefully at cancer studies. If we are moved to do something about environmental issues, we may look seriously at the studies on global warming. But few if any of us are motivated or able to think seriously about all the current developments in physics, computer science, biology, philosophy, brain science, history, linguistics, and so on.

Still, some of us find our interest piqued by developments in these areas. We may not be willing to take the time and effort to think deeply about them, but we do enjoy a few tastes now and then. This creates a big market for material that, as George W. Bush said of himself, "doesn't do nuance." Newspapers and magazines feed this market with the kinds of stories that scientists and other knowledge professionals complain about. The fact is that science and other intellectual work has become entertainment commodities for many of us. We want to be thrilled, amazed, titillated, awed, and charmed. Newspapers, magazines, and even science-related television shows are eager to help. The result is sensationalism. Of course, the more careful, balanced, complicated stuff is out there. In many cases, it has been made accessible by good popularizers. But getting to it often means reading entire books rather than short newspaper stories and most of us don't have enough time and interest for that. The point is that there is a large market for exaggerated, sensationalized, and otherwise unnuanced accounts of scientific and other intellectual developments. No matter how good their products, Knowledge Machines will have difficulty getting unadulterated versions of them to market. The inevitable result is significant public misunderstanding.

As much as they complain about this problem, some knowledge professionals contribute to it themselves. Some of them also have a tendency to sensationalize. They do this to get their fifteen minutes of fame and to stir up public support for and funding in their fields. They also do it simply because they are swept up in the grand drama of it all. It's exciting to believe one is on the verge of curing cancer, discovering the secrets of aging, or finding the genetic basis of every desirable and undesirable trait. It's hard to resist gushing about one's brilliant new idea that's now yielding such promising results (however preliminary). And there is something especially magnificent about being on the team that succeeds at what so many of the greatest thinkers have aspired to do: solve the deepest mysteries of the universe, discover the fundamental laws of nature, understand how life and the universe itself began.

This last – the thrill of it all – is, I think, primarily responsible for the confidence with which so many assert that we know what happened in the first 0.0000000000000000000000000000000000000001 second (or did I miss a zero?) in the history of the universe; that and perhaps an almost universal human need to have a story about how it all began. How else can one explain that confidence, given the magnitude of the problem, the paucity of our data base, the weakness and inconsistencies in our theories, the likelihood major theories will change, the need to posit "something I know not what" to account for 99.75% of the "stuff" in the galaxies, and so on. I think a similar impulse fuels the confidence of brain scientists that they have solved, or are on the verge of solving, the mystery of consciousness.

As we have seen, Knowledge Machines may mislead us in other ways as well. Because they want to be respected and speak authoritatively, they have an interest in appearing to be objective and value free. For this reason, they tend to de-emphasize the value dimension of inquiry (when there is one). In many cases, practitioners are probably not aware of that themselves. I have no idea how many psychiatrists recognize that they make value judgments when they declare people *enough* of a danger to themselves and others to warrant involuntary commitment. I also have no idea how many economists realize that they make value judgments when they treat utility (preference satisfaction) as *the* measure of a healthy economy (ignoring issues of distribution, such as the gap between the rich and poor, and also treating working conditions and eco-logical degradation as irrelevant). What is clear is that preserv-ing authority requires downplaying such things. That's because in some cases the value judgments in question would simply not be shared. If the value assumptions underlying economists' assessments of a healthy economy were made explicit, my guess is that most people would be shocked. Many of us would be willing to sacrifice consumer goods to reduce pollution, global warming, and other ecological degradation or to have more interesting and less dangerous work.

Of course, what gets delivered to the public can be no more accurate than the conclusions at which Knowledge Machines arrive. Knowledge Machines are successful only to the extent that they are organized in ways that help us avoid or correct our fallibilities as individuals. But sometimes the ways they are organized create new problems that skew their results. These social causes of belief impress sociologists of knowledge in general, and historians and sociologists of science in particular. Studies in the history of science and sociology of science, and certain philosophical considerations, have inspired some to conclude that the truth or falsity of a theory or claim is irrele-vant to its acceptance. The "fixation of belief," as they call it, is a social process entirely explicable in sociological terms. The explanation of how/why the scientific community or other knowledge-seeking community comes to accept a belief is the same whether the belief is true or false. There is not one social process for accepting true beliefs and another for accepting false ones. This cluster of claims raises complicated questions to which I can't do justice here. They also introduce reason for skepticism about science and feed into the conflict between post-modernism and science worship that I discuss in the following chapter.

CHAPTER 6

From Data to Conclusions: A Bit of Philosophy

How do Knowledge Machines get from data to conclusions? How do they differ in the way that they do this? And how can we determine the reliability of those methods? There are two popular and simple answers to these questions and both lead quickly to big philosophical issues. So does the alternative to them for which I will argue. As a result, this chapter will be more philosophical than its predecessors.

Descartes begins his famous *Meditations on the First Philosophy* by lamenting all the disagreement on the big questions of science and philosophy. History notwithstanding, he doesn't think it has to be like that. He thinks he has a method – one method – that not only provides answers to these questions, but can produce answers that are so clear and so compelling that all fair-minded, intelligent people cannot help but agree with them. This astonishing ambition – a single fool-proof method to answer all the big questions to everyone's satisfaction – is a recurrent philosophical dream. It is currently out of fashion in philosophy, but a more streamlined version of it survives among those who believe that science and only science provides us with knowledge of the world because science and only science has the right method, viz. the scientific method. This position is called "scientism." Scientism provides one popular answer to questions about how Knowledge Machines get from data to conclusions. It divides Knowledge Machines into two camps, those which use the scientific method and those which do not. Only the former are thought to produce reliable results.

The other simple and popular answer comes from post-modernists. According to post-modernists, it really doesn't matter to what degree Knowledge Machines differ in their methods. No methods produce objective knowledge of the world because all inquiry bears the mark of its cultural, historical, class, gender, religious, and even personal origins. Or, as they say, all inquiry is "situated." And, because all inquiry is situated, it simply provides us with one of an indefinite number of points of view. We cannot arrive at what Thomas Nagel calls "the view from nowhere." We must give up the idea that mind can mirror nature (a metaphor of Richard Rorty). The very idea of truth is obsolete. The most we can produce are useful discourses, which are simply discourses that serve our needs.

Both of these simple answers are mistaken. Reality is more complicated. Contrary to scientism, there is no method unique to the sciences or even shared by the sciences. With the exception of formal disciplines like mathematics and logic, all Knowledge Machines, including the sciences, employ a mix of familiar kinds of reasoning. Contrary to the post-modernists, some of these are more reliable than others, and some of them are very reliable indeed.

This complicates the problem of evaluating how Knowledge Machines move from data to conclusions. We can't just describe the methods characteristic of and unique to various Knowledge Machines – *the* method of physics, *the* method of history, etc. – and rank them in the order of their reliability. There are no such methods. With the exceptions noted, Knowledge Machines employ a mix of familiar types of reasoning, some of which are more reliable than others. As a consequence, the various conclusions of any given Knowledge Machine differ in their reliability. Some bits of physics, for example, are more reliable than others. As a consequence of *this*, we can't make sweeping generalizations about the relative reliability of Knowledge Machines with respect to one another. Some bits of history, for example, are more reliable than some bits of physics. The fact that George III was king when the American colonies declared their independence is much more reliable than the Big Bang Theory. To evaluate the reliability of the route from data to conclusion in any particular case, we need to trace that route itself. There are no shortcuts.

We will begin by discussing the two simple but popular answers to our questions: scientism and post-modernism.

Scientism and "the Scientific Method"

Scientism asserts that science and only science delivers knowledge because science and only science uses "the scientific method." The idea that there is a single method employed by and unique to science is a common feature of science texts for children and adolescents and is accepted uncritically by some science teachers. My high school chemistry teacher described that method as follows: (1) a scientist gets curious about something; 2) they formulate a question about it; (3) they develop a hypothesis that answers that question; (4) they figure out what observations or experiments will confirm or disconfirm that hypothesis; and (5) they make those observations or conduct those experiments. There are many things wrong with this description (for example, most science is not a response to random curiosity). What's important for our purposes is that there is nothing uniquely scientific about this procedure. It's simply what intelligent people do when they get curious about something and care enough about it to investigate. If we allow that getting curious can be motivated by practical concerns (as it often is in science), this method describes how car salesmen think about potential buyers, and how teenagers think about romantic prospects. There is nothing uniquely scientific about it.

It's not surprising that this and other popular accounts of the scientific method are simplistic. The fact is that few if any philosophers and historians of science now believe that there is such a thing as the scientific method. Recent work in the history and sociology of science instead finds important differences in method. Among other things, this makes it difficult to formulate a clear distinction between science and pseudo-science. This problem – the Demarcation Problem, as it is called – was a central theme in the work of Karl Popper and continues to be a major issue in the philosophy of science today. If there were such a thing as the scientific method, there would be no Demarcation Problem. Science would be distinguished from pseudo-science because it adheres to that method.

Of course, there are contrasts between scientific and nonscientific or unscientific approaches to the natural world. We get a good sense of that contrast by looking at the origins of scientific thought. Thales of Miletus (62?–546 BC) – generally regarded as the first philosopher and scientist in the Western tradition – declared that the first principle of all things is water. To understand why this is considered the first scientific theory in the Western tradition, we need to understand how the Greeks explained natural phenomena before Thales. As you might guess, those explanations were mythological. Particular events were explained by particular stories. Here are two examples.

Why do these two trees grow so closely together? One day a god, disguised as a beggar, appeared at the cottage of two very poor old people. Though they were poor, they invited him in and shared what they had to eat. Impressed by their generosity, the god revealed himself the following morning and offered to grant the old couple a wish. They wished to be together even in death. So when they died, he buried them together by the river and these two trees grew from their bodies.

Why does the flower of the hyacinth grow at a right angle to the stalk? One day the god Apollo was throwing the discus with a mortal lover named Hyacinthus. As a result of a momentary distraction one of the god's throws struck his beloved mortal in the throat, breaking his neck. As a memorial to his friend, the grieving Apollo created the hyacinth, a broken-necked flower.

These stories illustrate five important points about the pre-philosophical, pre-scientific approach to nature. First, explanations were ad hoc and particular. They consisted of particular stories about particular events or phenomena. There is no intention to generalize to other events of the same kind. *These* two trees are close together for the reason given, but the distance between *those* trees (or trees in general) have different explanations. Second, these stories are accepted entirely on the basis of tradition and authority. They are not based on observation. The old people and the god were alone and no one saw

Apollo hit Hyacinthus with the discus or create the new flower. There is no witness to either story and no one who heard these stories would be expected to ask for one. More generally, there is also no obvious way to confirm or disconfirm these stories by arguments or evidence and no obvious way to defend them against competing explanations ("Oh, no. Here's how I heard it. The couple wasn't old. They were young but the wife was dying . . ."). Third, these stories are straightforwardly and unabashedly anthropomorphic. They explain natural events in relation to the motives and intentions of human beings and gods (who are themselves modeled on human psychology). The natural world is understood in terms of the human world. Fourth, as this implies, there is no attempt to explain changes in the physical world exclusively in physical or material terms. Motives, intentions, and supernatural powers are at work. Finally, and relatedly, everything in these stories is familiar. There is nothing hidden or secret, no processes or forces comparable to electrons or electromagnetic force.

What, then, of Thales' theory that the first principle of all things is water? Given what scholars have to work with – mostly, what later philosophers say about Thales – we can't be completely sure what he meant by this. But, based on the work of his successors, the following seems very likely. First, Thales wanted to understand the natural world in its own terms (instead of anthropomorphically). To this end, he divided the stuff of the world into the most general categories he could, the elements earth, air, fire, and water (solids, gasses, liquids, and fire, not understood as a gas). Everything could be understood as one of these elements or as some combination of these elements. His task was then to describe the relationship between these elements and, more specifically, how each came to be. Based on various observations, he decided that water was the central element. All other elements are born of water and return to water. That is, earth, air, and fire are all transformations of water.

It's not clear what Thales observed to arrive at this conclusion. But there are many obvious examples of these transformations. Water turns to air as it boils or otherwise evaporates. Air turns to water when it rains, fogs, mists, or dews. Water turns to earth at river deltas and when it freezes. Earth turns to water at the mouth of springs and at the bottom of wells. Water turns to fire when we light oil lamps or other liquid fuels or during volcanic eruptions. Fire turns to water during lightning storms or when we extinguish torches in barrels of water. In addition, Thales lived at the edge of an island-filled sea. Looking out from a high place, one could see earth emerging from (or dissolving into) water. Also, as Aristotle later noted, the seeds of all things are moist. So water is also connected with life and hence perhaps with a kind of energy. This last is a bit of a stretch but it is connected with another fragment attributed to Thales, viz. "All things are full of gods." He could not have meant the Olympian gods of traditional Greek religion. Perhaps he was struggling for a metaphor that helped him explain *why* natural transformations occur. Certainly, this is what some of his followers did. (Empedocles, for example, thought that the elements mixed and separated because of the operations of "love" and "strife.")

What we have here, then, is a perfectly general theory (instead of ad hoc and particular stories). It is based on observation and evidence rather than authority and tradition. It forgoes anthropomorphism (at least the most obvious forms). It tries to explain transformations in the physical world exclusively in physical terms. And it is at least open to the possibility that there are hidden forces beneath the surface of appearances.

These are all important features of most science and they do help us to distinguish between scientific explanations and religious and mythological explanations. But nothing in this list of conditions justifies the claim that science is reliable or that science has a monopoly on knowledge.

Could we get an account of the scientific method by adding to this list? The most obvious candidates are reliance on mathematics and experimentation. The problem with this is that not all sciences are experimental or mathematical. Darwin didn't experiment or rely on mathematics. In fact, much of biology, ethology, geology, and astronomy is not experimental and much of anatomy and physiology is not mathematical either. Although some evolutionary biologists now sometimes conduct experiments, most evolutionary explanations of particular traits or behaviors are just likely stories about how those traits and behaviors conferred reproductive advantages on the creatures that developed them. In this respect, they are far more like explanations of the French Revolution than they are like explanations of chemical reactions.

Belief in the scientific method is not only central to scientism; it also helps create a popular illusion about science. Roughly, this is the illusion that all the accepted results of the sciences are equally reliable. This would be true if all these results were established in exactly the same way. But there are huge differences. We learn that plant species are spread by birds that eat seeds in one place and deposit them in another by observations that almost anyone can make and understand. Understanding these observations doesn't rely on a lot of specialized background theories or assumptions. This is very different from "observations" of subatomic particles and the inferences based on those observations. Those observations depend heavily on theory. And both of these are very different from the "discovery" of dark energy and dark matter. We posit dark matter and dark energy, among other things, to make the Big Bang Theory work. Without them, among other things, we can't explain the expansion rate of the universe. Beyond that, we have no idea what they are. As this suggests, some scientific conclusions are about things reasonably local in space and time (the birds and the bees, D.N.A., etc.), whereas others are about events that happened in the tiniest fraction of a second billions of years ago, and still others are about laws of nature that are supposed to hold for all time, everywhere in the universe.

Despite all these differences, the illusion of equal reliability is hard to shake. Echoes of it surface even in relatively sophisticated discussions about science. The apostles of both scientism and post-modernism exploit this tendency by picking examples favorable to their case and acting as if those are perfectly representative of all science. The post-modernists talk as if all science is like quantum mechanics and string theory (which, given the history of physics, are likely to be replaced as Newton was). The defenders of scientism pick examples closer to home and talk as if all science is like cell structure, D.N.A., and the birds and the bees. Both exploit the illusion of equal reliability.

Traces of this illusion are also present in general comparisons between science and nonscientific disciplines, especially disciplines in the humanities (for example, philosophy, literary criticism, and history). Science students and some scientists themselves sometimes talk as if their results are *always* more reliable than results in other fields (which are sometimes represented as mere matters of opinion or worse). But, given the differences in the reliability of scientific results and theories, and the relatively short shelf life of some of them, this is not credible. The fact that Abraham Lincoln was president of the United States during the American Civil War is about as certain as any bit of science and more certain than some (for example, the Big Bang Theory). Even philosophy can claim results more reliable than the Big Bang Theory (for example, that there is no universal method for answering all the big questions).

Post-Modernism

The term "post-modernism" has been tossed around with abandon during the last fifty years. Not surprisingly, it means different things to different people. I am interested here in the common threads that address the questions of this chapter. The resulting picture may not be true of all who have ever called themselves post-modernists.

Used in a purely descriptive way, "post-modern" is an adjective characterizing styles of architecture, art, poetry, fashion, academic work, journalism, even social relations. Used in this way it suggests a mix of disparate elements, surprising juxtapositions, and an absence of more traditional forms of order and sense (for example, collages that include classical and industrial themes and novels without linear storylines or coherent characters). But "post-modernism" is also the name of an intellectual movement that is skeptical of traditional forms of sense and order and that applauds, or at least accepts, the emergence of post-modern cultural forms.

Every version of the post-modernist intellectual movement defines itself explicitly in opposition to the Enlightenment. The Enlightenment was a powerful eighteenth-century (or, some say, seventeenth- and eighteenth-century) intellectual, political, and social movement that included some of the most important thinkers in the Western intellectual tradition. As post-modernists understand it, the Enlightenment was an unmitigated celebration of the powers of reason. On this view, Enlightenment thinkers believed that we can achieve a complete understanding of the natural and human world through the proper exercise of reason and/or the proper mix of reason and observation. Armed with this understanding, we can perfect our institutions and subjugate and exploit nature to our own purposes. What holds us back, on this account, are ignorance, superstition, religion, blind acceptance of authority, self-centeredness, and other forms of bias. Once freed of these burdens, once guided by reason and observation alone, we can arrive at objective, accurate, and complete pictures of ourselves and our world and use them to create a kind of paradise on earth.

Before describing the post-modernist critique of this account, I should warn the reader that this post-modernist portrait of the Enlightenment is ridiculously simplistic. For example, it makes a complete hash of two of the most important Enlightenment philosophers, David Hume and Immanual Kant. In most philosophical circles, Hume is not regarded as an apostle of reason. In fact, he is best known for his skepticism about both reason and observation. In opposition to the rationalists, he denies that we can understand the basic principles of the universe just by thinking about them. In opposition to the standard run of empiricists, he doesn't believe it's reasonable to generalize from observation either. For example, he thinks we have no good reason to believe that correlations that held between events in the past will continue to hold in the future (his famous problem of induction). Without that, he emphasizes, we have no good reason to believe that turning the door knob will open the door, drinking water will quench our thirst, putting our hand in a fire will burn us, etc. In fact, according to Hume, our belief that correlations that held in the past will hold in the future is simply a matter of "animal faith." We have no choice but to run our lives in accordance with habits that have no rational basis. Furthermore, in relation to ethics Hume famously argues that "reason is a slave of the passions." Yet Hume is among the most important figures of the Scottish Enlightenment.

Immanuel Kant is often portrayed as a poster boy of the Enlightenment. But Kant's most important philosophical project explicitly attacked the pretensions of reason in *defense of faith*. According to Kant, we have no hope of ever under-standing the world as it is in itself. The purpose of his most famous book – *The Critique of Pure Reason* – is to establish this claim. Although he very much admires science (in its place), he believes that science cannot settle the big questions and he tries to protect the *religious* ideas of God, freedom, and immortality against the incursions of both science and philosophy. Of course, some aspects Humean and Kantian thought better fit the post-modernist picture of the Enlightenment than these descriptions of their core views and central projects. The point is that, in their rush to contrast themselves to the Enlightenment, post-modernists ignore the complexity of the Enlightenment. They also fail to recognize that it contains the seeds of their own ideas. In his philosophi-cal capacity, no one was more deeply skeptical about our capacity to understand the world than Hume.

But this is just a historical point. We still need to address the post-modernist critique of what *they think* the Enlightenment represents. The most important theme of this critique is that we are all "situated" beings. We are members of a particular cul-ture at a particular period of history. We get our intellectual tools – our concepts and theories – from our time and place. We depend on these tools to reason about the world. And it is arro-gant to believe that these tools are better than all the possible alternatives or that they somehow enable us to "cut nature at the joints." In addition to time and place, we are also limited by the peculiarities of our own circumstances – for example, our religion, race, class, gender, family of origin, schooling, and other such contingencies. Finally, although everyone is situated in this way, our culturally authoritative pictures of the world are the pictures of the privileged and the powerful.

Understood as an account of the obstacles to knowledge – the problems we face as thinkers – there is a lot of truth to this picture. But most post-modernist thinkers use it to support more extreme conclusions. The literature of post-modernism is a litany of epistemic pessimism. We read that our situatedness is inescapable, objectivity is a pipe dream, truth is relative, it is impossible to hold our representations up to the world to see how well they capture it, the very idea of representing the world is obsolete, the idea of truth itself is obsolete, that all we have are the stories we tell ourselves and none of them has any more epistemic claim to our allegiance than any other, and that, in the end, it's all about loyalty and expediency. Perhaps not every post-modernist would assent to all of this, but there is no denying that the waters of skepticism everywhere run high and that nothing remains anchored in their wake. Science is washed away along with history, philosophy, and theology.

This kind of skepticism challenges the project of this book. If no narrative has any more claim to truth than any other, it's pointless even to try to guard against error. But not to worry. Considering the popularity of post-modern skepticism, it is an amazingly feeble philosophical position. The most obvious problem is that it hoists itself by its own petard by using sociological, historical, psychological, and philosophical arguments to show that no sociological, historical, psychological, and philosophical arguments or conclusions are trustworthy. If that's so, why should we trust the arguments and conclusions of the post-modernists? Radical post-modern skepticism undermines itself in the same way any argument that concludes one can't trust arguments undermines itself.

When philosophers point this out to post-modern evangelicals, they get two responses. Some post-modernists simply shrug them off as salvos in a turf war between what they take to be a narrow group of philosophers (so-called analytical philosophers) and the rest of the humanities and social sciences. That is, they take this criticism as expressing the complaint that they are practicing philosophy without a license. The truth is that most of them are practicing philosophy without a clue (that is, in almost complete ignorance of relevant episodes of the history of philosophy and of much of the relevant contemporary philosophical literature). The second response is, "Well, yes, I see the force of the criticism, but we have people working on that." Well, good luck.

Still, post-modernists are right to say that we are situated beings. It is an important observation and one that too many philosophers ignore (thinking that once they have made the obvious objection they can get on with business as usual). But how can anyone with any understanding of history, sociology, anthropology, or psychology deny that our situatedness creates obstacles and hazards on the road to knowledge? How can they simply ignore all the variations in basic beliefs between cultures, ethnic groups, social classes, genders, personality types, etc.? The real problem is to identify exactly what these obstacles and hazards are and to think about the degree to which and the methods by which we can transcend them. But neither the post-modernists nor their philosophical critics are interested in rolling up their sleeves and getting down to cases.

Both seem happier with their ritual dance of dramatic proclamations and balloon puncturing.

We can start thinking about the real problem by recognizing
that some forms of reasoning are not situated, but rather just
plain human. Every human group that trades does arithmetic.
Every human group that builds thinks geometrically. Every
human group that eats generalizes from examples. Every
human group that regulates behavior identifies particulars as
instances of rules. As human groups become larger and more
prosperous, they expand and develop these thinking skills.
Every known *civilization* has a number system, a calendar,
sophisticated engineering and building skills, a legal system,
and other technologies that demand planning and coordina-
tion. These are accessible to any intelligent person. People of
any class, race, and gender today can learn to do advanced
mathematics and science, to read history, to program computers, and so forth. And it's not as if Bantu, Maori, Japanese, or
Bedouin people have some special logic – some special, unique
methods of reasoning – that prevents them from learning these
things. We can all learn them because we have human brains
and these brains are remarkably reliable in some areas. They
provide us with pictures of the world on the basis of which we
build airplanes, computers, hydro-electric dams, and countless
other complex things. The fact that we can build things that
work doesn't *logically imply* that our theories are true, but that's
certainly the best explanation. If we were wrong about airfoils,
it would be an astounding bit of luck that airplanes fly.

Post-modernist writers respond that there are countless
ways to divide the world into types of things, countless possible systems of concepts and categories. The fact that our technologies work doesn't imply that our way of dividing the
world in thought is the best possible way, that it cuts nature at

the joints, or that it gives us the Best and Final Word on Things as they are in Themselves. It's not exactly clear what 'Things as they are in Themselves' means. Philosophers have struggled with that since Kant. But we don't need to worry about that in this chapter. Our concern here is with plain, old, ordinary garden-variety truth and reliability. Contrary to the way some post-modernists write, we don't need to categorize the world the way God would to have truth and reliability.

Here's a simple example. Instead of dividing animals into genera and species we could divide them in a much cruder way, say, according to their height (small, medium, and large, with fish measured from tail to head). That is hardly a candidate for cutting nature at the joints. For one thing, there is a lot we wouldn't discover about animals if we were limited to this tax-onomy. But, even given this taxonomy, we can use reliable (or unreliable) methods to make accurate (or inaccurate) statements about animals. We could say whether there are more small ani-mals than big animals, how the three kinds of animals are dis-tributed on the planet, which group has the lowest average lifespan, what proportion of each group is carnivorous, and so on. Again, we don't need a language that cuts nature at the joints to say things that are reliable and true about these matters.

The upshot of this discussion and the discussion of scientism is that the simple popular answers to the questions raised at the beginning of this chapter fail. It's now time to investigate some of the complexities further.

Our Cognitive Tools

As I said earlier, there are no special methods or logics charac-teristic of and unique to particular Knowledge Machines (with the exception of formal disciplines like mathematics and logic). Instead, all Knowledge Machines rely on types of reasoning more or less familiar to us all. This doesn't mean that they all have the same cognitive style. The mix of methods vary. Some Knowledge Machines rely on mathematical or statistical reasoning more than others; some are more experimental; some rely more heavily on interpretive reasoning. It just means that there is no such thing as *the* logic or method of biology, *the* logic or method of history, *the* logic or method of psychology, and so forth. I now want to flesh out this picture a bit by describing some of these familiar kinds of reasoning and the problems of reliability they face.

Deduction

All Knowledge Machines engage in deductive reasoning. Some familiar examples of valid deductive reasoning are: (1) "Socrates is a man and all men are mortal. Therefore Socrates is mortal." (2) "Tony Blair is a bachelor. Therefore Tony Blair is unmarried." The rules of deductive reasoning can be found in scores of introductory logic texts, so I won't spend much time with them here. Suffice it to say, *if* the premises of a valid deductive argument are true, their conclusions must also be true. As this suggests, the premise or premises of a valid deductive argument can be false (the Tony Blair example). Among other things, this allows us to reason *hypothetically*. But – unless we are lucky – a valid deductive with false premises will have a false conclusion (the Tony Blair example again). Here's an example of a "lucky" valid deductive argument with false premises and a true conclusion: "Tony Blair wears cowboy hats to state dinners. All prime ministers who wear cowboy hats to state dinners ally their countries with America.

Therefore Tony Blair allies his country with America." In any case, the rule with valid deductive arguments is garbage in, garbage out unless you get lucky. People do make mistakes when they reason deductively (one can find a list of fallacies in most beginning logic texts). But in most cases, false conclusions are a consequence of false premises. In academic disciplines, and other fields where published work must pass through several levels of editorial review, formal errors in deductive reasoning are generally caught.

Arithmetic calculations, statistical reasoning, and other applications of mathematics could be regarded as deductive arguments that use numerals and other kinds of notation instead of words. If the mathematical statements that we begin with are true, and we reason validly, our conclusion will also be true. Abuses of mathematics in general and statistics in particular are not uncommon, but this is not the place to review them. The interested reader will find many accessible, amusing, and instructive examples in John Allen Paulos's book *Innumeracy*.[1]

Induction

Most reasoning, however, is not deductive. In these cases we can reason perfectly well from true premises and still reach a conclusion that isn't guaranteed to be true. If I observe one thousand white swans and no swans of any other color on a trip through the U.K., I might reasonably conclude that all swans in the U.K. are white. If I read in the *New Scientist* that ninety-five percent of the world's helium balloons burst or deplete before reaching a certain altitude, I might reasonably conclude that the balloon I am about to release will burst or deplete before it reaches that altitude. But these conclusions are not logically guaranteed (I can affirm the premises and deny the conclusion without contradicting myself). These are examples of inductive reasoning. As it is usually characterized, inductive reasoning moves from instances (particular swans) to generalizations (all swans) or from generalizations (ninety-five percent of all helium balloons) to instances (the next balloon released).

Inductive reasoning assumes that correlations or regularities that have held in the past will continue to hold in the present and the future. That is, roughly speaking, it assumes that the present and the future resemble the past in some particular respect. But David Hume famously argued that we can't justify this assumption. We believe that the future will resemble the past only because it always has. That is, we think the future will resemble the past in the future because the future has always resembled the past in the past. But if we try to turn this into an argument, it is narrowly circular. That is, the move from "The future has always resembled the past" to "The future will continue to resemble the past" assumes what it is trying to prove, namely, that the future will resemble the past. Hume thinks our belief that the future resembles the past is not based on rational argument but is rather a matter of "animal faith."

Hume's left us with what philosophers call "the problem of induction." No one to my knowledge has successfully solved it. The best we have (in my view) is "the vindicationist" response, which is essentially pragmatic. Even though we can't justify our assumption that the future will resemble the past, it is reasonable to make that assumption because without that assumption we can't predict the future at all. That is, if the future is predictable at all, it is predictable on the basis of the past (and so far so good). So we are entitled to make this assumption because it is our only hope, the only game in town.

But this solution still leaves us with what I will call "the real problem of induction." The real problem of induction is to decide *exactly how* the future will resemble the past. After all, the future does not resemble the past in *every* respect. Things change. The trick is to determine which things change, which stay constant, and for how long. The climate in London has been reasonably constant for the last several hundred years. But it may change dramatically in the next fifty years owing to global warming. Many American deserts were once inland seas. And the earth has gone through many ice ages during the last few million years. These changes have big ecological consequences. Many plants and animals no longer occupy the same regions they occupied fifty thousand years ago. They evolve, migrate, or become extinct. In *these* respects, the future does not resemble the past. The real problem of induction is how to know when it will and when it won't.

Philosophers and scientists typically assume that causal laws – a.k.a. "the laws of nature" – remain constant. In this respect, they believe, the future resembles the past. Also, they think, we can use these laws to explain how the future resembles the past in other ways, and how it fails to do so. These laws of nature are supposed to hold for all time. But how do we *know* that there are such laws? And how do we *know* that we've found them? According to current estimates, baryonic matter, the kind of matter that is familiar to us, the kind made of sub-atomic particles, makes up just five percent of the matter in the universe.[2] The rest is called "dark matter" because we know nothing about it. Since we know nothing about dark matter, that is, ninety-five percent of the matter in the universe, it can hardly be said that we understand the laws of nature even in relation to baryonic matter. How can we assume that baryonic matter is somehow walled off in its own separate domain and operates according to laws that are entirely unrelated to laws governing the remaining ninety-five percent? Perhaps the laws we use to understand baryonic matter hold because baryonic matter is in some temporary relationship to certain kinds of dark matter (and/or dark energy), and when those relationships change – when the Milky Way Galaxy enters some new cosmic season – all bets are off. Of course, we have no reason to believe the universe is like this. But we have no reason to believe it isn't either. If we're going to get anywhere, we need to act as if the laws we've discovered are *the* laws of nature until we have reason to believe otherwise. But how about some humility? We are, after all, a bunch of hairless apes who have been around for an unimaginably short time in the history of the cosmos and have spent virtually all of it confined to an unimaginably small sector of it.

For all practical purposes, the real problem of induction isn't much of an issue in physics. If the current laws governing the behavior of matter remained constant for a few hundred thousand years, everything would continue to work as we expected it to and our species would die out before we knew the difference. When we move from physics to history or the social sciences, though, the real problem of induction is a more practical concern. For example, we know that relationships between kin, genders, ethnic groups, and social classes are quite variable across cultures and historical periods. The same holds for attitudes toward sex, violence, hospitality, mutual aid, foreigners, charity, minority religions, and lots of other things. Compare ancient Athens to ancient Sparta, to ancient Persia, to Aztec Mexico, to precolonial Polynesia, to modern Japan, to Elizabethan England – you get the idea. It would obviously be foolish to take any one of these cultures at some point in time and assume that the rest of human history will be like *that* in *these* respects. Some evolutionary biologists claim that evolutionary theory can provide us with a basic theory of human

nature and that the variations in question are just a manifesta-
tion of human nature under a specified set of environmental
circumstances. So far, though, this is mostly hand waving combined with a few likely stories. And no wonder. It's very hard
to create a theory of human nature which, in conjunction with
environmental circumstances, explains the wide variations in
kinship systems in the history of the world (and variations in
the structures of its languages, religions, gender relationships,
dietary taboos, etc.). If we knew that the future will resemble
the past in *those ways*, we could make predictions about these
variations under different ecological and environmental circumstances. We *can* make a few vague predictions (e.g. all
human groups will have languages, kinship systems, social
hierarchies, etc.). But we're a long way from explaining variations. In relation to understanding human history and human
societies, then, the real problem of induction is alive and well.
Even within a given society, it's hard to know which correlations and regularities will persist and for how long.

Explanation

Knowledge Machines not only make deductive and inductive
inferences. They also explain why things happen. Explanations
may use or be based on both deductive and inductive reasoning.
But their purpose is different. They do not try to justify or arrive
at some new fact or conclusion. Rather, they begin with a fact (or
alleged fact) and try to answer some "how" or "why" question
about it. Of course, explanations fail if that alleged fact is not in
fact the case. If dead ancestors don't really intervene in our lives,
there is no good explanation of why they are angry at us.

Philosophers offer different accounts of the nature of explanation. I won't review them here, since any useful discussion

gets technical fast (if you're interested, check the on-line *Stanford Encyclopedia of Philosophy* under "explanation"). Instead, I will discuss some issues that arise when we evaluate explanations.

The simplest scientific explanation of an event cites a law of nature that tells us why that event happened under the circumstances. These explanations have a deductive form. Given the law of nature and given the circumstances (which are called "initial conditions") as premises, we can deduce the event as a conclusion. Why did the water on the stove boil? Well, water boils at one hundred degrees Celsius under normal atmospheric pressure, the water on the stove was under natural atmospheric pressure, and the water on the stove reached one hundred degrees Celsius. When we explain events in this way we treat them as a particular example of a general regularity in nature. *This* water boils under these conditions because all water boils under these conditions. In effect, these explanations take the form, "Well, it just always happens this way." Some philosophers argue that all genuine explanation takes this form (this is called the Deductive Nomological Theory of explanation or D.N.).

Explanations of this kind are clear and straightforward. Their soundness depends on whether the law of nature they cite is true. This is something we can test. With a few slight changes, explanations of this form become predictions. Water boils at one hundred degrees Celsius, this water is at (or will be at) one hundred degrees Celsius, and therefore this water is boiling (or will boil). As we will see, this symmetry between D.N. explanation and prediction makes it difficult to think of all explanations as D.N. explanations.

We sometimes want more than an "It always happens this way" kind of explanation. But, according to defenders of D.N., this amounts to a desire to know why the law of nature involved in the explanation holds (for example, why water boils at one hundred degrees Celsius). We can explain these laws the same way that we explain events. Roughly speaking, they are consequences of more general laws under particular sets of circumstances. But we can't go on explaining laws in terms of other laws for ever. In the end, we bottom out. We reach laws for which we have no further explanation. All we can say in relation to these laws is, "That's just the way the universe is constructed; there is gravity." We may later find explanations for what we now take to be ultimate laws (as now seems to be happening with gravity). But at any point in time we will treat some laws as ultimate. So ultimately we're back to "it just always happens that way."

Of course, most interesting explanations are much more complicated than our boiling water example. They are not just directed at a single, simple event but cover a richer and more diverse set of facts. For example, among other things, the Big Bang Theory is supposed to explain not only what happened in the first tiniest fraction of a second in time, but also the distribution of matter and energy in the universe, the expansion rate of the universe, and so forth. Obviously, this isn't something we can do with a single law. The Big Bang Theory, then, involves many different laws to explain many different kinds of things. Since all explanations depend on the truth of the laws cited, all other things being equal, these more complicated explanations are more vulnerable to error than the simpler ones.

Also, many explanations don't seem to involve laws at all. For example, the rise of capitalism in Europe is an important part of the explanation of the rise of nation states, the displacement of rural populations, the growth of cities, the decline of craft guild standards, the rise of democracy, the standardization of weights and measures, and a whole lot of other things. It's not clear that anything like general laws of nature are part of this picture. First, it's hard to imagine what these laws would look like. If they were like the laws of physics, then, given a specified set of conditions, they would allow us to predict what happens when capitalism arises under those conditions (say, the conditions in late medieval Europe, in the former Soviet Union, in Japan after World War II, and, increasingly, in contemporary China). Of course, we can make some general points about that. But we have nothing comparable to precise laws with which to justify our conclusions. Since capitalism in fact arose under many different sets of circumstances, and since it created changes in *those* unique sets of circumstances, the task of discovering such laws is daunting. So is the prospect of discovering laws that would have enabled us to predict the rise of capitalism itself (given all the different circumstances under which it has arisen). Yet we can tell sensible stories about how capitalism arose under various historical circumstances, and also how it changed the circumstances under which it arose.

It's worth emphasizing that these kinds of explanations without precise laws also appear in science. Evolutionary biology is full of them. We have no laws in relation to which we can explain why *this* mutation in *that* particular set of ecological circumstances will come to predominate and *that* mutation will not. We can tell convincing stories but we have no way of saying *how much* reproductive advantage a given mutation confers. Without that we have no way of knowing how likely it is that it will spread, or how fast it will spread. The situation is further complicated by the fact that there is obviously a lot of luck involved. The carrier of the mutated gene might die of a disease, be eaten by a predator, be killed by a falling tree, etc. before it can reproduce. And so may its offspring.

This is how it is with most explanations. Once we leave certain areas of the sciences, our explanations are not supported by laws of nature, and we find ourselves telling likely stories. Some of these stories are very compelling. But there are no clear methods, procedures, or algorithms for evaluating most such explanations and showing that one is better than another. We do have some rough criteria. Perhaps most importantly, all other things being equal, one explanation is better than another if it explains more aspects of or facts about what it is trying to explain. When we evaluate explanations of the American Revolution, for example, we do so by looking at what facts or aspects of that event each of them explains well and/or fails to explain well. But we have no precise way of counting facts, comparing their importance, or measuring *how* well an explanation accounts for them. These are judgment calls and reasonable people often disagree. That is one reason there are competing explanations of so many things (historical events, marriage failures, crime rates, etc.).

Experimental reasoning is a close cousin of explanatory reasoning. If an experiment has a positive result, the hypothesis it tests explains the result that confirms it. If we test the hypothesis that the boiling point of water is one hundred degrees Celsius, and our experiment succeeds, the fact that the boiling point of water is one hundred degrees Celsius explains why the water in our experiment boiled at that temperature. Or at least this is true if we can rule out competing explanations that also explain the results. But this is not always done and is not always possible.

Here's an amusing example from social psychology (astonishingly, one included in an anthology celebrating important triumphs in the field).[3] The experimental subjects enter a room in which there are two platters on a long table. One contains radishes, the other cookies. They are told that they must eat from one and only one platter. The experimenters carefully note which platter each subject chooses. The subjects are then asked to sit at the table and draw a figure on a piece of paper without lifting their pencil from the page. The task is impossible. The experimenters carefully note how much time it takes for each subject to give up. As it turns out, there is a statistically significant difference between the quitting times of the radish eaters and the cookie eaters, the radish eaters tending to quit earlier. I invite you to take a moment to guess what the experimenters concluded from this result. That cookie eaters had more energy? That cookie eaters are happier people than radish eaters and happier people are more patient (or compliant)? That eating cookies puts people in better moods than eating radishes, which makes them more patient or compliant? Well, no. The hypothesis was that each of us carries around a certain quantity of willpower, like gas in a tank. The experimenters believed their results confirmed this hypothesis. The radish eaters quit early because they expended some of their willpower by resisting the cookies. The cookie eaters approached their task with fuller tanks.

Good explanations (and good experiments) attempt to rule out alternatives but in many cases it's difficult to imagine what the alternatives are. At any given point, we may even lack the conceptual resources to articulate them. This is a problem in physics and chemistry as well as in history and the social sciences. Newton described gravity as an ultimate law of nature (bodies attract). No one questioned this for two hundred years. There are now competing theories of gravity (that is, competing explanations of the phenomena gravity is supposed to explain). There may be more in the future. Newton's falling apple did not decisively settle the matter. In fact, whenever there are major changes in an area of science, many explanations need to be replaced by alternatives that were impossible to envision before the change happened. During much of the seventeenth and eighteenth centuries all combustible substances were supposed to contain the fluid phlogiston, which was released by burning. This was supposed to explain a number of facts including the fact that fire burns out in an enclosed space (the air is saturated with phlogiston) and why charcoal leaves very little residue when it burns (it is made mostly of phlogiston). It was difficult to imagine the alternative explanations we now accept until Lavoisier, in the late eighteenth century, discovered the role that oxygen plays in combustion.

Interpretation

Explanations try to tell us why or how something happened. Interpretations try to tell us what something is or means. The two are not entirely distinct. Historical explanations are sometimes called interpretations, and interpretations do play an explanatory role. We explain why Hamlet speaks to Ophelia as he does in relation to our overall interpretation of the play. A precise account of the relationship between explanation and interpretation is of little value for our purposes. It is also complicated, since it requires us to choose between a number of competing accounts of both. We can do well enough without one.

It is useful to think of interpretation in terms of parts and wholes. When we interpret something we say what it is or what it means. If it is a whole – *Hamlet* or a coded document – we do this by understanding the elements as part of a coherent whole. That's how literary critics interpret novels, poems, and plays and how historians interpret periods of history. The more elements an interpretation weaves together, the better the interpretation. On the other hand, we interpret an element – a passage from *Hamlet* or a particular coded passsage – by showing how it fits into a wider whole or system. That's what anthropologists do when they explain the meaning of rituals in relation to wider cultural themes and what historians do when they interpret documents in terms of wider historical movements. The strength of these interpretations depends on the strength of the larger interpretive framework and how well the element to be explained fits into it.

It is often said that interpretation is "subjective" because there are no clear criteria for deciding between competing interpretations. This, in turn, is used discredit the humanities as flaky. But as we have seen, there are no clear criteria for deciding between competing explanations either. This doesn't mean that either are *completely subjective*. It just means that they leave room for reasonable people to disagree. Also, there may be more than one good interpretation of an event, a play, a gesture, and so on. In the Lawrence Olivier film version of *Hamlet*, for example, the young prince is a poetic and philosophical figure burdened by indecision. In the Mel Gibson film version, he is a passionate youth driven by emotions he is barely able to control (this one could be called *Lethal Weapon in Denmark*). The Olivier and Gibson characters are obviously very different. But I for one think both interpretations make perfectly good sense of the text. This doesn't make them *completely subjective* because not every interpretation is as good as any other. *Hamlet* makes no sense as a romantic comedy, a detective drama, or a thriller (though there is a film version that flirts with the last).

As in the case of explanation, we can say some general things about what makes one interpretation better than another. One interpretation of a whole is better than another, for example, if it incorporates more of the elements of that whole. But just as we have no precise way to count the number of facts competing explanations explain, and to rank them in importance, so we have no precise way to count elements that interpretations weave into a coherent picture, and to rank them in importance. Certainly, the better interpretation is the one that gives us a more *coherent* picture of the whole. But philosophers, historians, literary critics, and others have spent more than a hundred years trying to develop criteria for deciding which of two or more systems of beliefs or interpretations is more coherent than the other, and haven't come up with much. Partly for this reason Larry Bonjour – the leading defender of the coherence theory of knowledge for much of the latter part of the twentieth century – has given up this position as hopeless.

Reflections

Philosophers have given up their quest for The Method. No one now believes that there is one and only one way to approach every question, problem, and subject matter. Philosophers also now widely agree that there is no single method even for the sciences. Evolutionary biology is a very different enterprise than quantum physics. The same holds even within particular sciences. Again, evolutionary biology is long on likely stories and short on experiment and observation. Molecular biology is not.

Very broadly speaking, human beings arrive at their conclusions about the world through observation and reasoning. In some cases – formal logic, mathematics, and much philosophy – we rely on reasoning alone. In logic and mathematics we rely on formal proofs. These proofs settle the matter. Because we have a proof of the Pythagorean theorem – the sum of the squares of the sides of a right triangle is equal to the square of the hypotenuse – we don't have to observe triangles in distant parts of the world to see whether it is true of them. Because we have a proof that there is no highest prime number, we don't have to continually check to see whether every known prime is followed by a higher one. It is a truly remarkable fact about us that we can know such things simply by thinking about them. Philosophers call this "a priori knowledge" and have wracked their brains for several hundred years trying to explain how it is possible and what it says about us and the world.

All Knowledge Machines rely on thinking, but most of them rely on observation as well. The mix depends on the subject matter and even the particular problem within the subject matter. But, since the meaning of an observation is heavily dependent on our preexisting beliefs and theories, observations themselves often owe their significance to prior thinking. Still, the degree to which observation is theory dependent varies from case to case. It is very strong in quantum physics, where our understanding of what we see – actually, what our instruments record – depends on a wide and complicated array of theories. It is much less strong in areas where science works with ordinary concepts. Some might argue that it doesn't exist in those cases at all. For example, it is a scientific discovery that birds distribute plants by eating seeds in one place and depositing them in another. This discovery assumes that plants grow from seeds and that seeds survive their journey through the digestive system of a bird. Whether this means that the observations of birds eating, depositing, and so forth are not theory dependent *at all* raises complicated questions we don't need to consider here. The important point is that theory dependence is a matter of degree. Some observations are dependent on a wider web of theories than others.

Observations that are relatively less dependent – those closer to the ground – often provide extremely strong evidence for the discoveries they support. In fact, it is almost impossible to imagine that they will someday be overturned (e.g. that the heart pumps blood, that the platypus reproduces by laying eggs, that birds and bees pollinate plants, and that water boils at one hundred degrees Celsius under atmospheric pressure at sea level). Thousands of discoveries are compellingly supported by observations in this way. In the face of this, the global skepticism about knowledge and science expressed by many post-modern thinkers seems a little crazy.

On the other hand, plenty of explanations and interpretations rest on less solid ground. For one thing, the observations that support some of them depend on theories that may prove to be false. For another, we don't have clear and precise criteria for saying that one explanation or interpretation is better than another. We do have rough and ready principles. For example, one interpretation is better than another if it weaves more elements into a coherent whole. But there is no clear way to apply these principles to cases and get definitive answers. For example, we have no way of counting elements or quantifying coherence. This means that there is plenty of room for reasonable people to disagree. Often, these cases generate considerable heat. Sometimes that's because they touch on issues related to our political or religious beliefs. But sometimes that's just because they've become big issues within a field, people have taken sides, and careers or bragging rights are at stake. In any case, as conflicts become more acrimonious, certainty often rises as evidential strength falls. The more our answers are underdetermined by the evidence, the more insistent we become that people on the other side are either fools or knaves.

Our attraction to one side or another of these controversies can only be explained in sociological and psychological terms. We might have some direct stake in the conclusion for career-related or other personal reasons (for example, reasons related to race, class, or gender). Or we may take a side because we hold certain theories about the world that are attractive to us for such reasons. In either case, as the post-modernists say, it is our situatedness that makes the difference. The history of the nature–nurture controversy in psychology, biology, and the social sciences is a good example of this. Most people now believe that everyone's character and behavior depend on some of each, that, in fact, nature and nurture interact (the environment influences the way our genes express themselves). But we still argue hotly about particular traits while the jury is out. People argued hotly about nature and nurture throughout much of the nineteenth and twentieth centuries, when we knew far less than we know now; that is, when our answers were even more underdetermined by the evidence. Often, informed outsiders are in a good position to realize that the jury is still out and sometimes they do. But they are usually ignored or shouted down by contestants and lose friends (as in other areas of life, the attempt to be fair and balanced is often a good way to do that). Partisans may be able to agree to disagree and forgo war, but in their hearts they know they're right.

Finally, partisans in these controversies sometimes discount theories on the other side on the ground that those theories reflect a situated point of view (for example, white, male, and dead). If the evidence for that theory is weak, if there are good independent arguments against it, or if there is an alternative that is equally well supported, this can be reasonable. But when it merely amounts to the claim that a particular theory advances the interests or reflects that outlook of a certain group, it is not an argument against that theory. The fact that a theory weakens the appeal of one's own political or religious outlook or the worldview of one's own group is not by itself a criticism. When it comes to the implications of scientific or other discoveries for politics or religion, the chips will always fall some way or other. If we are interested in an accurate view of the world, we must let the chips fall where they may. We cannot just assume that truth is on our side.

CHAPTER 7

Deciding What to Believe

The previous chapters detail the ways in which we are fooled by our own psychological tendencies, and the ways we are tricked, cheated, and unintentionally misled by trusted sources. But they also remind us (from time to time) of our achievements. That's important, since all this debunking could lead to an unwarranted, knee-jerk skepticism toward all established intellectual authorities. A healthy dollop of skepticism makes sense. But how much is enough? And in relation to what? We don't want to escape the grip of failed authority only to rush headlong into the arms of cynics or cranks. As Aristotle (and Goldilocks) emphasized, it's always possible to do, have, or be too little or too much of something. The trick is to find the right amount. But it's rarely possible to say what that is in some general and meaningful way. This certainly applies to degrees of skepticism. There is no algorithm for assigning appropriate degrees of doubt to our beliefs. But this much is true. Authoritative sources with strong track records have earned credibility. We should doubt them in particular cases only when we have good reason.

Reasons to Doubt

What are good reasons to doubt? There are at least nine candidates. As a matter of practice, we tend to doubt a conclusion of an authoritative source if: (1) we are competent directly to evaluate the arguments, evidence, methods, and assumptions that generate the conclusion, and find them wanting; (2) the conclusion conflicts with the conclusion of another trusted source; (3) we question the competence of the people who arrive at the conclusion; (4) we question the honesty of the people who arrive at that conclusion; (5) we question the objectivity or point of view of the people who arrive at the conclusion; (6) the conclusion conflicts with common sense; (7) the conclusion conflicts with our personal experience; (8) the conclusion conflicts with our intuitive judgment; and (9) the conclusion conflicts with our faith.

Ultimately, the credibility of a conclusion depends on the evidence and arguments in its favor, the methods by which it is generated, and the assumptions on which it rests. If we are competent to evaluate these things, that's what we ought to do. Most other reasons for doubting are just indirect indications that something is wrong with the evidence, arguments, methods, or assumptions. Often, it takes an expert to evaluate these things directly. But, surprisingly often, it doesn't. We've seen plenty of examples of that in psychology, survey research, medicine, cosmology, and so on. Mostly, though, laypersons don't know enough to evaluate conclusions in specialist literatures and must rely on indirect reasons for doubting.

One such reason is disagreement among experts. Sometimes the experts within a field disagree. And sometimes experts in one field disagree with experts in another on the same question (for example, the dispute between clinical psychologists and research psychologists on the issue of "recovered memories"). One response to such conflicts is agnosticism. But agnosticism is not always a practical option. We may need to decide who to trust in order to decide what to do. If we can't decide this directly (e.g. by evaluating the arguments) we may be able to decide it indirectly.

For one thing, we may consider the competence of our sources. Perhaps we have reason to believe that a particular doctor, journalist, psychologist, etc. doesn't know what he or she is doing (remember, fifty percent of all doctors finished in the bottom half of their class). Or perhaps we have reason to doubt the competence of most practitioners in a field, at least on *this* question. For example, since most science journalists are badly trained in science and many write stories in areas in which they have no training at all, we have reason to worry about the accuracy of any newspaper science stories on complicated questions. This is not just a reason to doubt a source when it conflicts with another source. It's also a reason to doubt on its own.

For another thing, we may evaluate the honesty and integrity of our sources. There may be reason to think the books are cooked, the data are faked, or conclusions are spun (recall the cases of science and accounting fraud). When authorities conflict, that may be all we have to go by. In that case, we need to ask who has the most incentive to lie, who has the most suspicious track record, who has the most effective safeguards in place against lying, and so forth. That is, our judgments are comparative. Where there is no conflict – when we're simply deciding whether to trust a conclusion – matters get trickier. Here we have to decide how much reason for suspicion is enough. For example, does the amount of fraud uncovered in research funded by drug companies justify skepticism about all drug-company-sponsored research? Do the cases of accounting fraud we've looked at mean we should never trust another big corporation's auditors' reports? It's hard to formulate hard and fast rules here. Reasonable people will disagree because some of us are just more trusting than others.

We may also doubt because we question the objectivity of the investigators. Although they may be honest and competent, they may have a stake in the outcome that affects their thinking. Or they may simply be looking for results that support a certain point of view. This is true, for example, of partisan political think-tanks. Often, for this reason, those on one side of the political spectrum simply dismiss the research of those on the other side as "advocacy research." The danger of this is that it leads to a closed-minded, blind allegiance to one's own point of view. On the other hand, engaging and evaluating all the research on the other side is more than a full-time job. Again, this is a question of balance. I will say more about this later.

In addition, our trusted authorities may reach conclusions that conflict with common sense. For centuries, common sense told us that the earth was flat. If it were round, people on the bottom would fall off (or, if they were kept in place by gravity, they would be upside down). Common sense also told us that solid objects were compact. Physics tells us they are mostly empty space. As these and other celebrated triumphs of science over common sense suggest, common sense is not a good reason to reject solid results in physics, chemistry, biology, and other hard sciences. Common sense has a somewhat stronger claim in sociological and psychological matters. There too it has led us astray. Only fifty years ago British and American common sense were bastions of racist and sexist ideas. But there are also cases in which common sense does better than the prevailing intellectual authorities. Recall that in the 1980s clinical psychologists convinced many Americans that people we had known and respected for years – neighbors, friends, relatives – had raped their own children, sometimes in Satanic rituals and drug-induced frenzies. In this case, common sense, abandoned by so many in favor of "expert" opinion, turned out to be right. So, although common sense is fallible in social and psychological matters, it should not be surrendered without good reasons. Fortunately, these are cases in which many of us can directly evaluate the arguments.

Like common sense, beliefs based on personal experience are sometimes wrong. As we've seen, we may be misled by perceptual illusions, problems with memory, and by heuristic-based thinking. If the conclusions of an authoritative source conflict with our personal experience, we need to look further at each. Are there *other* reasons to distrust the source? How likely is it that our own conclusion is skewed by problems of perception, memory, or thinking? This is not always an easy call. Generally, if there are no other reasons to distrust the source, the source is probably right. But not always. For many years, doctors and biologists discounted reports by bodybuilders that steroids built muscle mass, and physicists insisted that it is impossible for baseball pitchers to throw curve balls. Medical authorities currently tell us that many herbs and other alternative cures that seem to work for us are really just placebos. In this case, most of us trust personal experience, and I think we are right. Clinical tests of drugs, herbs, and other cures generally involve large populations. Usually, some people get better, some people get worse, and some people remain about the same. The overall test results average all this out. If there is no net gain, the cure is judged ineffective. But maybe there's a reason that the cure works for those who get better and fails to work for those who stay the same or get worse (blood chemistry, brain chemistry, whatever). Maybe we just don't know enough right now to know what that reason is. So if an alternative is working for you, you may be among those for whom it is biologically effective. Your doctor may insist that you are the beneficiary of the placebo effect. But even if she's right why should you care? The important thing is that you get better. Of course, things are more complicated if the medical establishment has an effective cure for your condition. It may be dangerous to reject that cure in favor of your alternative. The placebo effect may simply relieve your symptoms without addressing the underlying disease.

The conclusions of an authoritative source may also conflict with our intuitive judgment. Sometimes this is a good reason to doubt. If we are experts in a field and some widely accepted finding or theory just doesn't feel right to us, we should check it out (and perhaps even try to develop an alternative hypothesis). That's how progress is made in science and other intellectual areas. More generally, we have reason to take our intuitions seriously whenever they have a good track record (for example, if we predict rain more accurately than the weatherman). But few of us keep good records of the successes and failures of our intuitive judgments. Our impressions are based almost entirely on our memories, and our memories are vulnerable to distortions. Our intuitive judgments themselves are vulnerable to distortions as well. They may be based on inaccurate background theories, beliefs, or assumptions, they may be generated by unreliable heuristics (e.g. availability), and they may be affected by our hopes, fears, moods, and emotions.

Finally, many people also distrust authoritative sources when the conclusions of those sources conflict with their own faith-based beliefs. We will be discussing the claims of faith later in this chapter. For now, though, I will say only that faith-based belief is, by definition, belief without evidence. To believe something on faith is simply to choose to believe it. To doubt an authoritative source because it conflicts with a faith-based belief is to doubt it because one simply prefers to believe something else. I'm sorry but mere personal preference is not a good reason to reject the evidence-based finding of an authoritative source.

These reasons for doubting apply not only in relation to socially authoritative sources, but also in relation to the various alternatives that flourish as the established authorities lose their credibility – the conspiracy theorists, the spiritualists, the psychics, the crystal healers, the cults, and the rest. Strangely, many people judge these alternatives by less stringent standards than they judge the established authorities. This is partly because most of these alternatives are loosely associated with spirituality in people's minds, and spirituality is loosely associated with religion. When it comes to religion, the bar of credulity is set remarkably low. In fact, to the extent that religion rests wholly on faith, there is no bar at all. Again, believing on faith is believing without evidence. One believes simply because one chooses to believe.

We now have some idea of how to evaluate what our authoritative sources tell us. It's far short of an algorithm, but there is no algorithm for deciding what to believe. As in so many areas in life, there are just guidelines with a lot of gray areas where reasonable people may disagree.

An Ethic of Belief?

What should we do with this information? Do we need to examine *everything* we hear from authoritative sources to see whether there's some reason to doubt? More generally, how much time and effort should we spend trying to discover which of our beliefs are belief-worthy and which are not? We could all do more of this than we actually do. We spend time reading to our children, watching movies, playing computer games, taking walks, and making love when we could be at the library examining our beliefs. Are we slackers in the Republic of Reason? Socrates famously announced that the unexamined life is not worth living. But what of the constantly examined life? Is there a balance?

In the late nineteenth century, the English philosopher and mathematician W. K. Clifford wrote a paper called "The Ethics of Belief" in which he concluded that "it is a sin against mankind for anyone, anywhere to hold a belief without sufficient evidence." [1] William James responded to Clifford in a famous essay called "The Will to Believe" in which he argued that some beliefs can't be decided by the intellect alone, and in those cases we are entitled to believe what we like (assuming a couple of other conditions are met).[2] These essays by Clifford and James are staples of introductory philosophy anthologies. Strangely, the discussion of that issue has not advanced very far since their original exchange. That's a shame, since we all need to decide to what standards of evidence we should hold ourselves and others.

In effect, Clifford argues that we need to subject all our beliefs to close examination, and to reject those for which there is not sufficient evidence. If by "evidence" he means direct evidence, this is unrealistic. In this age of specialization, it is impossible for most of us to evaluate the direct evidence in favor of the claims of modern medicine, chemistry, physics, and so forth (for example, to look at the experimental results). Even where we could do this, it would be impossibly time consuming. Imagine examining the direct evidence for all your beliefs about history (for example, the letters, official documents, and newspaper reports).

For Clifford's proposal to get off the ground, he needs to allow evidence to include the testimony of authoritative sources. Even then he proposes an unrealistically demanding standard. Imagine what it would be like to evaluate the evidence for *all* your beliefs. You would need to list them – *all* of them – remember your reasons for accepting them, and evaluate those reasons. We just have too many beliefs for that. Try listing everything you believe about your own past, world geography, politics, personal relationships, medicine, sports, the meaning of every word you know, and so on. Now try remembering why you believe all this (even if it's just testimony). Now evaluate those reasons. Few if any of us could get even close. Do you remember, for example, why you believe that Shakespeare wrote the plays of Shakespeare, that vitamin C boosts the immune system, that "criterion" is a synonym of "standard," that bad cholesterol is bad, and that the tobacco industry suppressed studies of the dangers of smoking? Of course, you can *guess*; for example, that you read them in some book. But what book? And how reliable was that book? Clifford responds to this by saying that we should remain agnostic about all matters for which we lack sufficient evidence. But that is also unrealistic. We act on our beliefs about medicine, exercise, child-rearing, psychology, social interaction, word meanings, education, ethics, finances, and the rest every day. So we can't remain agnostic about them. If we did, it would be as if we based most of our decisions in life on mere guesswork. But if you plan to follow Clifford's instruction and look for sufficient justification for all such beliefs, say goodbye to your friends and loved ones, and have your mail forwarded to the library. No, forget the mail; you won't have time to read it.

What then? The examples in Clifford's classic essay suggest a different direction than his pronouncements. His principle tells us what to do, viz. find sufficient evidence for all our beliefs. His examples tell us what *not* to do, e.g. don't suppress our doubts, or let our beliefs be dictated by our prejudices or desires. This suggests a less demanding direction: trust your beliefs unless you have a reason to doubt them, and if you have a reason, investigate. This limits the number of beliefs we are asked to investigate. But it still leaves us wondering how much investigating we are supposed to do. Clifford's insistence on "sufficient evidence" suggests he sets a high bar. For example, most of us have a wide range of political and social beliefs, and we have our reasons for them. But we could have still better reasons if we simply spent a day doing library research. And we could have even stronger reasons if we spent six months on an issue (as people who write books on these topics do). How much is enough?

There is no general answer to this question. It's not as though we can simply assign probability values to our beliefs and declare we have sufficient evidence for them if the probability is high enough. What would the magic number be? (Ninety percent? Sixty-seven percent?) How do we go about assigning these numbers to our beliefs in the first place? (Try it with a few.) How much time and energy are we required to invest in the effort? More importantly, though, there is no standard of sufficient evidence – no magic number – that applies across the board. What counts as enough evidence depends on a lot of contextual variables. It's one thing for a diagnosis by an emergency room doctor and another for a diagnosis by internist (who can take her or his time). In general, we set the bar lower when we must decide under time constraints. What counts as enough in almost any emergency may not be enough in normal conditions. On the other hand, all other things being equal, the more that is at stake, the higher our evidential standards. What is enough to justify a belief about weeding is not enough to justify a choice between surgeries. Our standards may also vary depending on the abilities of the believer. Someone with very little intelligence is held to different standards than someone with a lot. In addition, the standards of evidence to which we are held vary with our responsibilities. If we are doctors or medical researchers, our beliefs need to be based on the research literature. If we are patients, we are entitled to trust what our doctors tell us (unless we have some specific reason not to). To make matters even more complicated, we have lives. The time and energy we put into examining our beliefs depend on what makes life meaningful or worth living for us. If we are highly driven physicists or artists, we may have little time or energy for examining much outside physics or art. If we are dedicated to *working* against world poverty (for example, by volunteering at refugee camps), we may have little time to master the scholarly literature on that topic. In short, the role of examination in our lives, what we examine and how much time and effort we spend examining it, will depend on who we are and in what circumstances we find ourselves. It will be one thing for Mother Theresa, another for John Cleese, and still another for Tony Blair. Since the time and effort we put into examining our beliefs will affect the amount of evidence we can get for them, our standards of evidence will depend on these factors as well. One-size-fits-all proposals like Clifford's ignore all this complexity.

In addition, the high bar Clifford sets for us is utopian. It would take a complete revolution in our values to implement Clifford's standard. Clifford's hope is to promote truth and squelch falsehood. But most of us just don't value truth as much as we value many other things (at least in First World nations). We think nothing of shading, spinning, and even utterly forsaking the truth to avoid hurting someone's feelings ("O Agnes, I love that hat"). Most of us also respect and even admire people who are well paid to spin, hide, and misrepresent the truth – P.R. people, super-salesmen, political speech-writers, ad writers, celebrities who endorse products they don't use, and so forth. When truth competes with feelings, money, prestige, career advancement, or even a good joke, we are often willing to sacrifice the truth. In addition, we are rarely *offended* by the mindless blather and ignorant ranting of blowhards and airheads. We may be bored or annoyed, but we don't usually feel slimed, abused, insulted, or disrespected. Many of us are more offended by people who are underdressed for a party. With just a few specific exceptions, we think it rude to chastise people publicly for expressing groundless or even idiotic beliefs. If we valued truth highly, we might chastise them the way, for example, we chastise someone who jumps a queue. All this makes calls for Clifford-like standards pipe dreams.

How Much Is Enough?

William James's response to Clifford is that some beliefs simply can't be settled "by the intellect alone" and that in some of these cases we have a right to believe without evidence. Before we get to that, though, we need to think a bit more about matters that can be settled by evidence and argument. If Clifford sets the bar too high in those cases, how high should we set it? As we've seen, if we were serious about seeking sufficient evidence for all of our beliefs – or even just the action-related ones – we would spend our lives in the library or online. Since we have lives, we are forced to have beliefs for which we don't have sufficient evidence. How much time and effort are we required to spend investigating those beliefs? And, given that time and effort, how should we distribute it across our beliefs. What do we owe to ourselves and what do we owe to others?

If we are to flourish in life, it's in our interest to have accurate beliefs about practical matters like health, finances, child-rearing, personal relationships, and other areas that affect our well-being. That doesn't mean we should spend all of our time thinking about them. We may have other needs, responsibilities, interests, and passions as well. We need to compare the benefits of pursuing these other things with the harms and risks of ignorance and misinformation about matters of health, personal relationships, finances, and so on. We may prefer bowling to reading, but we need to consider which serves us better. Sometimes the answer is bowling. What we owe to ourselves in pursuing knowledge about practical matters varies from person to person.

In addition to beliefs about practical matters, we also have beliefs about social, political, moral, spiritual, and religious matters. These beliefs may affect both ourselves and others. If we have racist or sexist beliefs, we may act in ways that harm others and that also make us unpopular in some circles and popular in others. Our beliefs about practical matters may affect others as well. We may give them bad advice. Or we may destroy our own health and finances, forcing them to support us. These impacts on others are, in fact, Clifford's main concern. The reason that he declared belief without sufficient evidence a sin against humankind is that he was acutely aware of the social and political mayhem produced by ignorance and superstition.

The question of what we owe to family, friends, neighbors, strangers, fellow citizens, and unknown people in distant lands is hotly disputed by philosophers and raises too complicated a set of issues to address in the few remaining pages of this book. But we can get some perspective on the question. Most of us identify our good with the good of others to some degree or other. We have concentric circles of concern. These circles may differ from person to person. Most people put themselves in the center (though some may put their children there, or even causes to which they are dedicated). For most people, family and friends come next, then neighbors, acquaintances, fellow citizens, etc. As a rough generality, proximity rules: the more closely involved we are with others, the more we care about them and the more we are willing to do for them (though some of us may care more about strangers we admire than neighbors or even family members). The more we care about others, the more reason we have to make our beliefs that affect them accurate. All other things being equal, we are willing to do more to assure the accuracy of beliefs that affect our friends than to assure the accuracy of beliefs that affect strangers. What makes things unequal is degree of impact. Depending on our degrees of caring, we may investigate beliefs that profoundly affect strangers more than we investigate beliefs that affect friends only a little. This is not to say how much we *ought* to care or *ought* to do from a moral point of view. We can't decide that until we decide how much one *should* care about others in these concentric circles. That takes us beyond the boundaries of our subject and into the dense thickets of ethics.

Instead of entering that terrain, I will close this section with an observation about the impact of our political and social beliefs on other people. For most of us, the impact seems minis-cule. That's one reason so many of us are so casual about our political and social beliefs. Since we don't occupy positions of power or authority, or influence the people who do, we assume that it does not much matter what we believe about global warming, globalization, Islamic terrorism, and so forth. The big decisions of the day are out of our hands. We may vote in elections, but so do tens of millions of other people. The fact that elections are won with money increases our sense of powerlessness (unless we're rich).

On the other hand, war, climate change, ecological degradation, and other big issues of the day affect billions of lives. When we think about our impact we also need to think about that. There is no algorithm for doing this, but here is a way to think about it. Imagine a tug of war with a million people on each side. Suppose that if the right side wins, a million lives will be saved. If you are an average tugger on that side, your responsibility for the outcome is one millionth, which is very small. But you also have a one-millionth part in saving one million lives. Arguably, that is equivalent to saving one life all by yourself. If we investigate an issue like global warming, join the right side, and win, our responsibility for the victory will be less than one millionth. But billions of lives will be affected by that outcome.

Believing Without Evidence

I argued earlier that Clifford's proposal – that we believe only on the basis of sufficient evidence – is unrealistic. William James makes a different kind of objection. James thinks we are entitled to hold some beliefs without any evidence at all. To the extent that the Clifford–James debate lives on in American academic philosophy, it focuses on James's claim. This is partly because faith-based belief plays such a powerful role in American culture.

James argues that many beliefs "can't be decided by the intellect alone." We are attracted to some of these, and may get important benefits by accepting them (for example, our religious beliefs may bring us peace of mind). Agnosticism and disbelief may each deprive us of those benefits. In these cases, James says, we have a right to believe whatever attracts us. (Actually, his view is a little more complicated, but this will do for present purposes.)

James doesn't say that everyone *should* believe under these circumstances. He is not evangelical about it. He thinks that whether or not we choose to believe depends on our cognitive style. He thinks that those of us who are error-phobic will suspend judgment on matters that can't be decided by the intellect alone, while those who are more interested in finding truth than avoiding error will take leaps of faith. He doesn't argue that one attitude is more reasonable than the other. Despite a few nod-nod-wink-winks, his official claim is only that it is reasonable to take the leap of faith (and by no means a sin against humankind).

Unfortunately, James never clarifies the meaning of "can't be decided by the intellect alone." Presumably, he doesn't want to include all doctrines we can't *prove* to be false. That's much too inclusive. There's a lot we can't prove to be false. For example, we can't *prove* it to be false that the leaders of the world are remotely controlled by aliens, that the King James version of the Bible – and only that version – was inspired by God, or that there is a planet revolving around Alpha Centauri that is inhabited by hermaphrodites who dress like circus clowns. So, if "you can't prove it false" were the standard, there would be very little prior intellectual constraint on beliefs that can't be decided by the intellect alone. On the other hand, many of us reject these hypotheses because we think there is no argument or evidence in their favor. But if we take *that* as our intellectual constraint, we can't have any non-evidentially grounded beliefs at all (since non-evidentially grounded belief is by definition believing without evidence or argument). Any prior intellectual constraint James adopts must fall somewhere in between these two criteria. That is, it must disqualify more beliefs than "you can't prove it false" does and fewer beliefs than "there is no evidence or argument in its favor" does. Here is a suggestion James might (or might not) want to accept. As a first approximation, a doctrine can't be decided by the intellect alone if (1) there are no strong arguments or evidence for it and no strong arguments or evidence against it, or (2) the arguments for or against it are about equally weighty.

These criteria need some fleshing out. For one thing, we need to make it clear that in some cases the fact that there is no evidence for a claim is itself an argument against it; for example, claims for which there almost certainly would be evidence were they true ("At the time of the dinosaurs, three-headed monkeys were as plentiful as pteradactyls"). But we don't need to fill in all such blanks for our purposes. A more serious concern is James's use of the definite article in "the intellect." That suggests he wants to limit his claim to doctrines for which there *can be* no conclusive evidence or argument. But if we're trying to provide advice to real people, that's too restrictive. People differ in their intellectual talent and training; that is, we differ in what we can decide by our intellects alone. We need to decide what, if anything, we have a right to believe about issues that exceed our capacity to decide. Most of us are in this position in relation to some beliefs – we are not experts, the experts disagree, and our indirect criteria are indecisive. In addition, we may not have the talent to become experts. What, if anything, do we have a right to believe in such cases?

With or without these refinements, criteria (1) and (2) do place prior intellectual constraints on non-evidentially based beliefs. Although the Alpha Centauri hypothesis remains an option, the belief that the King James version of the Bible is written by God does not. It fails the first criterion, since we have historical and linguistic reasons against taking the King James version to be God's own truth. The first criterion also rules out many other faith-based beliefs for the same reason. These include one of the most important doctrines of Judaism, Christianity, and Islam, namely, that God is perfect (that is, that God is both all-good and all-powerful). This doctrine seems to conflict radically with the way the world is made. On the face of it, God's work ("creation") does not seem to be the work of an all-good, all-powerful being. If God were all-good, he would want the best for his creation. If God were all-powerful, he could make that happen. So one would expect an all-good, all-powerful creator to produce the best of all possible worlds. But ours seems to have its imperfections. Why, for example, does it hurt so much when we break a limb? Of course, the pain has a purpose. It keeps us from moving the limb, which prevents further injury and promotes healing. But surely there are less painful ways to do *that*. Half the pain would work just fine. And why does there need to be any pain at all? That is, why didn't God design our limbs so that they were simply temporarily paralyzed when broken (and temporally restored to mobility when absolutely necessary). For that matter, why did he design limbs that are so easy to break in the first place and that take so long to heal? Why can't we heal in a matter of hours and simply regenerate severed limbs the way salamanders regenerate severed tails? Once we start thinking this way, it's obvious that the problem is bigger than limbs. Why aren't our eyes and ears more sensitive? Why does our hearing fail with age? Why didn't God design babies with horrible genetic defects like Tay–Sachs syndrome? And what about cancer? Or, to broaden our concern, why is there so much pain and carnage in the animal world? Why did God design a nature red in tooth and claw? Why all those terrified prey desperately and futilely thrashing about in the jaws of predators? Why all the panicky little fish continually chased and eaten by big fish? Surely God could have limited the animal world to herbivores.

All theologians agree that these are strong arguments. They have labored to answer them for nearly two millennia, and they're still trying. That's because their answers never manage to convince religious skeptics, or adherents to other religious traditions. It's no wonder: these answers barely manage even to convince believers. The question of natural evil arises anew for believers with every drought and tsunami and every still-born child. How can God allow *that* to happen? Of course, natural catastrophes are consequences of the laws of nature, but God is supposed to have designed the laws of nature. In the end, most believers fall back on the solace that God works in mysterious ways. Our finite minds are incapable of understanding his infinite intellect. This conflict between reason and the faith is settled simply by new affirmations of faith; that is, by choosing to believe something else without evidence.

If we take him at his word, this is not a problem for James. As far as religion goes, his official goal in the "Will to Believe" is to defend what he calls "the Religious Hypothesis," which demands much less than a full-blooded religion. James's first description of the Religious Hypothesis asserts only that there is an eternal aspect to the universe and that we are all better off believing that. A couple of pages later, James adds that that eternal aspect is person-like (a Thou). Although there is no evidence or argument in favor of this, there is also no evidence or argument against it. According to the first criterion, it can't be decided by the intellect alone and so we are entitled to believe it without evidence (since it also satisfies James's other conditions).

Beliefs that satisfy the second criterion are neglected by both Clifford and James and have had relatively little attention from English-language philosophers in general. But at some point almost all of us find ourselves trying to decide between beliefs the arguments for which seem equally strong to us (be they direct or indirect). Clifford says we should remain agnostic in these cases. But this can be quite costly. Suppose you are gravely ill and your doctors disagree about the most effective cure. You need to choose. You could choose on pragmatic grounds while remaining officially agnostic. For example, you could choose the one that least interfered with things you like to do while remaining doubtful that it is otherwise better than the other. But you might feel better about the whole thing if you could manage to convince yourself that your choice is not the horrible mistake one of your doctors keeps saying it is. Believing might also improve your chances of success (the placebo effect). So, unless there's a serious downside to believing, it's hard to see why you shouldn't choose to believe or try to convince yourself (if you can). In general, unless there is a serious downside to believing, it seems foolish to deny ourselves and each other the benefits of belief in these cases. (Of course, it's an open question to what extent we can convince ourselves.)

The main downside of non-evidentially based belief is the wrongful harm it can bring to others. Suppose someone wants to add to James's Religious Hypothesis that the "Who" – the personal eternal aspect of the universe – commands us to kill all adulterers, Jews, and homosexuals by 10/10/2010. Since there are no strong arguments for or against what the "Who" commands, this can't be settled by the intellect alone. But that doesn't give anyone a right to believe it, even if he calls it a faith-based belief. Most faith-based believers recognize this and constrain their faith by their moral beliefs. But a minority are astonishingly audacious in the privilege they claim for themselves. "Because I choose to believe something without any evidence at all, you, Martha, cannot have sex with a woman!" Or worse, "Because I choose to believe something without any evidence at all, you, infidel, must be driven from the Holy Land!"

Despite what some of them say, most religious people don't base most of their religious beliefs on faith alone. When challenged or when evangelizing they make philosophical arguments, look for archeological evidence, inspire each other with testimonials, appeal to their own personal experience, and so on. As much as I'd like to discuss all that, there is no space for it here. The topic of religion came up because faith-based belief is the most important example of non-evidentially based belief.

James worried that if we deny ourselves (and each other) the right to believe under the relevant circumstances, we impover-ish our lives. The reader may be wondering what's at stake here. What does it mean to have a right to believe, and why does it matter? The short answer is this. Since what we believe affects others, belief is an ethical matter. What's at stake, then, are the ethical standards to which we hold ourselves and each other. These standards guide our conduct and our judgment. Other things being equal, we think well of those who comply with them and think badly of those who don't (including our-selves). In theory, at least, this mobilization of public attitude changes our behavior.

If enough of us came down heavily on people who believed without evidence, fewer people would do it. Because we don't come down heavily on people who lie and otherwise distort the truth for a living, more people do it.

The Final Frame

In the end, the picture looks like this. Most of us have different levels of justification for our beliefs. We can make better cases for some of them than we can for others. This is inevitable. We can't thoroughly investigate and evaluate everything we believe.

We also differ as individuals in what it makes sense for us to investigate. We have different lives: different needs, interests, responsibilities, and passions. So we have greater and lesser need for accuracy in different areas. People with children need to investigate child-rearing theories more diligently than people without them. In general, the amount of time and effort we owe it to ourselves to invest in our beliefs, and the way we diversify that investment, depends on what we are like. In the end, what we owe to ourselves is to live well. That means investigating to the extent that best contributes to our well-being.

Since what we believe affects others, there is also the matter of what we owe to them. Again, that raises a nest of difficult ethical questions I'm not able to address here. But this much seems clear: the more the lives and welfare of others depend on the accuracy of our beliefs, the higher our standards of evidence should be.

Once we make peace with the fact that some of our beliefs are based on relatively little evidence, and that's okay, the thought that we are entitled to believe without evidence in certain cases may seem less shocking. I've argued that we do have such a right, subject to two strict requirements. First, the issues must be ones we can't decide on the basis of the evidence and arguments (even when evidence includes what the experts say). Second, our adopting the belief in question must present no significant risk or harm to others.[3]

Some might take these conclusions as an endorsement of intellectual laziness. But they're not. I'm just being honest about the fact that few of us have the time, energy, need, or capacity to carry out Socratic missions. This is not to say we don't need more people like Socrates (or the child who declared the emperor naked). As the last six chapters have illustrated, the world is rife with charlatans, cheats, flimflam artists, incompetents, unscrupulous careerists, and fools in high places (often with big egos). In addition, the intellectual world is not immune to politics or fashion. At times it stampedes and at times it circles the wagons. As a result, bad things happen. We've seen plenty of examples. So we need our skeptics and iconoclasts, our unmaskers and our sticklers for the truth. We should build monuments to these whistle-blowers in the fields of knowledge and create an annual holiday in their honor. Above all, we should listen to what they say (without losing sight of how often our trusted sources also get things right).

But most of us are ill-equipped to walk in Socrates' sandals, and most of the rest don't want to. As we learned from Socrates, unmasking false experts can be hazardous to one's health. It usually involves speaking truth to (or about) power, and power didn't become power by turning the other cheek. What happened to Socrates is extreme by today's Western democratic standards, but, with the exception of stand-up comics, serious iconoclasts and unmaskers have a harder life than the rest of us (unless they are extraordinarily gifted, like Richard Feynman). As the old saw says, you have to go along to get along, and they don't. Insider whistle-blowers, in particular, have a harder row to hoe than their more compliant and complacent peers. Exposing the weakness of a major research program in one's field makes one unpopular with colleagues invested in that enterprise. And exposing fraud by a respected or well-liked colleague may even seem traitorous. The fact that our unmaskers and debunkers risk all that is precisely what makes them heroes.

Notes

Chapter 1

1. Oliver Howes, "Hypochondriasis: An Overview with Reference to Medical Students," *studentBMJ*, 7, 1999, p. 394.
2. Jerome Brunner and Leo Postman, "On the Perception of Incongruity: A Paradigm," *Journal of Personality*, 18, 1949, pp. 206–223.
3. H. J. McQuay, D. Carroll, and R. A. Moore, "Injectived Morphine in Postoperative Pain: A Quantitative Systematic Review," *Journal of Pain and Symptom Management*, 17, 1999, pp. 164–174.
4. Michael Brooks, "13 Things that Do Not Make Sense," NewScientist.com News Service, March 19, 2006, www. newscientist.com/news.ns.
5. Brian Reid, "The Nocebo Effect: Placebo's Evil Twin," *Washington Post*, April 30, 2002, p. HE01. For a more general discussion of the nocebo effect, see A. J. Barsky, R. Saintfort, M. P. Rogers, and J. F. Borus, "Nonspecific Medication Side Effects and the Nocebo Phenomenon," *Journal of the American Medical Association*, 5, 2002, pp. 622–627.
6. I. M. Klotz, "The N-Ray Affair," *Scientific American*, 242, 1980, pp. 122–131.
7. "Resolution on Facilitated Communication by the American

Psychological Association," Adopted in Council, August 14, 1994, Los Angeles California. This resolution includes references to thirteen papers demonstrating the problems with this method.

8. D. Beukelman and P. Mirenda, *Augmentative and Alternative Communication: Management of Severe Communication Disorders in Children and Adults* (Baltimore: Paul H. Brookes, 1998).

9. E. F. Loftus and G. R. Loftus, "On the Permanence of Stored Information in the Human Brain," *American Psychologist*, 35, 1980, pp. 409–420.

10. M. Garry, E. F. Loftus, S. W. Brown, and S. C. DuBreuil, "Womb with a View: Memory Beliefs and Memory-Work Experiences," in *Intersections in Basic and Applied Memory Research*, ed. D. G. Payne and F. G. Conrad (Hillsdale, NJ: Erlbaum, 1997), pp. 233–255.

11. R. S. Nickerson and M. J. Adams, "Long-Term Memory for a Common Object," *Cognitive Psychology*, 11, 1979, pp. 287–307.

12. J. D. Branford and J. R. Franks, "Sentence Memory: A Constructive versus Interpretive Approach," *Cognitive Psychology*, 3, 1972, pp. 193–209.

13. An excellent summary of this research can be found in D. G. Payne and J.M. Blackwell, "Truth in Memory: Caveat Emptor," in *Truth in Memory*, ed. S. J. Lynn and K. M. McConkey (New York: Gilford Press, 1998), pp. 32–62.

14. U. Neisser and N. Harsch, "Phantom Flashbulbs: False Recollections of Hearing the News about Challenger," in *Affect and Accuracy of Recall: Studies of "Flashbulb Memories,"* ed. E. Winograd and U. Neisser (Cambridge, UK: Cambridge University Press, 1992), pp. 9–31.

15. Elizabeth Loftus, "Make Believe Memories," *American Psychologist*, 58, 2003, pp. 864–873.

16. F. Gabbert, A. Memon, and K. Allan, "Memory Conformity: Can Witnesses Influence Each Other's Memory for an Event?" *Applied Cognitive Psychology*, 17, 2003, pp. 533–543.

17. D. J. Dooling and R. E. Christianson, "Episodic and Semantic

Aspects of Memory for Prose," *Journal of Experimental Psychology: Human Learning and Memory*, 3, 1977, pp. 428–436.

18. M. Snyder and S. W. Uranowitz, "Reconstructing the Past: Some Consequence of Person Perception," *Journal of Personality and Social Psychology*, 36, 1978, pp. 941–950.

19. G. B. Markus "Stability and Change in Political Attitudes: Observe, Recall and 'Explain'," *Political Behavior*, 8, 1986, pp. 21–44.

20. G. R. Goethals and R. F. Reckman, "The Perception of Consistency in Attitudes," *Journal of Experimental Social Psychology*, 9, 1973, pp. 491–501.

21. E. Eich, J. L. Reeves, B. Jaeger, and S. B. Graff-Ratford, "Memory for Pain: Relation between Past and Present Pain Intensity," *Pain*, 23, 1985, pp. 275–279.

22. L. M. Collins, J. W. Graham, W. B. Hansen, and C. A. Johnson, "Agreement between Retrospective Accounts of Substance User and Earlier Reported Substance Use," *Applied Psychological Measurement*, 9, 1985, pp. 301–309.

23. C. McFarland, M. Ross, and N. DeCourville, "The Relation between Current Impressions and Memories of Self and Dating Partners," *Personality and Social Psychology Bulletin*, 21, 1987, pp. 736–746.

24. D. Holmberg and J. G. Holmes, "Reconstruction of Relationship Memories: A Mental Models Approach," in *Autobiographical Memory and the Validity of Retrospective Reports*, ed. N. Schwartz and S. Sudman (New York: Springer-Verlag, 1994), pp. 267–288.

25. S. J. Read and M. B. Rosson, "Rewriting History: The Biasing Effects of Attitudes on Memory," *Social Cognition*, 1, 1982, pp. 240–255.

26. A long, autobiographical account of this appears in *False Memory Syndrome Foundation Newsletter*, January/February 1998 and April 1998.

27. You can find them at www.religioustolerance.org/rmt_prof. htm.

28. E. Loftus and J. E. Pickrell, "The Formation of False Memories," *Psychiatric Annals*, 25, 1995, pp. 720–725.

29. I. E. Hyman, T. H. Husband, Jr., and F. J. Billings, "False Memories of Childhood Experiences," *Applied Cognitive Psychology*, 9, 1995, pp. 181–197.

30. K. Oates and S. Shrimpton, "Children's Memories for Stressful and Nonstressful Events," *Medicine, Science, and the Law*, 31, 1991, pp. 3–10.

31. L. Rudy and G. S. Goodman, "Effects of Participation in Children's Reports: Implications for Childrens's Testimony," *Developmental Psychology*, 27, 1991, pp. 527–538.

32. Descriptions of these and other studies on this topic can be found in Payne and Blackwell, "Truth in Memory," pp. 48–50.

33. Norbert Schwartz, "Retrospective and Concurrent Self-Reports: The Rationale for Real-Time Data Capture," in *The Science of Real-Time Data Capture: Self-Reports in Health Research*, ed. A. A. Stone, S. S. Shiffman, A. Atienza, and L. Nebeling (Oxford: Oxford University Press, 2007).

Chapter 2

1. Malcolm Gladwell, *Blink: The Power of Thinking without Thinking* (New York: Back Bay Books, Little Brown, 2005).

2. You also need to understand enough about formal logic to recognize the limits. Roughly speaking, the rules of logic tell us how to move from one sentence or set of sentences to another; that is, they tell us what implies what. But they do that for sentences in an artificial language, where both the sentences and connections between sentences are represented by symbols. If you work comfortably with symbols – for example, if you are good at formal mathematics – translating English sentences into logical notation can be helpful in some cases. But it can also be very misleading. A key symbol in formal logic is the arrow symbol (sometimes also represented in other ways, for example, as a horseshoe). This symbol is generally expressed in English as "if . . . then . . ." But the arrow (horseshoe, etc.) connection in logic is not the same as the

"if . . . then" connection in English. In elementary logic, the arrow represents a connection between sentences, which are represented by variables (usually, lower-case letters). Where "p" and "q" represent sentences, the compound sentence "p → q" is false in logic in only one case: when p is true and q is false. That means it's true *whenever* both p and q are false; in fact, it's true whenever p is false. Students in logic classes are often asked to translate "if . . . then" statements in English as "p → q" statements in logic. If we do, the following sentences are true according to the rules of formal logic: "If George Bush is a literary genius, the moon is made of green cheese" and "If Margaret Thatcher is a man in drag, Margaret Thatcher is a woman." As the second example shows, the truth of a compound English sentence (for example, the truth of an "if . . . then" sentence) does not always depend only on the truth of its components. In formal logic, compound sentences always depend only on the truth of their components. This doesn't mean formal logic is useless in helping us understand arguments in English. It just means that one needs to know a lot about it and do a lot of exercises before it becomes useful. It's impossible to provide that in just one chapter or a section of a chapter. Readers who are interested in learning formal logic can find scores of logic books with exercises included.

3. A. Tversky and D. Kahneman, "Judgment under Uncertainty: Heuristics and Biases," in *Judgments under Uncertainty*, ed. D. Kahneman, P. Slovic, and A. Tversky (Cambridge, UK: Cambridge University Press, 1982), pp. 3–23.

4. Ibid., pp. 4–5.

5. For a collection of such studies, see L. Heath, R. S. Tindale, J. Edwards, E. J. Posavac, F. B. Bryant, E. Henderson-Kind, Y. Suarez-Balcazar, and J. Myers, eds, *Applications of Heuristics and Biases to Social Issues* (New York and London: Plenum Press, 1994).

6. For an excellent discussion of these issues and references to these studies see D. M. Eddy, "Probabilistic Reasoning in Clinical Medicine: Problems and Opportunities," in *Judgments under Uncertainty*, ed. D. Kahneman, P. Slovic, and A. Tversky (Cambridge, UK: Cambridge University Press, 1982), pp. 249–267.

7. Ibid., p. 254.
8. Tversky and Kahneman, "Judgment under Uncertainty," p. 12.
9. Ibid., p. 12.
10. There are examples of this in nearly every paper in Heath et al., *Applications of Heuristics and Biases to Social Issues*.
11. P. Slovic, B. Fischhoff, and S. Lichtenstein, "Rating the Risks," *Environment*, 21, 1979, pp. 14–20, 36–39; and "Facts versus Fears: Understanding Perceived Risk," *Judgments under Uncertainty*, ed. D. Kahneman, P. Slovic, and A. Tversky (Cambridge, UK: Cambridge University Press, 1982), pp. 463–492.
12. Steven Schwartz, "Medical Judgment and Decision Making," in *Judgments under Uncertainty*, ed. A. Tversky and D. Kahneman (Cambridge, UK: Cambridge University Press, 1982), pp. 50–51.
13. Tversky and Kahneman, *Judgments under Uncertainty*, pp. 11–12.
14. C. G. Lord, L. Ross, and M. R. Lepper, "Bias Assimilation and Attitude Polarization: The Effects of Prior Theories on Subsequently Considered Evidence," *Journal of Personality and Social Psychology*, 37, 1979, pp. 2098–2109.
15. S. E. Asch, "Forming Impressions of Personality," *Journal of Abnormal and Social Psychology*, 41, 1946, pp. 258–290.
16. E. E. Jones, L. Rock, K. G. Shaver, G. R. Goethals, and L. M. Ward, "Patterns of Performance and Ability Attribution: An Unexpected Primacy Effect," *Journal of Personality and Social Psychology*, 10, 1968, pp. 317–340.
17. L. Ross, M. R. Lepper, and M. Hubbard, "Perseverance in Self Perception and Social Perception: Biased Attributional Processes in the Debriefing Paradigm," *Journal of Personality and Social Psychology*, 32, 1975, pp. 880–892.
18. M. R. Lepper, L. Ross, and R. Lau, "Persistence of Inaccurate and Discredited Personal Impressions: A Field Demonstration of Attributional Perserverance," unpublished manuscript, Stanford University, Stanford, CA, 1979.
19. R. Hyman, "Cold Readings: How to Convince Strangers That You Know All about Them," *Skeptical Inquirer*, Spring/Summer 1997, pp. 79–95.
20. Ibid., p. 84.

21. D. Koehler, L. Brenner, and D. W. Griffin, "The Calibration of Probability Judgments in Theory and Practice," in *Heuristics and Biases: The Psychology of Intuitive Judgments*, ed. T. Gilovich, D. W. Griffin, and D. Kahneman (Cambridge, UK: Cambridge University Press, 2002), p. 692.

22. P. C. Wason and D. Shapiro, "Reasoning," in *New Horizons in Psychology*, ed. B. M. Foss (Harmondsworth, UK: Penguin Books, 1966), pp. 135–151.

23. William James, "The Will to Believe," in *The Will to Believe and Other Essays in Popular Philosophy* (New York: Dover, 1956).

24. Tory Higgins, "Emotional and Evaluative Effects on Regulatory Focus: Promotion and Prevention as Distinct Motivational Systems," in *Feeling and Thinking: The Role of Affect in Social Cognition*, ed. J. P. Forgas (Cambridge, UK: Cambridge University Press, 2001), Chapter 12.

25. M. S. Clark, "A Role for Arousal in the Link between Feeling States, Judgments and Behavior," in *Affect and Cognition*, ed. M. S. Clark and S. T. Fiske (Hillsdale, NJ: Lawrence Erlbaum, 1982), p. 264.

26. L. L. Martin and G. L. Clore, *Theories of Mood and Cognition* (Mahwah, NJ: Lawrence Erlbaum, 2001), p. vii.

27. Herbert Bless, "Mood and the Use of General Knowledge Structures," in *Theories of Mood and Cognition*, ed. L. L. Martin and G. L. Clore (Mahwah, NJ: Lawrence Erlbaum, 2001), p. 9.

28. P. H. Ditto, J. A. Scepansky, G. D. Munro, A. M. Apanovich, and L. K. Lockhard, "Motivated Sensitivity to Preference-Inconsistent Information," *Journal of Personality and Social Psychology*, 75(1), 1998, pp. 53–69.

29. Z. Kunda, "Motivation and Inference: Self-Serving Generation and Evaluation of Evidence," *Journal of Personality and Social Psychology*, 53, 1987, pp. 636–647.

30. Z. Kunda, "The Case for Motivated Inference," *Psychological Bulletin*, 108, 1990, pp. 480–498.

31. D. C. Moldon and T. Higgins, "Motivated Thinking," in *The Cambridge Handbook of Thinking and Reasoning*, ed. K. J. Holyoak, Jr. and R. G. Morrison (Cambridge, UK: Cambridge University Press, 2004), p. 304.

Chapter 3

1. H. Munsterberg, *On the Witness Stand* (Doubleday: New York, 1908).

2. G. L. Wells, R. C. L. Lindsay, J. W. Turtle, R. S. Malpass, R. P. Fisher, and S. M Fulero, "From the Lab to the Police Station: A Successful Application of Eyewitness Research," *American Psychologist*, 58, 200, p. 581.

3. R. Buckhout, "Eyewitness Testimony," *Scientific American*, 231(6), 1974, pp. 29–30.

4. *United States* v. *Moore*, 786 F.2d 1308, 1312 (5th Cir. 1986).

5. *United States* v. *McGinnis*, No. 05-30317 (5th Cir. September 28, 2006).

6. Buckhout, "Eyewitness Testimony," pp. 27–29.

7. N. M. Steblay, "Social Influence in Eyewitness Recall: A Meta-analytic Review of Lineup Instruction Effects," *Law and Human Behavior*, 21, 1997, pp. 283–298.

8. Wells et al., "From the Lab to the Police Station," p. 586.

9. D. Yarmey, "Eyewitness Identification: Guidelines and Recommendations for Identification Procedures in the United States and Canada," *Canadian Psychology*, 44, 2003, pp. 181–189.

10. Perhaps the best-known list is in E. Bass and L. Davies, *The Courage to Heal: A Guide for Women Survivors of Child Sexual Abuse* (New York: Harper & Row, 1988). According to Maryanne Garry and Elizabeth Loftus, Therapist Karen Ratican offers a checklist of sixty-five symptoms in eleven categories. ("Repressed Memories of Childhood Sexual Trauma: Could Some of Them Be Suggested," *USA Today*, 122, January 1994, findarticles.com/p/articles/mi_m1272/is_n2584_v122/ai_14741884/p3).

11. The statements from professional organizations quoted in this paragraph can be found at www.Religious Tolerance.org. This website includes passages from many other professional organizations that are not mentioned here as well as references to these

statements: www.religioustolerance.org/rmt.htm. One can also find links to all of these statements on the webpage of the False Memory Syndrome Foundation: www.fmsfonline.org/.

12. J. Rachels, "Active and Passive Euthanasia," *New England Journal of Medicine*, January 9, 1975, pp. 78–80.

13. See, for example, "The Wisdom of Repugnance," *New Republic*, June 2, 1997, pp. 17–26.

14. M. Philips, *Between Universalism and Skepticism: Ethics as Social Artifact* (Oxford: Oxford University Press, 1994).

15. There is a concise and accessible discussion of these issues on the Investorhome website (www.Investorhome.com).

16. For a somewhat technical review of the academic literature see Kian-Kuan Lim, "The Efficient Market Hypothesis: A Developmental Perspective," in *Pioneers of Financial Economics: Vol. II*, ed. Geoffrey Poitras (Cheltenham, U.K.: Edward Edgar, 2007), Chapter 9.

17. *Science News Online*, 186(5), 2004, p. 72.

18. The latest version of F.A.C.S., by Paul Ekman, Wallace V. Friesen, and Joseph Hager, is available at the Human Face e-Store (Face-and-emotion.com/dataface/estore/main.jsp).

19. "NIH Consensus Statement Online, November 3–5, 1997," *Acupuncture*, 15(5), pp. 1–34. These findings are repeated in National Center for Complementary and Alternative Medicine, *Get the Facts on Acupuncture* (National Institutes of Health, 2004), nccam.nih.gov/health/acupuncture/acupuncture.pdf.

20. Noam Chomsky, "A Review of Skinner's *Verbal Behavior*," *Language*, 35(1), 1959, pp. 26–28.

Chapter 4

1. W. L. Rathje and W. W. Hughes, "The Garbage Project as a Nonreactive Approach: Garbage in . . . Garbage out?" in *Perspectives on Attitude Assessment: Surveys and Their Alternatives*,

ed. H. W. Sinaiko and L. A. Broedlins (Washington: Smithsonian Institution, 1975).

2. H. Pope, Jr., *Psychology Astray: Fallacies in Studies of "Repressed Memories" and Childhood Trauma* (Boca Raton, FA: Upton Books, 1997), pp. 67–68.

3. L. H. Rogler, D. K Mroczek, M. Fellows, and S. T. Loftus, "The Neglect of Response Bias in Mental Health Research," *Journal of Nervous and Mental Disease*, 189(3), 2001, pp. 182–187.

4. K. M. Mazor, B. E. Clauser, T. Field, R. A. Yood, and J. H. Gurwitz, "A Demonstration of the Impact of Response Bias on the Results of Patient Satisfaction Surveys," *Health Services Research*, 37(5), 2002, pp. 1403–1417.

5. R. McDonald and S.-J. K. Ho, "Social Desirability Response Bias in Accounting Ethics Research," *Social Science Research Network*, Social Science Electronic Publishing, 2007, www.ssrn.com/.

6. Both studies are in W. A. Belson, *Validity in Survey Research* (Aldershot, UK: Gower, 1986), p. 13.

7. J. Fee, "Symbols and Attitudes: How People Think about Politics," Ph.D. dissertation, University of Chicago, 1979.

8. H. Clark and M. Schober, "Asking Questions and Influencing Answers," in *Questions about Questions*, ed., Judith Tanur (New York: Russell Sage Foundation, 1992), p. 31.

9. Ibid., pp. 31–32.

10. Belsen, *Validity in Survey Research*, p. 111.

11. Ibid., p. 18.

12. Clark and Schober, "Asking Questions and Influencing Answers," p. 39.

13. J. Bachman and P. M. O'Malley, "When Four Months Equal a Year: Inconsistencies in Student Reports of Drug Use," in *Survey Research Methods*, ed. E. Singer and S. Presser (Chicago: University of Chicago Press, 1989), pp. 173–185.

14. E. Loftus, K. Smith, M. Klinger, and J. Fielder, "Memory and Mismemory of Health Events," in *Questions about Questions*,

ed. Judith Tanner (New York: Russell Sage Foundation, 1992), pp. 102–135.

15. A.A.U.W. Initiative for Education Equity, *Shortchanging Girls, Shortchanging America: A Call to Action* (Annapolis Junction, MD: A.A.U.W. Sales Office, 1992).

16. A. Adams, "Scientific Fraud Unpreventable Donald Kennedy Warns," *Stanford News*, January 25, 2006, amps-tools.mit.edu/tomprofblog/archives/2006/03/705_scientific.html#more.

17. *New Scientist*, March 18, 2006, p. 7.

18. P. Dizikes, "Under the Microscope," *Boston Globe*, January 22, 2006, p. E1.

19. D. Goodstein, "In the Matter J. Hendrik Schon," *Physicsweb*, Institute of Physics Publishing, November 2002, physicsworld.com/cws/article/print/11352.

20. W. P. Whitely, D. Rennie, and A. W. Hafner, "The Robert Slutsky Case," *Journal of the American Medical Association*, 272, 1994, pp. 170–173.

21. Onlineethics.org, "Ethics in the Science Classroom, Case Study 1: Overly Ambitious Researchers—Fabricating Data," Online Ethics Center for Engineering and Science at Case Western Reserve University, August 30, 2004, www.onlineethics.org/CMS/edu/precol/scienceclass/sectone/cs1aspx.

22. L. K. Altman and W. J. Broad, "Global Trend: More Science, More Fraud," *New York Times*, December 20, 2005, nytimes.com/ref/membercenter/nytarchive.html.

23. Responsible Conduct of Research, "Research Misconduct," Columbia Center for New Media Teaching and Learning, Columbia University, 2003–4, ccnmtl.columbia.edu/projects/rcr/rcr_misconduct/foundation/index.html.

24. L. Marsa, "Scientific Fraud," *Omni*, June 1992, pp. 38–43.

25. J. Barnoya and S. A. Glantz, "The Tobacco Industry's Worldwide ETS Consultants Project: European and Asian Components," *European Journal of Public Health*, 16(1), 2006, pp. 69–77.

26. *NewScientist.com* news service, May 30, 2003.

27. Dizikes, "Under the Microscope."

28. Marsa, "Scientific Fraud," pp. 40–41.

29. Ibid., p. 39.

30. For a brief and accessible account of such practices see Zeke Ashton, "Recognizing Revenue: Games People Play," *Financial Journalist Newsletter*, 11, 2002, www.newswise.com/articles/view/?id=FJMay2.IMR.

31. D. A. Moore, P. E. Tetlock, L. Tanlu, and M. H. Bazerman, "Conflicts of Interest and the Case of Auditor Independence: Moral Seduction and Strategic Issue Cycling," *Academy of Management Review*, 31(1), 2006, p. 13.

32. Ibid., p. 15.

33. P. Patsuris, "The Corporate Scandal Sheet," *Forbes.com*, August 26, 2002, www.forbes.com/; and *Answers.com*, "Accounting Scandals 2002," www.answers.com/topic/accounting-scandals.

34. *Answers.com*, "Accounting Scandals 2002."

35. For all but Computer Associates: *Citizenworks.org*, "The Corporate Scandal Sheet," March 29, 2003, www.citizenworks.org/enron/corp-scandalphp. For Computer Associates: *U.S. Security and Exchange Commission*, sec.gov/news/press/2004-134.htm. The reader can find multiple articles on all of these scandals at *Answers.com* by entering the name of the relevant corporation in the search dialog box, followed by "scandal 2002."

36. *Citizenworks.org*, "The Corporate Scandal Sheet."

37. Stanford Law School, "Securities Class Action Clearinghouse," April 23, 2007, securities.stanford.edu/companies. html.

38. A. Dyck, A. Morse, and L. Zingales, "Who Blows the Whistle on Corporate Fraud?" Law and Economics Workshop, University of Michigan Law School, Ann Arbor, December 1, 2005.

39. Moore et al., "Conflicts of Interest and the Case of Auditor Independence," p. 28.

40. "Oversight Systems Corporate Fraud Survey Finds Sarbanes–Oxley Effective in Identifying Financial Statement Fraud; Few Feel the Heightened Push for Institutional Integrity and

Fraud Prevention by Business Leaders Will Continue in the Long Run," Oversight Systems, November 1, 2005, www.oversightsystems.com/news_events/release_051001.php.

41. Elizabeth MacDonald, "Where Were the Auditors?" *Forbes.com*, November 6, 2006, www.forbes.com/2006/11/03/accountants-back-dating-options-biz-cx_emd_1106auditors.html.

42. There is a very comprehensive account of these events complete with a large bibliography in "Killian Documents," *Wikipedia*, en.wikipedia.org/wiki/Killian_documents.

43. "FOX's Garret Repeated Bogus Suggestion that Dems Are Perpetrating Voter Fraud," *Media Matters for America*, October 25, 2004, www.mediamatters.org/items/200410250006.

44. Ibid.

45. F. Foer, "The Source of the Trouble," *New York Magazine*, June 7, 2004, nymag.com/nymetro/news/media/features/9226/.

46. "Frequently Asked Questions," *Center for Science and Medical Journalism*, Boston University, www.bu.edu/com/jo/science/faq.htm#1.

47. Richard Lee Colvin, "Improving Education Journalism: Educate the Writer Too," *Carnegie Reporter*, 2(5), 2004, backpage.

48. "Improving the Education of Tomorrow's Journalists," *Carnegie Corporation of New York*, www.carnegie.org/sub/program/initiativedocs/Exec_Sum_Journalism.pdf, p. 7.

49. *Wikipedia*, "Journalism Scandals," en.wikipedia.org/wiki/United_States_Journalism_scandals (click on "United States Journalism Scandals" under the list of items offered).

50. Dee Korber and John Hill, "Bee Publishes Results of Griego Erwin Probe," *Sacramento Bee*, June 26, 2005, p. B1.

51. *Wikipedia*, "United States Journalism Scandals," section 1.19. There is a link to an informative article on this scandal in the *New York Times*, May 11, 2003.

52. *Wikipedia*, "United States Journalism Scandals," section 113. There is a link to an informative article in *Slate.com*.

53. Robert Kolker, "The Great Pretender," *New York Magazine*,

February 25, 2002, www.nymag.com/nymetro/news/media/
features/5740.

54. *Wikipedia*, "United States Journalism Scandals," section 2.2.

55. A list of Glass's articles and further information on other journal-
    ism scandals can be found on Rick Mcginnis's webpage under
    "Glass Index," www.rickmcginnis.com/articles/Glassindex. htm.

56. Institute of Medicine, National Academies of Science, *To Err Is
    Human: Building a Safer Health System* (Washington: National
    Academies Press, 2000), pp. 26–48.

Chapter 5

1. M. Philips, *Between Universalism and Skepticism: Ethics as Social
   Artifact* (Oxford: Oxford University Press, 1994), Chapter 3.

2. Jonathan Amos, "Dark Matter Comes out of the Cold," *BBC
   News Online*, February 5, 2006, news.bbc.co.uk/1/hi/sci/tech/
   4679220.stm.

3. Richard Lewin, "Is Your Brain Really Necessary?" *Science*,
   December 1980, p. 1232.

4. To get a sense of other possibilities, see *Wikipedia*, "Knowledge
   Management," en.wikipedia.org/wiki/Knowledge_Management.

5. *Online Ethics Center for Engineering and Science*, "Roger Boisjoly
   and the Challenger," Case Western Reserve University,
   temp.onlineethics.org/moral/boisjoly/RB-intro.html.

6. Feynman's Appendix to the Roger's Commission Report can be
   found at www.ralentz.com/old/space/feynman-report.htm.

7. This is all on the Jefferson Center website: www.Jefferson-
   Center.org.

8. J. Surowiecki, *The Wisdom of Crowds: Why the Many Are Smarter
   Than the Few and How Collective Wisdom Shapes Business, Economies,
   Societies and Nations* (New York: Doubleday, 2004).

9. Ben Goldacre, "Don't Dumb Me Down," *Guardian*, September 8,
   2005, www.badscience.net.

10. Denise Brehm, "Science Journalism in D Minor," *MIT Tech*

Talk, November 20, 2002, web.mit.edu/newsoffice/2002/journalism-1120.html.

11. J. Hart and R. Chappell, *Worlds Apart: How the Distance Between Science and Journalism Threatens America's Future* (Nashville: First Amendment Center, 1997).

12. E. Singer, "A Question of Accuracy: How Journalists and Scientists Report Research on Harzards," *Journal of Communication*, 4, 1990, 102–115.

13. Sara Robinson, "Math and the Media: A Disconnect, and a Few Fixes, Emerge in San Diego Session," *Siam*, August 26, 2002, www.msir.org/people/members/sara/articles/mathandmedia.html.

14. Goldacre, "Don't Dumb Me Down."

15. Ben Goldacre, "Publish or Be Damned," *Guardian*, August 4, 2005, www.badscience.net.

16. Chris Mooney, "How 'Balanced' Coverage Lets the Scientific Fringe Hijack Reality," *Columbia Journalism Review*, November/December 2004, www.cjr.org/issues/2006/6/mooney-science. asp.

Chapter 6

1. John Allen Paulos, *Innumeracy: Mathematical Illiteracy and its Consequences* (New York: Hill & Wang, 1988).

2. "What Is Dark Matter?" *Usenet Physics FAQ's*, math.ucr.edu/home/baez/physics/index.html.

3. R. Abelson, K. P. Frey, A. Gregg, and A. P. Gregg, *Experiments with People: Revelations from Social Psychology* (Mahwah, NJ: Lawrence Erlbaum, 2003), pp. 115–116.

Chapter 7

1. W. K. Clifford, *Lectures and Essays: Volume II, Essays and Reviews* (London: Macmillan, 1879), pp. 163–176.

2. W. James, "*The Will to Believe and Other Essays in Popular Philosophy* (Boston: Longman, Green, 1897), pp. 26–34. This essay can be found in many beginning philosophy anthologies.

3. One could also say where the promise of benefits outweighs the expected burdens. The choice between these formulations raises some tricky questions about whether we should treat harms and benefits symmetrically in ethics: roughly speaking, should benefits count as much as harms when we construct our moral principles?

Index